THE MAKING OF AN ALL-AMERICA CITY

EAST ST. LOUIS AT 150

Mark Abbott, Editor
Harris-Stowe State University

EAST ST. LOUIS SESQUICENTENNIAL SERIES

The Making of an All-America City:
East St. Louis at 150

Series Editor:	Andrew J. Theising, Ph.D., SIUE Institute for Urban Research
Volume Editor:	Mark Abbott, Ph.D., Harris-Stowe State University
Editorial Board:	Jeffrey Smith, Ph.D., Lindenwood University
	Nancy Thompson, Saint Louis University
	Debra H. Moore, Ph.D., Adjunct Faculty, Washington University in St. Louis, The George Warren Brown School of Social Work
Managing Editors:	Christen Gates (2009), SIUE
	Delia Major (2010), SIUE
Layout/Page Design:	Vamsi Kammili, SIUE
Digital Imaging:	Virginia Stricklin, SIUE
Index:	Delia Major, SIUE
Off-site Photography:	Stephanie Powell, Powell Photography
IUR Staff:	Hugh Pavitt, SIUE
	Rhonda Penelton, SIUE
Contract Support:	Trisha Simmons, SIUE
Publisher:	Virginia Publishing, www.stl-books.com

Southern Illinois University Edwardsville
Institute for Urban Research
Box 1246
Edwardsville, IL 62026-1246

TABLE OF CONTENTS

CHAPTER 3: FACING THE CHALLENGES OF DE-INDUSTRIALIZATION

CHAPTER 4: PATHS CHOSEN

EPILOGUE

Acknowledgements

The Institute for Urban Research at Southern Illinois University Edwardsville acknowledges the hard work of many people who have made this volume possible. The editors are grateful to all of these people, and have attempted to provide a complete list. For any omission or error, the editors extend their heartfelt apology.

Mark Abbott spent many hours shepherding the many authors to completion. His editorial board consisted of Jeffrey Smith, Nancy Thompson, and Debra Moore who did an amazing job of supporting the authors and polishing their essays. Of course, the contributors each deserve thanks and honor for their thoughtful pieces. They should be proud of this remarkable collection.

Administrative support was provided by Christen Gates and Delia Major. Trisha Simmons managed contracts and payments. University support was provided through the leadership of Steve Hansen and Jerry Weinberg.

Technical support and layout was provided by Vamsi Kammili. Steve Kerber and Virginia Stricklin provided digital imaging of archival material. Stephanie Powell did an outstanding job as the off-site photographer. Jeff Fister of Virginia Publishing provided considerable technical and administrative guidance.

Finally, to the good people of East St. Louis past and present, the editors extend their admiration and appreciation. Happy anniversary!

…a place called East St. Louis

I t was April Fool's Day, and the people went to the polls…again. They had just gone there a month before to approve a new charter for the place that had been known as Illinois Town. They had settled on a new government. They had new boundaries. Now, they were deciding on a new name. A few different choices were discussed, but "East St. Louis" was the name that was ultimately put forward, and the people approved it by a vote of 183 to 89.

So, on April 1, 1861, there was a new place on the map—a place called East St. Louis. In the 150 years that have passed since that day, much has happened. It has been a place of boom and bust, of triumph and tragedy, of joy and pain. From its ranks have risen global beacons of sound, and song, and dance, and motion.

The centennial celebration of that event, held in 1961, was an occasion to remember. Many alive at that time recall it as the city's finest hour. It was a double celebration because, in 1960, the place called East St. Louis was honored with *Look Magazine*'s All-America City designation. There were flags and banners, beautification campaigns, and lots of media attention. That celebration melded right into the year of centennial celebrations, where there were parades and contests. Men grew beards and women wore bonnets. The newspaper published the local history and many businesses took the opportunity to document their own histories in the place called East St. Louis. (There is a fine collection of ephemera from this event in SIUE's Bowen Archive.)

Southern Illinois University Edwardsville, which traces its beginning to classrooms in the old high school building in East St. Louis, is pleased to recognize the 150th anniversary of a place called East St. Louis by sponsoring a series of books over the course of the sesquicentennial year. *The East St. Louis Sesquicentennial Series* will release several volumes (both digital and print) that examine the city's impact over 150 years, document and preserve its history, and provide meaningful reference for historians to come.

Dr. Mark Abbott of Harris-Stowe State University begins the series with a thoughtful selection of essays on the city that had once been held up for all of America to see. A wonderfully diverse group of contributors examines the community from many different angles and helps discern the lessons from the city's 150 years of existence. It is a fitting start to a year-long examination and reconsideration of this place called East St. Louis.

Andrew J. Theising, Ph.D.
Series Editor
Institute for Urban Research
Southern Illinois University Edwardsville

THE
MAKING
OF AN
ALL-AMERICA
CITY

EAST ST. LOUIS
AT 150

Mark Abbott, Editor
Harris-Stowe State University

EAST ST. LOUIS SESQUICENTENNIAL SERIES

Introduction

Every year the National Civic League names ten cities as its "All America Cities." In 1960 East St. Louis received the award. When many people hear this now, they think it was some kind of joke. After all, HUD has called East St. Louis the "most distressed small city in America." However, neither East St. Louis nor its previous designation as an "All America City" is a joke. On the contrary, East St. Louis may be the most "American" city in America. Whatever is right or wrong with contemporary American society and culture is written large in East St. Louis. While the media and academia have well-chronicled the horrors of de-industrialization and racism that have plagued the city over the last half generation, there is another East St. Louis story which never seems to get as much attention. This story involves the heroic struggle of the East St. Louis residents who have stayed and their valiant successes in trying to reclaim their city.

This book is about both these stories. It attempts to explain and interpret the causes of East St. Louis' decline since 1960 and why it continues to encounter incredible obstacles in its efforts at recovery. But it is also about the human spirit and the power of community. The fifteen essays and the one prose poem contained in this book tell both these stories in a spirit of candor and celebration as the residents of East St. Louis approach the commemoration of its sesquicentennial.

In chapter one, "A City by the River", the four essays speak to the power of place and how the Mississippi River has shaped (and continues to shape) East St. Louis. Joseph Galloy, an archeologist with the University of Illinois, notes that East St. Louis has always been a suburb even in the thirteenth century. Then it was a suburb of the great Mississippian metropolis of Cahokia located to its north and was far more important than a smaller settlement across the river to the west. His essay describes his research and his amazing discoveries about this earlier East St. Louis culture. Michael Allen, an architectural historian, traces the architectural evolution of East St. Louis before the Great Depression and how East St. Louisans were forging a style of their own independent of St. Louis. On the other hand, Preston Lacy of Southwest Illinois Conservation and Resource Development tells how East St. Louis and the surrounding communities were literally St. Louis' dumping ground. Picking up on a theme first explored by Andrew Theising in *Made in USA: East St. Louis: The Rise and Fall of an Industrial Suburb*, Lacy details the environmental devastation that unfettered industrialization inflicted upon East St. Louis and its neighbors and how it was perhaps the most obvious example of environmental racism in America. Bryan Werner, a planner with the Metro East Park and Recreation District, and Les Sterman, an engineer with the Southwestern Illinois Flood Prevention District and former long time Executive Director of the East-West Gateway Coordinating Council, end the chapter talking about how the river is currently both a challenge and an opportunity for East St. Louis and the region. They outline the enormity of the task now facing East St. Louis and the American Bottom communities as they attempt to block the potential decertification of the eastside levees by the Army Corps of Engineers and the ramifications if they fail. However, they also point to how the river is actually the core of the Jefferson National Expansion Park and how the current campaign to improve the park grounds on both sides of the river which could have a tremendous beneficial impact on the future of East St. Louis.

Chapter two, "The Question of Race and Culture", explores the complexities of race and racism in the East St. Louis experience. Charles Lumpkins, a scholar at Pennsylvania State University and the author of *American Pogrom,* recounts the horrors of the 1917 race riot and how its legacy continued to haunt the city to the 1950s and beyond. But Kimberly Curtis, a historian at Harris-Stowe State University in St. Louis, talks about how Katherine Dunham was able to overcome the limitations of racism to become one of the greatest American dancers of all time and how her educational center continues to be a source of strength for the black community. Lillian Parks, the retired superintendent of the East St. Louis Public Schools, recounts the story of African American perseverance in the face of racism and records the many successes of the East St. Louis black community. Drawing on the work of Carter G. Woodson and his famous work, *The Mis-Education of the Negro*, Dr. Parks suggests that the media distorts East St. Louis' lack of progress and the degree of corruption that takes place there to "mis-educate" the city's black community into thinking that they are incapable of taking control of their lives. On the other hand, Billie Turner's essay is literally a "love song" to East St. Louis. Although Turner, who is the Community Liaison with the East St. Louis Action Research Project (ESLARP), acknowledges her own personal struggles with racism in the city, she celebrates the strength of African Americans in East St. Louis in overcoming adversity and the tremendous sense of community that is present among black East St. Louisans.

Chapter three, "The Challenges of De-industrialization", examines the causes of industrial decline. In my essay, I explore the 1920 East St. Louis Comprehensive Plan that was prepared by the noted urban planner Harland Bartholomew in the wake of the 1917 Race Riot. What I argue is that even though Bartholomew's plan for East St. Louis literally became a "template" for the planning profession in how to create a comprehensive or a "master" plan, it did not adequately address the city's industrial and social problems. Joseph Davis, a colleague at Harris-Stowe and a former resident of East St. Louis who worked in the city's rail yards, looks at the transformation of the rail industry during the mid-twentieth century and its impact on East St. Louis. Taking a position counter to mine, he maintains that there was nothing that East St. Louis could have planned for or done to prevent the departure of the railroads. It was simply a matter of changing technology and transportation practices. Andrew Hurley, chair of the Department of History at the University of Missouri at St. Louis, studies the issue from a slightly different perspective. Instead of focusing on the causes of East St. Louis' industrial decline, he compares East St. Louis to other failed industrial suburbs and investigates potential explanations for why some other industrial suburbs like Camden (Philadelphia) and Hoboken (New York City), New Jersey, were both able to remake themselves and while East St. Louis has not. He concludes that it has not been a failure to act on the part of East St. Louis and its other industrial neighbors. Rather, he maintains, it is the result of regional stagnation. In situations where industrial suburbs have been able to reinvent themselves, the impetus has been regional growth. In St. Louis where the region as a whole has been stagnant, this stimulus has been absent. However, Hurley does hold out a glimmer of hope. What East St. Louis and the older east side industrial suburbs have in their favor is affordable housing prices and that this may eventually draw residents and businesses back into the area.

Chapter four, "Paths Taken", considers choices that have been made—and choices that need to be made—by East St. Louisans. In the first essay, Andrew Theising, Director of the Institute for Urban Research at Southern Illinois University Edwardsville and the author of *Made in USA*, the definitive work on the history of East St. Louis, examines the choices made by three early East St. Louis leaders who dominated the city's political scene for sixty years between 1860 and 1920. Each of these three men took East St. Louis down a different path and each was important in shaping East St. Louis continuing legacy. James Ingram, a local reporter and columnist, tackles one of these legacies head on, the question of corruption in East St. Louis. For Ingram, the state of corruption in East St. Louis is merely learned behavior. Coming of age politically under the tutelage of generations of corrupt white political bosses who could be traced back to the time of one of Theising's politicos, Locke Tarlton, black politicians have simply followed in their mentors' footsteps. According to Ingram, political corruption is as "American as Cherry Pie" and that it will not stop in East St. Louis—or anywhere else in America—until East St. Louisans become "sick and tired of being sick and tired" of corruption and decide to do something about it. Yet according to Anne Flaherty, political science professor at Southern Illinois University Edwardsville, not all the paths taken in East St. Louis have been bad or corrupt. In fact, she contends the decision to build the casino was a good one and that it perhaps saved the city from financial ruin. Yet Debra Moore, who is also a political scientist and the current

Executive Director of the St. Clair County Intergovernmental Grants Agency, argues that until the city chooses to abandon its legacy of political rule that is steeped in personal aggrandizement and adopts a rational approach to decision-making, it will remain a failed city and an economic backwater. In her mind, East St. Louis politics' orientation around personal relationships has kept it and will continue to keep it from acquiring the organizational capacity to ever rebuild itself.

In the epilogue, Eugene Redmond, the poet laureate of East St. Louis, uses his poem that he composed for this occasion to rejoice in the history of East St. Louis. Using two south side streets—Bond and Piggott—as metaphors for the incredible vitality of the city, Redmond chronicles both the exploits of the cultural giants that have emerged from East St. Louis as well as the throbbing pulse of everyday life in East St. Louis.

The authors of these essays come from varying backgrounds. Some have lived in East St. Louis their entire lives, others are merely observers. Some are African American, others are white. Some write for a living, while for others this was their first essay. But all of their voices are authentic and provide insight into the past, present, and future of this remarkable city as it is poised to celebrate its 150th birthday. This is an important book not just because of what it has to say about East St. Louis, but because of what it has to say about America.

Mark Abbott, Ph.D.
Editor
Harris-Stowe State University

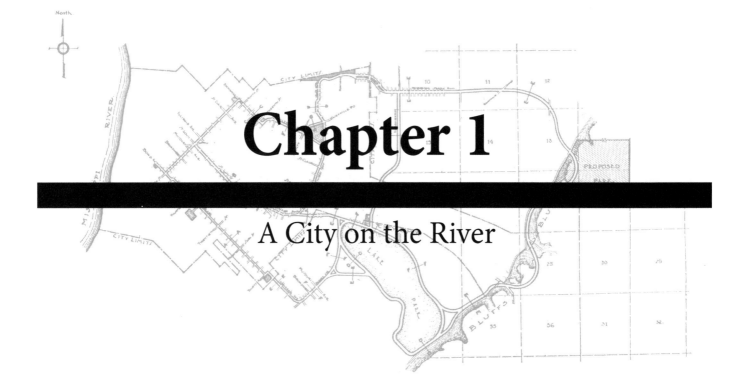

Chapter 1

A City on the River

A Once and Future City: The Splendor of Prehistoric East St. Louis

Joseph M. Galloy, Ph.D.

Illinois State Archeological Survey

University of Illinois at Urbana-Champaign

The young man had just passed his fifteenth summer. Apprenticed to his much older brother, a master flintknapper, he had himself begun to perfect the craft of shaping useful things out of stone. When he was younger, he had spent many of his days at the quarry, where he mined slabs of chert, a low grade flint, along with the other village boys. Saddling some of the stone on his dogs, and the rest of it on his back, he hauled it a short distance to his brother's workshop, one of several in their village. There the chert would be chipped into blades for digging and cultivating tools, which were always in high demand. The best knappers also made finely crafted knives and other special objects. Usually, his brother's handiworks would be brought to local traders for food, clothing, jewelry, utensils, and other necessities, but this time—for the first time—he would accompany his older brother on a special trip to exchange them at market. Their journey would take them more than 100 miles up the Mississippi River to a great riverside marketplace. Afterwards, they would see the wonders of Cahokia, the great City of the Sun.

Monk's Mound, 2004 Theising Photo

The river was low, as there had been little rainfall that summer. Nevertheless, paddling against the river's flow remained a difficult challenge, and in a few places where the current was strongest they were forced to portage their canoe. As they made their way north, the river was flanked with familiar sights: families tending agricultural fields, young men fishing the river, and old men collecting firewood from its banks. Small homesteads and farming villages dotted the highest floodplain ridges, avoiding the worst of the river's wrath.

Eventually the floodplain widened, signaling that their tiring four-day journey was almost over. The trees that grew along the river's edge had begun to run thin, and then disappeared completely as the air became heavy with smoke. Across the expanses of floodplain, they saw scattered towns with large earthen mounds. Some of these mounds were topped by temples and by dwellings of the powerful.

It was late afternoon when they arrived at their destination. They turned into the mouth of Cahokia Creek and paddled to a landing, where some passing boys helped them bring their canoe ashore. They fixed their heavy cargo to their backs, and began trudging towards the market. The path underfoot was so well worn that the young man was able to concentrate instead on the enormous ridge-top mound in the distance. He knew that Cahokian ridgetop mounds marked the burial place of the wealthy and powerful, but this one, at 40 feet high, dwarfed all other mounds that he had ever seen. As they drew closer, they came upon an

enormous level area, the center of which was marked with a massive wooden post that was much taller than the mound. This plaza was defined by several other mounds, some of which served as platforms for huge wood-and-thatch buildings. A few more mounds were still under construction, with foremen watching over and shouting at their teams of workers. Many people milled about the plaza: nobles, warriors, priests, merchants, builders, potters, and farmers. For the first time in his life, he saw a man (who was obviously crippled) begging for food. The market was alongside the plaza, and the activity there was also hectic with dozens of people haggling over a bewildering array of goods: finely crafted clay pots, wooden bowls, and baskets, ear ornaments, colorful cloth, dyes, furs, tobacco, meats and fish, iron and lead pigments, marine shells, and many others.

After exchanging their stone handicrafts for blankets, necklaces, and some salted deer meat the brothers returned to their canoe and continued their journey up Cahokia Creek. As they paddled away to the northeast, they gazed upon the city's earthen pyramids. Many of these mounds, including the largest one, were arranged in a straight line along the southern end of the plaza. After a short while, the creek bent to the north and another straight line of mounds was visible in the distance. These mounds overlooked a huge area containing most of the city's residential neighborhoods, which contained several hundred houses. There, on a much larger scale, were the familiar sights and sounds

of village life: children playing games, women grinding corn and tending their household gardens, and men lounging under open-walled sunshades discussing politics and the coming harvest season. It was now dusk, and many people were coming home from their daily activities. Never had the young man seen so many people in one place.

The brothers stopped at a small town a short distance upstream to stay for the night. As they pulled the canoe ashore, the young man thanked his brother for taking him on the journey. He told him that he had always thought that his brother's stories were full of exaggeration, but now that he had seen the City of the Sun, he knew for himself how wondrous it truly was. His brother began to chuckle, and then erupted in laughter. "That's not the City of the Sun!" he told him. "That is one of Cahokia's two port cities, located on each side of the river." He slapped his brother on the back, and said, "Cahokia is still farther up the creek, and its temples reach to the heavens. Ten times as many people live there, brother. There, the Great Sun resides, lord and ruler of the three cites. We'll see Cahokia tomorrow." The young man's embarrassment at his naïveté didn't dampen his growing excitement. Sleep was difficult for him that night.

The essence of this story—a person from a civilization's hinterlands discovering the wondrous size and splendor of its greatest cities—has surely been repeated countless times across the ages, from 5,000-year-old Bronze Age cities in the ancient Near East to modern behemoths like Tokyo, Mumbai, or New York. What will surely come as a surprise to most Americans is that such a scenario could have taken place one thousand years ago in the country's heartland. An ancient Native American civilization, replete with the accoutrements of urban life, once thrived at the confluence of the Mississippi and Missouri rivers near modern-day East St. Louis, Illinois. For well over a century, archaeologists working in St. Louis Metro East have been uncovering the remnants of an ancient civilization known as "Mississippian."

The Mississippian civilization flourished from roughly 1000 to 1600 CE and was once spread over much of the American Southeast, Mid-South, and lower Midwest. The Mississippians were the most complex of the prehistoric societies north of Mexico, and their civilization left behind many archaeologically visible cultural traits. Principally, these traits include a reliance on

maize (corn) agriculture and an associated settlement focus on large river valleys, large nucleated populations, hierarchical and centralized sociopolitical and settlement systems, extensive exchange networks, and monumental ceremonial and mortuary structures including earthen pyramids.[1]

Cahokia Mounds, the well-known archaeological site located near East St. Louis in Collinsville, Illinois, represents the remains of the earliest and largest city in the Mississippian world.[2] At its peak, Cahokia was home to an estimated 15,000–20,000 inhabitants. While small by modern standards, Cahokia was larger than contemporary London, England, and remained the largest city in American history until Revolutionary War-era Philadelphia overtook it. Monumental architecture, a characteristic of civilizations everywhere (the St. Louis arch is a modern example), is exemplified at Cahokia by Monks Mound, the

100-foot-tall earthen pyramid at the heart of the site that was itself topped by a five-story-tall wooden building. A marvel of prehistoric earthwork engineering, it covers an area equal to that of Egypt's Great Pyramid of Giza. Furthermore, it was one of at least 120 mounds, many of them quite large themselves, that were spread over an area of roughly six square miles. Cahokia's landscape is also characterized by other monuments such as post circles (Woodhenges), borrow pits, palisade fortifications, and by extensive residential neighborhoods. However, Cahokia is only the most noticeable manifestation of this ancient culture's presence on the landscape. Smaller cities and towns with several mounds, as well as smaller settlements with only a few mounds, are scattered across the landscape of the Mississippi floodplain and the adjacent uplands.

Farming villages and isolated homesteads without any mounds

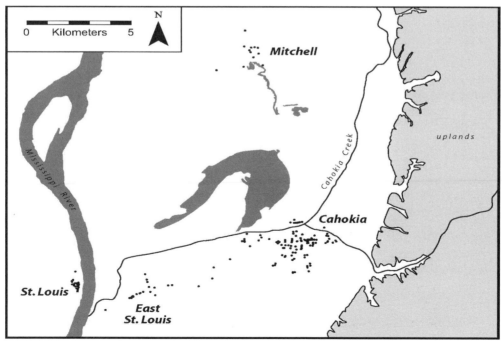

Figure 1: Cahokia and Nearby Mound Centers. Galloy image

are even more abundant and widespread throughout the region, yet are essentially invisible to those without a trained eye and a sense of where to look for them.

After Cahokia, the next largest or "second-tier" cities in the region were located in the same spots as modern East St. Louis and St. Louis, Missouri. The East St. Louis Mound Center was situated to Cahokia's west and downstream along Cahokia Creek, and the St. Louis Mound Center opposite East St. Louis on the Mississippi River bluffs (Figure 1). Considered individually, East St. Louis and St. Louis ranked among the largest cities in the Mississippian world. East St. Louis was second only to Cahokia in the number of mounds, and St. Louis trailed the third largest city of Moundville in Alabama.[3] Significantly, it is difficult to draw an exact dividing line between Cahokia and East St. Louis because the outlying mounds of both cities overlap. Because of this, archaeologist Timothy Pauketat views Cahokia,

East St. Louis, and St. Louis not as distinct entities, but as parts of the "central administrative complex" of the Cahokian polity.[4] Both St. Louis and East St. Louis are strategically located on high ground along the Mississippi, and during the historic period they both functioned as river ports and manufacturing centers, possibly echoing similar roles in antiquity. They also likely served as symbolic and literal expressions of Cahokian power over human activities on the Mississippi River.

The first descriptions of the East St. Louis site appeared in travel accounts dating from 1811, 1837, and 1841, well before East St. Louis' modern emergence. These descriptions indicate that the site originally contained about 45 to 50 mounds before they began to be leveled for borrow.[5] The first professional archaeologist to become interested in East St. Louis was Charles Rau, a German immigrant and self-taught archaeologist. Around 1860, Rau discovered what he thought was

the residue of ancient pottery manufacturing—clay mining pits and large amounts of potsherds—while walking along the banks of Cahokia Creek.[6] His interest in the site occurred at a time when East St. Louis began to experience rapid urban and industrial growth. Sometime around 1865, in an effort to document the site's disappearing mounds, Belleville dentist and amateur archaeologist John J. R. Patrick located 17 of them on a street map (Figure 2).[7] This map would later prove to be a useful guide to future archaeologists looking for the remaining traces of the site.

East St. Louis's populace at this time seemed indifferent to the destruction of the mounds, although local newspapers did describe the dismantling of the site's largest mound in 1869 and 1870.[8] Known locally as "Cemetery Mound," this ancient tumulus measured an estimated 300 feet long and 40 feet high. Its summit was shaped like a ridge, indicating that it marked an elite

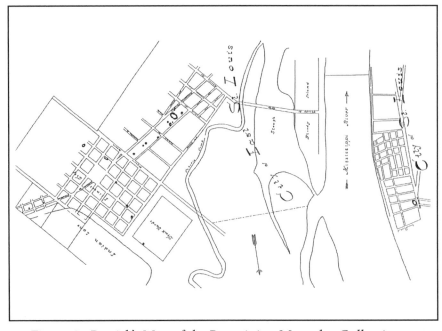

Figure 2: Patrick's Map of the Remaining Mounds. Galloy image

burial site. Thus—after workers removed American, French, and/or historic Indian burials that intruded into the mound—they uncovered stone-capped burial vaults and a collapsed burial chamber at the mound's center, which contained masses of poorly preserved human bone. All sorts of burial offerings including ceramic vessels, marine shell beads, and stone tools were carted off by workers and onlookers. Another account from this era describes the accidental discovery of a storage pit that contained 70 to 75 chert hoes.[9] The pit was found during grading for Sixth Street near Pennsylvania Avenue in the 1860s, and other nearby pits contained masses of marine-shell beads and boulders of chert and igneous rock.

After Rau, the next professional archaeologist to take interest in East St. Louis was Warren King Moorehead. In the 1920s, Moorehead attempted to relocate the pottery production areas described by Rau, but he was unsuccessful because there were almost no undeveloped areas to examine. He complained that "In Rau's time, East St. Louis was a small place. Today, the buildings, pens, tracks, streets, etc. ... must cover at least 500 acres."[10] Nevertheless, Moorehead proceeded with test excavations in a garbage dump as well as about 30 to 40 residential backyards in an attempt to locate prehistoric deposits.[11] Although he was successful in doing so, Moorehead's field methods were less than rigorous even for the 1920s, so he neglected to record where he dug or what artifacts he found. Regardless, Moorehead's work was significant because

it conclusively established that some portions of ancient East St. Louis had survived the near-total destruction of its mounds and ongoing urban-industrial development. Oddly, much later in the 20th century, most archaeologists failed to consider Moorehead's discoveries, and simply assumed that the ancient city had been completely destroyed.[12] This false assumption became a self-fulfilling prophesy in the early 1960s when Interstate 55/70 was under construction. No archaeologist thought to monitor the grading work that cut a swath right through the middle of the site's downtown "civic-ceremonial precinct."[13]

Fortunately, the destruction wrought by the interstate's construction was not total. After passage of the National Historic Preservation Act in 1966, performing archaeological investigations before highway construction was no longer limited to hurried "salvage" excavations of small portions of large and important sites. Instead, the new law mandated careful, methodologically sound excavations with the goal of producing high-quality archaeological data. As a result, from 1991 to 1992 and again from 1999 to 2000, archaeologists working under the auspices of the Illinois Department of Transportation (IDOT) conducted excavations of the existing Interstate 55/70 right-of-way prior to widening of the interstate and other planned improvements.[14] There they found extensive and very complicated Mississippian deposits on both sides of the interstate, including even the lower portions of mounds. This

discovery exploded the persistent myth that the ancient city had been destroyed by development.[15]

What was it that preserved the archaeological deposits in these cases? The short answer is "fill."[16] After devastating nineteenth century floods and decades of wrangling over the issue, the East St. Louis City Council finally passed the High Grade Act in 1874. This act was designed to reduce the risk of flooding by elevating the city with a blanket of fill, so about 3 to 10 feet of fill was placed along streets and in many (but not all) residential neighborhoods. Similar filling was also performed in rail yards, and in some cases the fill was clearly borrowed from the site's mounds.[17] Filling buried the ancient Mississippian archaeological deposits and helped protect them from further damage by construction.

The IDOT investigations along I-55/70 provided an astonishing peek at the civic and ceremonial core or "downtown" of this ancient city (Figure 3).[18] Despite the fact that the excavated areas were fairly narrow (only about 30 feet wide) more than 400 archaeological features were revealed. These reflect public works projects on a truly monumental scale: the basal remnants of a handful of mounds, reclaimed borrow pits, a stockade or wall, large rectangular and circular buildings, and dozens of huge pits that held massive marker posts. The site's central plaza was also identified. This earthwork was constructed by filling and leveling an area the size of 8.5 football fields. There was also a sprawling compound containing huts that likely stored the food (and likely other) wealth of the city's elite residents.

The excavations also showed that the Mississippians often reused the same space for different purposes, reflecting evolution of the city plan over the 12th century (Figure 3). Interestingly, the recovered artifacts show that most of the earthwork construction in this downtown area began 50 years after Cahokia's emergence c. 1050 CE. Instead, nearly all of this activity occurred from 1100 to 1200 CE, when parallel construction projects were undertaken at other mound centers throughout the region. Oddly, there was hardly any evidence that the downtown area was occupied after 1200 CE. It therefore appeared, similar to modern East St. Louis, that the city had a fairly brief (in an archaeological sense) pulse

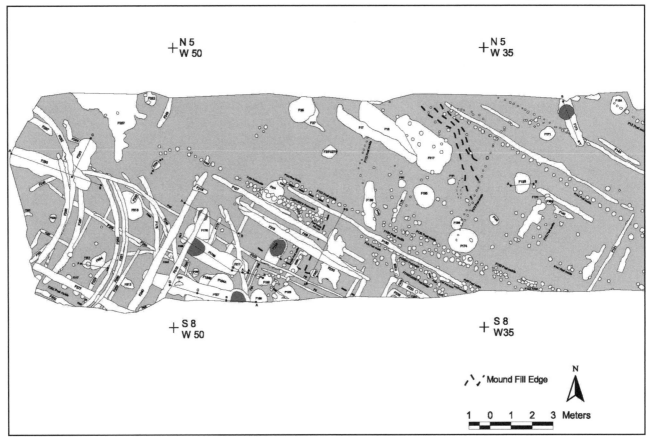

Figure 3: Outlines of Mississippian Architecture within the I-55/70 Excavations. Galloy image

of rapid growth followed by abandonment shortly thereafter.[19]

However, this view of ancient East St. Louis has been challenged by new excavations by the Illinois State Archaeological Survey (ISAS)[20] for the construction of the new Mississippi River Bridge and Interstate 70 Connector. This work, again sponsored by IDOT, began in 2008. This time, a much larger portion of the East St. Louis site is under investigation, primarily within the now-defunct St. Louis National Stockyards (in Fairmont City, Illinois) and adjacent areas. Although it was known that Moorehead had recovered artifacts from the stockyards, and that a large mound once stood in its eastern half, this area had never been seriously investigated. Thus, the stockyards constituted a big unknown when ISAS began work there in September 2008.

To the delight of the ISAS team, Mississippian archaeological deposits were found intact underneath most of the area to be affected by the bridge project. It was immediately clear that these deposits were fundamentally different from those in the downtown area; instead, they represent a huge residential zone. This residential area largely rests upon a broad north-south trending rise and is estimated to encompass an area of more than 100 acres.[21] As of July 2010, roughly 20 percent of the site area to be impacted by the project has been stripped. Within that area, 227 prehistoric structures have been excavated, along with 480 storage pits and 22 marker-post pits.[22] Based on topography and the area remaining to be excavated, it is estimated that as many as 300 to 400 additional structures will eventually be uncovered and excavated. This represents the largest contiguous slice of a Mississippian city ever excavated, and should provide rich data regarding the emergence and development of this civilization.

One of the most significant discoveries so far is that most of the dwellings and other features date from the very earliest part of the Mississippian period (1050–1100 CE), which was almost entirely absent in the downtown area. This also means that both East St. Louis and Cahokia were developing simultaneously. Our preliminary population estimates indicate

that at least 3,000 people lived there at that time.[23] The artifacts recovered from this residential neighborhood reflect the typical remains of Mississippian daily life. Community plans were often characterized by the presence of large marker posts. These posts were generally pulled a few decades later, reflecting changes in the neighborhood plan. Very often, buildings were erected over the former post locations.

From 1100 to 1200 CE, the time when downtown East St. Louis was being built, the residential zone seems to have witnessed a sharp reduction in population by perhaps one-half to two-thirds. This decline is consistent with those witnessed by other Mississippian cities in the area (including Cahokia) reflecting a trend towards decentralization of the populations away from cities

and into more rural settings.[24] One interesting find from the 12th-century residential zone consisted of a few pieces of distinctive pottery that were made by people of the Great Plains "Mill Creek" culture from western Iowa. Only a few other examples of this pottery have been found before in this region, but they all remind us that Cahokia and her subordinate cities were the center of socioeconomic power in an ancient Midwest that drew people of many different cultures together. Another rare find is a 3.5-inch-tall stone figurine that was found on the floor of a structure that had burned to the ground (Figures 4 and 5). Luckily, although the back of this statuette was charred, it had not been heated to the point of cracking. It also narrowly avoided being churned to the surface several decades ago when a trench for drain tile was dug right next

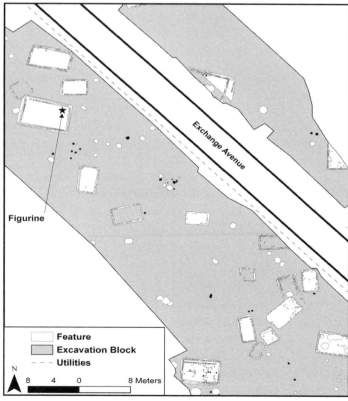

Figure 4: A Portion of the Residential Zone showing the Figurine Location. Galloy image

to it. Made of Missouri flint clay (a soft stone that is easily carved), the figurine depicts a kneeling female who is holding a cup or dipper fashioned from a large marine snail shell. A handful of similar flint clay statues have been found at nearby Mississippian sites. The symbolism of these other figurines, which depict supernatural females, evoke fertility and life renewal themes and were typically found in ritually burned temples.[25]

No occupation of this residential zone appears to have lasted beyond 1200, which is around the same time that the downtown area was also abandoned. So, what led to the demise of prehistoric East St. Louis? At present, this question is extremely difficult— if not impossible—to answer definitively. Although Cahokia was also continuing to experience a decline in population, it did cross the 1200 CE threshold with some of its population intact. Ominously, however, this is also around the time when Cahokia constructed an enormous defensive palisade around its civic-ceremonial core surrounding Monk's Mound and when East St. Louis built its own palisade. Also around the same time, villages in the northern part of the region erected their own fortifications.[26] Together, this evidence indicates that Mississippian settlements at around 1200 CE faced deadly serious threats, possibly from groups that lived to the north.

In this context, it is not hard to imagine that warfare may have hastened East St. Louis' demise. This has been suggested before by others, because the elite storage hut compound in the downtown area was

destroyed in a conflagration that occurred at around that time.[27] From the stockyards residential zone, several additional contemporaneous structures had also burned down. In both cases, there was evidence that some people continued to occupy the site, especially the downtown area, but this appears to have been relatively short lived, perhaps no more than 10 to 20 years. This evidence tantalizingly suggests that the ancient city was struck a fatal blow in a successful raid, but more supporting details are needed to say this with greater confidence. If such were the case, some of the population might have relocated to small rural villages and farmsteads, but it seems plausible that most would have abandoned the region altogether.

After East St. Louis was vacated, nature began the long process of transforming its mounds and plazas into earthen ruins. Erosion started to reshape the tallest of the mounds, and grasses and trees likely took hold in the plazas and residential neighborhoods. Nevertheless, Mississippians continued to have a significant presence in the region. Cahokia remained occupied, although by this time it was reduced to around a few thousand people.[28] This rendered prehistoric East St. Louis an abandoned ruin for two centuries before the last Mississippians left the region and the Oneota people began filtering in from the north. When the French began to settle the area in the late 17th century, they encountered bands of Illini Indians who were not related to the Mississippian masters of only a few centuries before.

Ironically, one of the Illini tribes, the Cahokia, lent its name to the Mississippian Leviathan.

In 1811, Henry Marie Brackenridge provided the first description of the Mississippian mounds at the place where East St. Louis would later emerge.

He recounted:

I crossed the Mississippi at St. Louis, and after passing through the wood which borders the river … entered an extensive open plain. In 15 minutes, I found myself in the midst of a group of mounds, mostly of a circular shape, and at a distance, resembling enormous haystacks scattered through a meadow … Around me, I counted forty-five mounds, or pyramids, besides a great number of small artificial elevations; these mounds form something more than a semicircle, about a mile in extent, the open space on the river.[29]

Decades later, due to its riverfront location and the economic shadow cast by St. Louis—similar to the one once cast by Cahokia—East St. Louis would rise again, to

Figure 5: The Exchange Avenue Figurine. Galloy image

eventually claim its position as one of America's foremost industrial cities. In the process, East St. Louis would also become something completely unique in American cultural history: an ancient city that was completely overprinted, but not totally destroyed, by a modern one.[30] Will this be repeated in 200, 500 or 1,000 years? The odds seem to be in East St. Louis favor.

End Notes:

1. James B. Griffin, "Eastern North American Archaeology: A Summary," *Science* 156, no. 3772 (1967); ———, "Changing Concepts of the Prehistoric Mississippian Cultures of the Eastern United States," in *Alabama and the Borderlands: From Prehistory to Statehood*, ed. R. Reid Badger and L. A. Clayton (Tuscaloosa: University of Alabama Press, 1985); Bruce D. Smith, "Archaeology of the Southeastern United States: From Dalton to De Soto, 10,500-500 B.P.," *Advances in World Archaeology* 5 (1986); Vincas P. Steponaitis, "Prehistoric Archaeology in the Southeastern United States, 1970-1985," *Annual Review of Anthropology* 15 (1986).

2. The archaeology of Cahokia is a vast subject and there is no shortage of books on the subject. Up to date introductory works include William R. Iseminger, *Cahokia Mounds: America's First City* (Charleston, South Carolina: History Press, 2010), and Timothy R. Pauketat, *Cahokia: Ancient America's Great City on the Mississippi* (New York: Viking, 2009). More scholarly recent summaries include books such as George R. Milner, *The Cahokia Chiefdom: The Archaeology of a Mississippian Society* (Washington, DC: Smithsonian Institution Press, 1998), and Timothy R. Pauketat, *Ancient Cahokia and the Mississippians* (Cambridge: Cambridge University Press, 2004).

3. Pauketat, *Ancient Cahokia and the Mississippians*.

4. Ibid. With or without political integration, I propose that this cluster of cities bears some resemblance to a modern megalopolis, similar to America's northeastern seaboard, albeit on a much smaller scale.

5. John E. Kelly, "The Archaeology of the East St. Louis Mound Center: Past and Present," *Illinois Archaeology* 6 (1994).

6. Charles Rau, "Indian Pottery," in *Annual Report of the Smithsonian Institution for 1866* (Washington, D.C.: Smithsonian Institution, 1867).

7. John J. R. Patrick, "Map of East St. Louis Mounds," (St. Louis: Missouri Historical Society, 1880).

8. Kelly, "The Archaeology of the East St. Louis Mound Center: Past and Present."

9. Charles Rau, "A Deposit of Agricultural Flint Implements in Southern Illinois," in *Annual Report of the Smithsonian Institution for 1868* (Washington, D.C.: Smithsonian Institution, 1869).

10. Warren K. Moorehead, "The Cahokia Mounds: Part I, a Report of Progress on the Exploration of the Cahokia Group," *University of Illinois Bulletin* 21, no. 6 (1923).:39–40

11. ———, "The Cahokia Mounds: Part I, Explorations of 1922, 1924, and 1927," *University of Illinois Bulletin* 26, no. 6 (1929).:25

12. Kelly, "The Archaeology of the East St. Louis Mound Center: Past and Present."

13. Fred A. Finney, "Historical Background and the History of Site Investigations," in *The Archaeology of the East St. Louis Mound Center, Part II: The Northside Excavations*, ed. Andrew C. Fortier, *Transportation Archaeological Research Reports No. 22* (Illinois Transportation Archaeological Research Program, University of Illinois at Urbana–Champaign, 2007).

14. Andrew C. Fortier, ed., *The Archaeology of the East St. Louis Mound Center, Part II: The Northside Excavations*, Transportation Archaeological Research Reports No. 22 (Illinois Transportation Archaeological Research Program, University of Illinois at Urbana–Champaign, 2007), Timothy R. Pauketat, ed., *The Archaeology of the East St. Louis Mound Center, Part I: The Southside Excavations*, Transportation Archaeological Research Reports No. 21 (Illinois Transportation Archaeological Research Program, University of Illinois at Urbana–Champaign, 2005).

15. Unfortunately, this cannot be said for the St. Louis Mound Center directly across the Mississippi River. In St. Louis, nineteenth-century construction leveled nearly all of the mounds and the areas underneath and around them were largely borrowed away. Recent archaeological investigations in this area by the Missouri Department of Transportation suggest that these deeper impacts erased the ancient city at St. Louis.

16. Finney, "Historical Background and the History of Site Investigations.", Kelly, "The Archaeology of the East St. Louis Mound Center: Past and Present."

17. Joseph M. Galloy and Michael L. Kolb, "Transposed Mound Fill in the CSX Railyard, East St. Louis Mound Center (11S706)," *Illinois Archaeology* 20 (2008).

18. Fortier, ed., *The Archaeology of the East St. Louis Mound Center, Part II: The Northside Excavations*, Pauketat, ed., *The Archaeology of the East St. Louis Mound Center, Part I: The Southside Excavations.*

19. Galloy and Kolb, "Transposed Mound Fill in the CSX Railyard, East St. Louis Mound Center (11S706)."

20. ISAS is an intergovernmental program formed by the Illinois Department of Transportation and the University of Illinois to perform transportation-related archaeological work across the state.

21. Jeffery D. Kruchten and Joseph M. Galloy, "Uncovering the Early Cahokian Residential Zone at East St. Louis" (paper presented at the Annual Meeting of the Society for American Archaeology, St. Louis, Missouri, April 15–18, 2010).

22. The ISAS team has also been excavating several dozen privy (outhouse) vaults associated with people who lived around the stockyards between around 1880 and 1930. This work will open a window onto working-class life in the shadow of one of America's great industrial cities.

23. Kruchten and Galloy, "Uncovering the Early Cahokian Residential Zone at East St. Louis".

24. Timothy R. Pauketat and Neal H. Lopinot, "Cahokian Population Dynamics," in *Cahokia: Domination and Ideology in the Mississippian World*, ed. Timothy R. Pauketat and Thomas E. Emerson (Lincoln: University of Nebraska Press, 1997).

25. Thomas E. Emerson, Brad Koldehoff, and Timothy R. Pauketat, "Serpents, Female Deities, and Fertility Symbolism in the Early Cahokian Countryside," in *Mounds, Modoc, and Mesoamerica: Papers in Honor of Melvin L. Fowler*, ed. Steven R. Ahler, *Scientific Papers Series* (Springfield: Illinois State Museum, 2000).

26. Pauketat, *Ancient Cahokia and the Mississippians*.:148–149

27. Fortier, ed., *The Archaeology of the East St. Louis Mound Center, Part II: The Northside Excavations*, Pauketat, *Ancient Cahokia and the Mississippians.*

28. Pauketat and Lopinot, "Cahokian Population Dynamics."

29. Henry M. Brackenridge, *Views of Louisiana; Together with a Journal of a Voyage up the Missouri River, in 1811.* (Pittsburgh: Cramer, Spear, and Eichbaum, 1814).:187

30. Galloy and Kolb, "Transposed Mound Fill in the Csx Railyard, East St. Louis Mound Center (11s706)."

ACKNOWLEDGEMENTS

Nearly everything that we know about ancient East St. Louis is due to the Illinois Department of Transportation's unwavering commitment to the letter and spirit of the laws that protect our nation's cultural patrimony. IDOT's Chief Archaeologist Dr. John Walthall and the Illinois State Archaeological Survey's Director and Principal Investigator Dr. Thomas Emerson deserve special mention. Both have ably guided the East St. Louis investigations over the course of the last two decades. As with any large undertaking, there are scores of other individuals at IDOT and elsewhere who have made this work a success. For the sake of brevity, they cannot be mentioned individually but all have my heartfelt thanks. The figures accompanying this essay are provided courtesy of the Illinois State Archaeological Survey.

The Second Skyline: Downtown East St. Louis' Unique Architecture

Michael R. Allen

Preservation Research Office,

St. Louis, Missouri

In the first three decades of the twentieth century, two cities were growing rapidly on the banks of the Mississippi River below its confluence with the Missouri. With the fame and fortune of St. Louis already well assured, its neighbor across the river, East St. Louis, was an insurgent urban force. The emergence was staggering: in 1900, East St. Louis had a mere 29,734 residents, but by 1930 that number was 74,397. Such explosive growth brought with it full urbanization and development of the built environment on a massive scale. There is no surprise that at the pinnacle of East St. Louis' emergence as an important American city, it generated an architectural expression much different than that of St. Louis. But nonetheless, what signaled East St. Louis position as a financial and industrial center were impressive modern buildings: massive warehouses, mighty packing plants, foundries, office buildings, a hospital, churches and eventually a movie palace to rival the best in St. Louis.

Collinsville Avenue, c. 1915   Bowen Archives, SIUE

Between 1907 and 1928, downtown East St. Louis was remade from a modest city center into a central business district built on a scale anticipating future growth. The core of downtown East St. Louis gave rise to buildings of as much architectural refinement as contemporary buildings in St. Louis, but with a distinctly local mark. Few of the buildings built by East St. Louis' elite that came to proclaim the city's emergence were to be designed by St. Louis architects, despite proximity and the wide regional recognition that St. Louis architects were some of the best in the country. Instead, East St. Louis' embrace of urban modernity would be shaped by local designers like Albert B. Frankel and J.W. Kennedy, as well as Kansas City's Boller Brothers. Even when St. Louis architects were used, their contributions were largely omitted from the popular press, which freed them to to produce original, not derivative, works. As a result, the architecture of downtown East St. Louis shows signs of open experimentation, like the Murphy Building's bakery brick façade, the Ainad Temple's boldly Moorish style, and the Sullivanesque ornamentation of the Spivey Building. Although some of its commercial expressions were occasionally awkward, early twentieth century East St. Louis architecture eventually developed against the strong Beaux Arts influence prevalent in St. Louis to develop a unique style very much its own.

By 1930, downtown East St. Louis could boast a modern air-conditioned movie palace seating over 1,700; a hotel capable of

hosting statewide conventions; a skyscraper employing the design tenets of the progressive Prairie School; a large and modern hospital; well-designed banks; office buildings of all sizes and styles; a beautiful City Hall; department stores and other retailers; and even a filling station with banks on pumps facing two major arteries. Surrounding downtown were other hallmarks of modernity, including fireproof warehouses and factories of reinforced concrete, elegant brick churches with graceful spires, beautiful mansions in revival styles and tasteful bungalows for working-class homeowners. And if visitors to East St. Louis approached the city from the west, they came over the Eads Bridge, one of the hallmarks of modern architectural engineering, and would catch a view of the region's powerful new Cahokia Power Plant. Downtown East St. Louis had all of the architectural marks of an emerging major city.

Although the city had started the twentieth century moving toward greatness, fate would lead East St. Louis in another direction, and that direction has been the subject of much study. Consequently, history has not recorded much information about the architecture of modern East St. Louis. Many volumes discuss the industrial build-up of the city, abandonment, the Model City renewal program and other aspects of East. Louis' built environment, but none chronicle the architectural history of a city that built a second skyline at St. Louis. This essay attempts to sketch a partial history of one aspect of that history by examining some of the major downtown buildings

and the pattern of architectural distinction that emerged as the city built up a modern downtown. Such a history may prove useful in the near future, since East St. Louis retains much of its landscape of architectural modernity. Downtown East St. Louis has lost many buildings, but the major works of the early twentieth century still stand with few exceptions. The two-block run of Collinsville Avenue from Broadway north to Martin Luther King Drive is nearly intact, providing a hopeful sense of the layers of past density. The architectural history here exists as past, but the buildings exist as present and, with stewardship and imagination, as future.

A Modern Downtown Emerges

The May 14, 1907 edition of the *St. Louis Republic* devoted the front page to the rise of East St. Louis. The title of the article was "Industrial East St. Louis" and featured a panoramic photograph of the city as well as picturesque renderings of tall buildings and smoke plumes rising to form a stylized skyline.[1] The article called East St. Louis the "Second City of Illinois" and noted its industrial prowess. However, the images chosen to illustrate the article depicted not industrial work, laborers or even individual factories. The images showed the Eads Bridge and an envisioned skyline that was as much metropolitan as it was industrial. These perceptions from the larger neighbor matched East St. Louis' own aspirations.

Certainly, industry was the key to the city's identity and economy.

The completion of the Eads Bridge in 1874 gave East St. Louis a modern entrance, but its chief purpose was movement of goods. Factories and the National City stockyards were the chief sources of local pride and regional recognition. Physical development of the city proper to that point was modest. Moreover, the downtown had a distinct obstacle, too: the former Bloody Island. Bloody Island, scene of at least four major duels, was a sandbar in the Mississippi River close to the bank at Illinoistown. In 1837, Lt. Robert E. Lee, working for the Army Corps of Engineers, devised a plan to gradually divert waters away from the channel between Bloody Island and Illinoistown, thereby dredging the riverbank next to St. Louis. By 1856, the island was attaching to the bank, and by the time that East St. Louis was incorporated in 1861 the land was becoming the city's riverfront. Yet the land was prone to flooding and unsuitable for extensive construction. Consequently, East St. Louis' commercial heart was somewhat distant from St. Louis' – a remove of great consequence today.

Nonetheless, development of downtown East St. Louis rose after the opening of the Eads Bridge. A pivotal architectural moment was the completion of the East St. Louis City Hall (demolished) in 1900. The symmetrical four-story building was a grand structure in the French Renaissance Revival style, with a high mansard roof, tall central cupola and limestone walls. Architecturally, City Hall was the finest building built in East St. Louis to that point. The construction was during the

administration of Mayor Malbern Stephens, whose commitment to the public good brought East St. Louis into a new era of respectability.[2] City Hall was a fitting home for a government that would steward development of a great American city. The style and plan, however, were not unlike that of St. Louis City Hall, completed in 1898. East St. Louis City Hall was a fine accomplishment for a young city, but its design showed that it was still under the clear architectural influence of St. Louis.

Subsequent years saw construction of two stone bank buildings, the Union Trust Company Building at the northwest corner of Collinsville and Missouri Avenues (1901), and the Southern Illinois Trust Company Building at 313 E. Broadway adjacent to City Hall (1903, demolished). These two buildings showed that East St. Louis banks had sufficient wealth to build architect-designed, stone-faced classical buildings that conveyed a necessary sense of security. The banking lobbies were tall, voluminous spaces with mezzanine levels and large windows. At the same time, these

buildings showed limits to the city's wealth. The two-story buildings provided floor space to the bank operations only. The banks lacked the capital to fund extra floors of speculative office space, as their St. Louis counterparts often did.

The next major downtown building, The Cahokia Building (1907) provided a breakthrough even though it demonstrated continued architectural linkage to St. Louis. (The building is now known as the First National Bank Building.) The six-story building at the northeast corner of Collinsville and Missouri Avenues was East St. Louis' first tall office building, and it was also the home of the First National Bank that built it. The architects were Mauran, Russell & Garden, one of St. Louis' best-regarded and most prolific firms of the period. John L. Mauran, Ernest J. Russell and Edward G. Garden were architects employed in the St. Louis office of Shepley, Rutan and Coolidge, successors to the office of master architect H.H. Richardson. After Shepley, Rutan and Coolidge closed the St. Louis office in 1900, Mauran organized a new firm with

The new city hall, 1900   Bowen Archives, SIUE

his colleagues.[3] The firm's earliest work included a prominent industrial design, the Laclede Power Company, built in 1901 on the St. Louis riverfront. The firm's quick rise parallels Mauran's acumen as a leader among St. Louis architects; Mauran was elected president of the St. Louis chapter of the American Institute of Architects in 1902 and 1903.[4] By 1906, when hired to design the Cahokia Building, the firm was enjoying the completion of the Butler Brothers Warehouse at 1717 Olive Street in St. Louis, a large reinforced concrete structure

The Cahokia Building, c. 1915
Bowen Archives, SIUE

that enjoyed national attention for its structural application of concrete. Thus, the Cahokia Building's design provenance was both a show of the city's importance and a reminder of its status as an architectural satellite of St. Louis. While East St. Louis relied on a prominent St. Louis firm for the design of the Cahokia Building, the accomplishment was

not second-rate. The building had an interesting scale, with the wide elevation of seven bays facing Collinsville Avenue and a single bay facing Missouri Avenue. The base was clad in buff terra cotta above a gray granite base that contained the first two levels. The corner had granite entrances on each face, and each bay consisted of a large round-arch opening with keystone and foliated surround. Single windows filled the openings that included both floors, a feature which was echoed in the design of the Union Trust Building across the street. Above this refined base were four floors of offices adorned in brick adorned only by band courses above the windows. At the top, dark bricks created a diamond pattern under a projecting bracketed terra cotta cornice topped by acanthus arrangements. The bank expanded the building to the west in 1927 with four bays built that mimic the original section save the brick pattern work.

The Cahokia Building fits well among Mauran, Russell & Garden's other works. There was a harmonious interplay between Beaux Arts principles articulated in pliant terra cotta and the modern commercial form articulated through simple brick masonry. The firm's designs from the early 1900s exploited the expressive range of simple masonry, often using contrasting brick colors—many newly available due to innovations in the brick industry—to create patterns. Yet the firm maintained a classical sensibility and did not boldly embrace modern design trends. Mauran, Russell & Garden's work was well-suited for East St. Louis,

which still had to prove itself as an important city. Yet the city was a modern industrial city, and its downtown architecture would soon shift away from classically-influenced design. The architects leading the way would be the city's own.

The Murphy Building: Developing an Architecture of East St. Louis Own

Completion of the Cahokia Building changed the face of East St. Louis, and provided the impetus for rapid development of the downtown core. Collinsville Avenue overtook Main Street and Missouri Avenue as the city's primary downtown commercial artery, although the entire downtown was full of the hustle and bustle of early modern life. In 1909, the G.C. Murphy Construction Company announced plans to build a second modern office building on Collinsville Avenue, across the street from the Cahokia Building. The company was the city's largest builder and had acquired a substantial downtown site. There, the G.C. Murphy

A. B. Frankel, 1923
Bowen Archives, SIUE

Construction Company would build its eponymous building, a six-story modern office building with a gleaming white facade. The architect selected for this major edifice was immigrant A.B. Frankel of East St. Louis, who had never designed a major commercial building before.

Albert Brur Frankel (usually billed as A.B. Frankel) was born in Stockholm, Sweden in 1868. His parents immigrated to the United States in 1871 and later moved to East St. Louis.[5] Albert Frankel attended the University of Illinois, where he studied architecture. Upon graduation, Frankel spent three years traveling in Texas before returning to East St. Louis. However, city directories list the young architect as a draftsman in 1891 and as an architect (office at 636 N. 8th Street) in 1892. Frankel's office in 1909 was at 206 Collinsville Avenue. His work was varied, but included numerous major public buildings in East St. Louis and southern Illinois. Frankel designed Irving, Horace Mann and Webster Annex schools as well as the Washington Place United Presbyterian, First Methodist and Plymouth Congregational churches.[6] Surviving work outside of East St. Louis can be found in Hillsboro and Waterloo, Illinois as well as the house at #4 Lewis Place in St. Louis. While Frankel's career is largely not documented, it is certainly worthy of further historical appraisal.

Perhaps Frankel's lack of experience with large commercial design trends spurred his creativity with the Murphy Building, or perhaps the client wanted to show off its own abilities as a builder. Whatever the cause, Frankel had created one of the region's best-proportioned and coherently articulated office buildings when construction was finished in 1910. The classicism of the ornamentation was very freely selected and employed, in contrast to the restraint widely seen in contemporary St. Louis office buildings. The Murphy Building's front elevation was clad in white bakery brick, a modern material not widely used for cladding large buildings.

The brick was a fine backdrop for delicately detailed buff terra cotta. The entrance had an arched window at the second floor with cartouche at center, and two female figures that projected out of brackets on each side to support massive blocks under light standards. Admittedly, the entrance was somewhat ostentatious, but otherwise terra cotta was used smartly. The third through fifth floors were

Murphy Building, c. 1911
Bowen Archives, SIUE

articulated as an arcade, with recessed spandrels, Corinthian capitals on the piers and elaborate arch hoods with keystones. Terra cotta was used to surround the sixth floor and to form the projecting cornice with foliated brackets.

Frankel maximized the floor volume by utilizing narrow light wells – one at center and two at the ends of the buildings. The walls of these wells were clad in bakery brick to amplify daylight. In form and scale, the Murphy Building was typical for its time. Stylistically, the Classical Revival ornamentation was also within the bounds of convention. Yet the use of bakery brick on a large scale for an outside elevation and the sensitivity to the massing of the front elevation gave the Murphy Building a definite modern character. But the real importance of the Murphy Building was that it showed that East St. Louis had clearly come into its own architecturally. It demonstrated that the city could build up in a unique way using strong local talent. As East St. Louis forged an architecture of its own, Frankel would lead the way and would design the city's crowning architectural achievement seventeen years later.

Snubbing Ittner: Downplaying the St. Louis Connection

World War I interrupted construction around the nation, and East St. Louis' growth slowed somewhat. Yet major projects downtown resumed with the construction of the National Catholic Community House at 422 St. Louis Avenue in 1919. The completion of this building started the boom of the 1920s construction that would bring downtown East St. Louis to its most modern and completed state. Perhaps what most clearly articulated the state of East St. Louis architecture during this time was the construction of Union Electric Company's mighty Cahokia Power Plant which was largely completed in 1924 (though not fully completed until 1938). Although it was actually located south of the city limits, it was visually very much a part of the city. Designed by Mauran, Russell & Crowell (successor to Mauran, Russell & Garden), the gigantic power plant with its six tall smokestacks was a soaring structure that drew the eyes of St. Louis eastward.

While the huge Union Electric plant was the largest construction project on the East Side in the twenties, there was much new commercial and institutional architecture to see as well. The

Concept drawing of the Cahokia Power Plant, c. 1923
(the actual construction had only six smokestacks) Bowen Archives, SIUE

East St. Louis Journal would have at least one article on construction or architecture per week from 1920 through 1928, and the citywide details are far too vast to even summarize here. What happened downtown was happening all over East St. Louis. Ironically, the one project that signaled the city's desire to stake out its own architectural style was a project with a strong St. Louis connection, the Ainad Temple at 615 St. Louis Avenue on the western end of downtown. Completed in 1923, the lavish temple remains an architectural jewel of extraordinary imagination. Like fraternal clubs in urban centers around the nation enjoying membership growth, the local Grand Lodge of Ancient Free and Accepted Masons needed larger quarters. After raising $550,000 for construction, purchasing a full city block for construction and commissioning a design, the Masonic lodge laid the cornerstone on November 24, 1922.[7] Work was completed by October 1923, and the dedication ceremony that took place on October 26, 1923 included a parade of 5,000 masons from around the state.[8]

The large building was designed in an exotic Moorish Revival style unlike anything seen on such a scale in the region. (St. Louis' large exotic Moolah Temple would not be completed until 1925 and, although built on a larger budget and grander scale, shows the influence of the earlier temple across the river.) The Ainad Temple was clad in contrasting bands of red and dark red brick and its form was a rather prosaic expression of the layout inside. In contrast, the entrance was dazzling: an arcade of yellow polychromatic terra cotta under a red tile roof with copper cupola, with a recessed entrance wall whose base was clad in polychromatic blue terra cotta tiles. Terra cotta elsewhere

formed arches of Moorish patterns, and at the top of the shaped parapet on the auditorium was a terra cotta scimitar and star. The interior was equally impressive, with a 3,600 seat auditorium replete with a stage measuring 78 by 30 feet, 2,200 seat lower-level banquet hall, a private dining rooms and various offices and meeting rooms. The auditorium had a three-manual electric pipe organ that cost $15,000.[9]

While the temple was the most magnificent piece of architecture that East St. Louis had produced by the early twenties, it showed that the city was still not quite ready to produce its own style. To design this beautiful structure, East St. Louis had turned to the noted St. Louis architect, William B. Ittner. (1864-1936). Ittner

designed the Ainad Temple in collaboration with Albert B. Frankel but was largely responsible for the exterior design and spatial program. Ittner who was one of the most prolific and celebrated St. Louis architects of the time served as Commissioner of St. Louis Public Schools from 1897 until 1910. The position made Ittner responsible for the design of every new school building and several additions during that period. Ittner acquired a national reputation having designed many noted St. Louis schools, such as McKinley and Soldan High Schools. In his school designs, Ittner introduced to American educational architecture the use of ample natural light, large hallways and open classroom plans. Once he returned to private practice, Ittner continued to design for the

The Ainad Temple, 2010 Powell Photo

St. Louis district but also designed schools across the country in cities ranging from Washington, D.C. to Long View, Washington. Altogether Ittner designed 86 schools for the St. Louis Public Schools and over 230 throughout the United States.[10] In addition to his work with schools, Ittner had also established a reputation for designing impressive fraternal buildings, such as the Missouri Athletic Club Building (1916, with George F.A. Brueggemann) and the Scottish Rite Cathedral (1921) in St. Louis. His Moorish Revival Shriner's Hospital (1923) is a peer in style and date to the Ainad Temple.

Given the tremendous reputation that Ittner enjoyed in his own time, there was some hubris in the *East St. Louis Journal*'s coverage of the Ainad Temple. Trying to minimize the St. Louis connection, the *Journal* ignored Ittner's contribution. His name did not appear once in the paper's coverage of the project—not when the building was announced, not at the cornerstone laying and not at completion. On the dedication date, the building received a full section of the newspaper with the proclamation "City's Finest Building Being Dedicated Today." A lengthy account of construction, "All Work on Ainad Temple Performed by Local Crafts," credits the building to contractor Jesse I. Gedney and reports in great detail the costs and materials of the building. Although the article listed the suppliers of materials in great detail and even the companies that issued the insurance policies for construction, it never gave the the name of the Ainad Temple's architect. By contrast, when officials dedicated St. Mary's Hospital at 129 N. 8th Street in 1926, the *Journal* published a rendering of the building with local architect J.W. Kennedy's name and praised the architect's skill in an accompanying article.[11] Kennedy was skilled but not even as prominent as Frankel, let alone Ittner. While who was credited and who was not may seem rather insignificant, it clearly showed that the city was at a point in its development that it had a desire to come into its own architecturally. The final three major downtown buildings of the 1920s certainly demonstrated that it was indeed ready.

The City's First Modern Hotel

Completed in 1927, the Broadview Hotel was the only large hotel ever built in East St. Louis. Standing seven stories tall and having 260 rooms as well as a large dining room and ballroom, the Broadview helped solidify the status of East St. Louis as

The Broadview Hotel, c. 1940   Bowen Archives, SIUE

Illinois's largest downstate city. In 1926, a group of investors organized the Central Hotel Corporation in order to develop a large hotel in downtown East St. Louis.[12] The leading hotel in East St. Louis was the National Hotel at the Stockyards, remote from downtown. The developers purchased a site between Fourth and Fifth streets on the north side of Broadway in the heart of downtown. At that point, East St. Louis lacked a modern, large hotel capable of hosting conventions. The city's commercial activity and position as the regional economic center of southern Illinois demanded a grand hotel. The March 28, 1926 issue of the *East St. Louis Journal* carried the bold headline

"East St. Louis to Have 260-Room Hotel." The sub-title was "Home to Future Conventions."[13] The article contained a rendering of a seven-story fireproof hotel in the Classical Revival style designed by Widmer Engineering Company of St. Louis. The cost would be $1,350,000. Reeb proudly told

the newspaper that "[t]he hotel is a cinch" and that the answer to Central Hotel Corporation's issuance of stock was quick. [14] The hotel was relatively modest compared to large hotels in bigger cities at the time, but it had parallels to "economy" hotels being built in other cities, including St. Louis.

Notable features mentioned in the article were the fact that each room would have its own bath, that there would be a rooftop garden open to the public, that the hotel would have a large ballroom on the top floor and a restaurant. These were all expectations not just of guests but of those using the hotel as a meeting space for dinners and larger affairs. Reeb made it clear that he wanted to rectify East St. Louis' inability to provide such entertainment, which made it difficult to attract business conventions. Major cities had to offer such amenities to lure convention groups looking for hotels that could offer in-house entertainment. The city was keeping pace with the Broadview

investors' ambitions, however, because that same day's newspaper contained an article mentioning that there had been $340,000 worth of reported construction costs on building permits issued in East St. Louis in March 1928.[15]

The choice of the Widmer Engineering Company to design the Broadview is odd given that the company's largest achievements were structural rather than architectural. Up until this time Widmer's greatest accomplishment was generating the structural specifications of the Railway Exchange Building in St. Louis (1913, Mauran, Russell and Garden), which at completion was the largest reinforced concrete structure in the world besides the Panama Canal.[16] While cost certainly may have been an issue behind the use of Widmer Engineering Company, the result was that the city's major hotel bore little resemblance in style or massing to any of its contemporaries in St. Louis. Again, East St. Louis owners employed St. Louis designers to

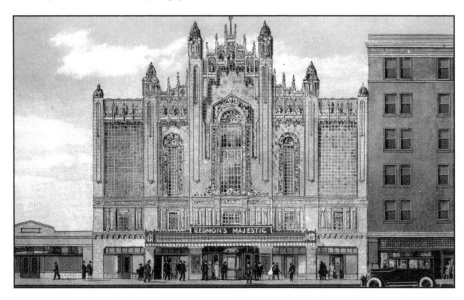

Illustration from invitation to Majestic Theater's opening, February 25, 1928
Bowen Archives, SIUE

create a distinct architectural work rather than to mimic a design seen across the river.

The vision of the investors was realized when the Broadview opened on October 5, 1927 to host the annual meeting of the prestigious Illinois State Convention of Realtors.[17] The grand opening took place on October 15, 1927, and by the end of the year the large Cahokia Room dining hall was operational. Advertisements for the hotel in 1928 list the Cahokia Room, a rathskeller, private dining rooms and the 600-person ballroom as amenities along with free parking for guests.[18] While it was a striking fulfillment of East St. Louis' ambitions, the hotel opened at the onset of the 1929 stock market crash. East St. Louis would not build another large hotel until the Casino Queen Hotel opened nearly 75 years later.

A Modern Movie Palace

A tragic fire led to East St. Louis' construction of a modern movie palace on Collinsville Avenue. In June 1927, the Majestic Theatre adjacent to the Murphy Building caught fire, and owner Harry Redmon had it demolished.[19] Redmon seized the opportunity to build a new "Million Dollar Majestic," which was announced in the *Journal* by June 26, 1927. On July 10, 1927, the paper published a rendering of the new theater.[20] The elaborate new theater in the Spanish Gothic style would be taller than the Murphy Building. Like movie palaces being built around the country, the Majestic would be exotic in form and ornament. There would be air conditioning (not installed until 1929 but part of the original

plans), a marble lobby, and seats for 1,700 people. Along with a modern hospital, the new hotel, tall office buildings and the Ainad Temple, East St. Louis would now have a fine modern movie theater.

The design came from a nationally-renowned architectural firm whose work consisted exclusively of theaters, the Boller Brothers of Kansas City Originally from St. Joseph, Missouri Brothers Carl (1868-1946) and Robert Boller (1887-1962) established their firm in Kansas City. After working for several years for other architects in Kansas City, Carl opened his own office specializing in theaters in 1902. The much younger Robert came to work for Carl in 1906, and by 1921 there was so much work for the firm nationally that Carl moved to Los Angeles to supervise a new office there. Robert was responsible for the firm's vast portfolio of Midwestern commissions, including the Majestic.[21] Several of the theaters that the firm designed in the period used the same Spanish Gothic style and similar massing as the Majestic, but few of the over 100 theaters attributed to the firm made such dramatic use of the polychromatic terra cotta that made the Majestic so distinctive.

East St. Louis had no problem giving the firm proper credit, in contrast to the earlier treatment of William B. Ittner. Perhaps coincidentally, before the Majestic, the Boller Brothers never had a major St. Louis-area commission. But because this was their first commission in the St. Louis region, the national reputation of Boller Brothers & Co. allowed East St. Louis to enjoy an architectural achievement that, although not

the work of a local mind, avoided any semblance of reliance on St. Louis. Furthermore, by introducing the concept of an "atmospheric" house to the region, where the ceiling of a theater was lit to simulate dusk at the start of a movie, nightfall and night time during the run, and morning at the end, the Majestic further enhanced East St. Louis' reputation as an architectural star in its own right.

A. T. Spivey, 1923
Bowen Archives, SIUE

The Murphy Building and the Majestic Theatre remain delightfully contrasting neighbors. The Majestic now has lost its original upper spires and its marquee, but most of its facade is as intact as it was upon completion. Six rising piers of buff terra cotta form pinnacles and frame the bays. The center bay projects and rises above the others. A projecting terra cotta surround, composed of detailed Spanish patterns, frames two central windows. Exotic, colorful polychromatic terra cotta clads the bays. The inside bays have plain tiles of nearly-pastel shades, which had not been used in the St. Louis region prior to construction of the Majestic. The outer bays' tiles, however, are even more unusual: grids of pattern blocks that utilize multiple colors on each block. The building's style may have been a revival, but the terra cotta patterns and colors represents the height of the development of the material – just as the Murphy Building's bakery brick had represented the height of brick masonry. The Million Dollar Majestic was yet another step on the city's march to build a downtown of architectural distinction.

At Last, A Skyscraper City:

The Spivey Building Rises

The Great Depression would end significant twentieth century development of downtown East St. Louis, but the city built its first skyscraper before the boom ended. Allan T. Spivey, owner of the *East St. Louis Journal*, enjoyed a record profit of $80,000 in 1927 due to increased circulation of the paper.[22] Spivey sought to use some of his wealth to give the city its tallest building as symbol of his publishing power and the city's projected rise into the tiers of major American cities. Spivey purchased a site on Missouri Avenue across the alley from the Murphy Building and hired its architect, A.B. Frankel, to design the new skyscraper.

A.B. Frankel's intriguing design showed the architect's evolution in the nearly twenty years since he designed the Murphy Building. Frankel envisioned a tall, narrow 13-story steel-framed building with very straightforward

fenestration arranged in a simple grid. The first two floors would measure 80 by 132 feet, but the upper levels formed a shaft measuring 80 by 46 feet—truly a very narrow building.[23] Because of Frankel's use of dimensions, what could have been a bland boxy building attained a soaring dramatic form. Frankel gave the building the three-part division of a base, shaft and crown

Spivey Building, 2010
Powell Photo

popularized by the Chicago School of architecture as well as a soaring vertical emphasis. The stark dark brick body was punctuated by buff terra cotta spandrels between the windows. The top two floors carried seven projecting brick and terra cotta piers that form pinnacles above the roofline connected by balustrade. The ornamentation, especially the spandrel panels and the cornice above the second floor, was clearly inspired by the work of Louis Sullivan. Yet the

geometry of the crowning piers and balustrade was almost Gothic in character, and little about the building form shared much in common with Sullivan's work. Frankel's building was a pragmatic essay in emphasizing height through the use of ornament, and seemed to share a vocabulary with early Art Deco skyscrapers. For instance, the Southwestern Bell Building (1925) and the Missouri Pacific Building (1928), both setback skyscrapers with Art Deco elements in St. Louis designed by Mauran, Russell & Crowell, make use of projecting piers that rise to form pinnacles in a manner similar to the Spivey Building.

The End of the Era

Although the Spivey Building was only thirteen stories tall—much shorter than what would pass as a tall building in 1920s St. Louis— the building emphatically was a skyscraper in every inch of its rise. The Spivey Building's strong verticality became the peak rather than the precedent, though, since no taller building was ever built in East St. Louis. The East St. Louis building boom that remade the city's downtown into a modern urban business district ended with the Great Depression, and never resumed.

While subsequent years have removed much of the downtown urban fabric, most of the city's proudest architectural accomplishments still stand. Although East St. Louis never became a peer of its neighbor across the river, there is no doubt that the city produced a second skyline of high architectural merit and distinct identity. The range of buildings exhibited important tendencies in commercial design of the period, including use of modern ceramics, plain expression of form, development of exotic styles like Moorish and Spanish revivals and the influence of Louis Sullivan and the Prairie School. Without established precedents and lacking architects with elite education, East St. Louis between 1900 and 1930 was in some ways more open to experimentation in commercial design than was St. Louis. The major downtown buildings that remain continue to give the city an indelible character, and their preservation is advantageous as East St. Louis reinvents itself. The collection of remaining downtown buildings ensures that the city will never be lost to the eyes of the world.

End Notes:

1. Andrew Theising, *Made in USA: East St. Louis, the Rise and Fall of an Industrial River Town*. St. Louis: Virginia Publishing, 2003. p. 96.

2. Ibid., p 87 and p. 198.

3. Carolyn Hewes Toft, "John Lawrence Mauran, FAIA (1866-1933)." *Landmarks Association of St. Louis* <http://www.landmarks-stl.org/architects/bio/john_lawrence_mauran/>. 1 July 2010.

4. Ibid.

5. Newman Bateman et al, *Historical Encyclopedia of Illinois* (Volume 2). Chicago: Munsell Publishing Company, 1907. p. 1015.

6. Ibid.

7. Bill Nunes, *East St. Louis, Illinois: Year-by-Year Illustrated History*. Dexter, Mich.: Thomson-Shore, Inc., 1998. p. 146

8. "Dykeman Praises Ainad at Dedication." *East St. Louis Journal*, 26 October 1923. 1.

9. "Oriental Architecture of Ainad Temple Fit Setting for Nobles in Far East Garb." *East St. Louis Journal*, 26 October 1923. 1-A.

10. Henry F. Withey and Elsie Rathburn Withey. *Biographical Dictionary of American Architects*. Los Angeles, Calif.: New Age Publishing Co., 1956, p. 316.

11. "1,600 Bricks Used." *East St. Louis Journal*, 19 September 1926. 5-D.

12. "Hotel Company Makes Call for First Payments," *East St. Louis Journal*, 9 April 1926.

13. "East St. Louis to Have 260-Room Hotel." *East St. Louis Journal*, 28 March 1926.

14. Ibid.

15. "March Permits List $340,000 Construction," *East St. Louis Journal*, 28 March 1926.

16. Ibid, 8.14.

17. "Broadview to Be Opened at 5:00 P.M. Today," *East St. Louis Journal*, 5 October 1927.

18. Advertisements in *East St. Louis Daily Journal*, 1928.

19. William Reichert and Margaret M. Dodson, National Register of Historic Places Inventory Form: Majestic Theatre. Washington, D.C.: Department of the Interior, 1985. p. 8:2.

20. "Architectural Drawing of New Majestic." *East St. Louis Journal*, 10 July 1927. p. 1.

21. Sheri Piland, "Boller Brothers: A Kansas City Architect." *Historic Kansas City Foundation Gazette*, May/June 1982.

22. Nathan Parienti, National Register of Historic Places Inventory Form: Spivey Building. Washington, D.C.: Department of the Interior, 2002. p. 8.

23. Ibid. p. 1.

A History of Pollution and the Struggle for Environmental Justice

Preston Lacy

Southwestern Illinois Resource Conservation and Development

The root of East St. Louis' unsurpassed successes as well as its most serious crises can be traced back to its beginning as an industrial city even before it was incorporated in 1861. Factories brought jobs, income, opportunities to buy homes and start families, trips to the theater and to go shopping. These same factories and employment centers also discharged environmental pollutants to the surrounding air, water, and soil that continue to plague the city to this day. Natural systems know no jurisdictional boundaries. Likewise, pollutants, whether they enter the air, water, or soil, also are not aware of these lines on a map as they contaminate the surrounding environment. This thought is important to consider when one chooses to take an action that directly impacts the environment and one's neighbor, whether in a positive or negative manner. Health problems due to these pollutants have lead to higher rates of asthma and lead poisoning than other areas in the region. Though some would say any industrial city is going to have prolonged environmental hazards that may affect the local population, East St. Louis is unique in that it has a number of historical and present day environmental and social elements that have compounded the long term negative effects of industrial pollution on both former and current residents.

Cahokia Creek, 1914 Bowen Archives, SIUE

Many former and existing partnerships at the federal, state, regional, and local level have already taken great strides toward providing resources and assisting existing community organizations when needed. However, after a long history of nonexistent and later poorly enforced regulations, current East St. Louis residents have been handed a disproportionate burden of environmental health hazards. The need for continued expansion of regional advocates who support the current and future grassroots leaders, the citizens, of East St. Louis is evident as a newcomer to the region. These broader collaborations are imperative to understand and overcome former race and class driven institutional and market barriers that have historically deprived residents' equitable and sustainable solutions to these environmental injustices.

The effects of environmental pollution continue to harm the health and livelihood of East St. Louis residents today and only an increase in citizen action, pollution abatement, and sustainable redevelopment will create a healthier future for all of the city's residents and the region as a whole. The need for a regional environmental justice movement that further engages and empowers the community and surrounding communities is a necessity when considering a history of corporate and governmental corruption, and the corresponding years of unregulated pollution that comes with it. The current largely economically distressed African American population did not create these conditions nor should they have to live in them.

Industrial History

East St. Louis was incorporated in 1861 in order to serve as an industrial suburb for the city of St. Louis. The subsequent industrial powers that located and grew in and around East St. Louis in the latter half of the nineteenth century can be explained by a number of factors that made the east side of the river a new industrial powerhouse. Three main factors were identified early by social observers and entrepreneurs, which included cheap land near downtown St. Louis, a large network of railroad facilities, and proximity to an available labor supply across the river. There were also unique factors that gave a young East St. Louis an advantage over its neighbor across the river that many other industrial suburbs of larger cities did not enjoy, including: cheap fuel in the form of coal from Southern Illinois, cheap water at nearly half the cost of St. Louis, and fewer environmental regulations such as the lack of early smoke regulations or enforcement of nuisance laws.[1]

The lack of political interest in protecting citizens from corporate interests was established even before the city's founding due to changes in the state constitution. In 1848, Illinois passed a constitution that strictly limited the amount of spending the state could authorize after nearly bankrupting itself subsidizing railroad construction.[2] This constitutional amendment set the political climate in East St. Louis and its soon to be new neighbors. In effect, the amendment "shifted economic and development responsibility (and the power that goes with it) to the local level."[3]

This provided tremendous power to local business leaders and gave them authority to make decisions that were clearly not in the public's overall interest for health, safety, and welfare. New cities like East St. Louis became "tools of these entrepreneurs and, as such, enjoyed laissez-faire atmosphere from higher government".[4]

The only remaining impediment to further industrial growth was the frequent and unwelcome occurrence of flooding. Though this was not the first large human settlement in the American Bottom, it was the first to have the technological capacity to control the river with levee systems. The East Side Levee and Sanitary District was established after the 1903 Mississippi River flood and began planning and constructing an extensive levee system. With the levees came rapid industrial expansion and the near permanent end of a thriving wetland and bottomland forest ecosystem that relied on the pulsing floodwaters and a shifting river to create oxbow lakes and meander scar wetlands in the Bottom.[5]

The historic unwavering support for industry in early East St. Louis has left lasting and rippling repercussions on the city's current residents. In the book *Made in USA: East St. Louis*, Andrew Theising explains that every city needs a "social contract," or a government with the primary function of serving its people by means of public policies that protect citizen's rights and welfare. Because industrial suburbs like East St. Louis were primarily interested in protecting the interests of private industries, there was little concern for a social

National Stock Yards entrance, 1911   Theising image

contract to protect local citizens.[6] And when the city did begin to set regulations and provide limited protections, new industrial suburbs were incorporated adjacent to the city in order to circumvent laws and policies inherent to protect citizens.

Power Players and New "Communities"

The East St. Louis area provided a prime location for nuisance industries to relocate in order to avoid nuisance lawsuits on the Missouri side of the river.[7] In 1872, the National Stock Yards became the first major industry and located north of town. Other industries included "flour and grist mills, chemical and paint works, rolling mills, foundries, machine shops", meat packing, glass works, lumber companies, tanneries, and oil companies.[8]

Employees of these industries began moving across the river and the demand for basic public services started to grow. Potential industries considering locating in the city wanted to make sure they would not be subject to future regulations or increasing taxes due to the expansion of government services for residents.[9] With relaxed incorporation laws at the state level, industries began incorporating their own towns around East St. Louis in order to avoid existing and future taxes and environmental regulations.[10]

These communities had their own local government, which consisted mostly of employees from the community's major industry. East St. Louis provided a large workforce for these new industrial towns while the new towns "strangled the city government" by restricting future annexation and property tax base expansion for public services like trash collection, streets, sewers, health and emergency services.[11]

The new industrial communities included National City, Fairmont City, Monsanto later renamed Sauget, Washington Park, and Alorton. Each community had unique large-scale industries with one company often dominating the municipality and the local government. National Stockyards was the first major industry in the American Bottom and, in 1907, became incorporated as National City. American Zinc located in Fairmont City along with seed plants. Emerson Electric located in Washington Park with fertilizer plants. Aluminum Ore Company incorporated Alorton. Monsanto Chemical Company incorporated Monsanto (Sauget) with enough extra acreage to draw a host of oil, chemical, metal, and munition companies.[12] Many of these industries reflected national trends around the turn of the century as mergers and vertical integration allowed increased production through economies of scale and subsequent increased political control in the community.[13]

While East St. Louis still had significant industries along the

Standard Oil's Metro East refinery, c. 1917   Bowen Archives, SIUE

railroads, it was being forced into a bedroom community for the new "towns." Workers could easily access these new adjacent industrial suburbs by streetcar. Likewise, new sources of pollution could also easily access East St. Louis via creeks, groundwater, and air. Because the new communities were intricately tied to East St. Louis on nearly every level except by political jurisdiction, it is necessary to consider their negative impacts on the city's environmental history as well. This history consists of numerous forms of pollution that have impacted the air, water, and soil of East St. Louis. While some pollution and waste disposal issues have been addressed, many others remain and continue to adversely impact the health of the city's residents.

Air Pollution

Prevailing winds often indicate where air pollution is traveling. Because of East St. Louis'

geographical location, the city's residents have historically had to breathe air pollutants emitted from St. Louis as well as those emitted in the American Bottom. During stagnant weather patterns, river valleys accumulate higher densities of pollution that linger and subsequently degrade air quality until a weather system either blows the pollution away or rain brings particulate matter down to the soil and surface water.

Neighboring and upwind, St. Louis was known as a city with poor air quality due to the widespread use of cheap coal with high sulfur and ash found mostly in Southern Illinois. Black Tuesday, an infamous day in St. Louis' history, occurred November 28, 1939, when the streetlights in the city stayed on all day due to the heavily polluted skies. By the next year, St. Louis had passed an ordinance requiring low sulfur fuel to be used by industry and residents alike.[14] This new fuel was actually a higher quality coal from

Arkansas mines.[15] Even though this notable achievement in St. Louis led the nation in local clean air policy, the new regulations as well as previous semi-enforced policies only caused several industries to relocate in Illinois to avoid these laws.[16]

Industries had another early reason to move across the river--cheaper coal transportation costs. The Terminal Railroad Association charged fifty-two cents to deliver a ton of coal across the river to St. Louis, but only charged thirty-two cents to any location in Illinois.[17] These incentives increased the number of coal spewing industries and the level of smog in East St. Louis. Another form of air pollution that directly impacted the city came from the National Stock Yards to the north where thousands of animals were slaughtered on a daily basis. Meatpacking businesses began to relocate to National City adding to the air quality contamination.[18] The amount of raw animal waste in the wetlands and in adjacent Cahokia Creek allowed "the stink of death and rot and animal waste [to] spread south across St. Clair Avenue into downtown East St. Louis until it permeated the air".[19] When National City developed its own sewer system to the Mississippi River, odors from Cahokia Creek decreased.

As sewer and electric utility infrastructure continued to expand, some of the early quantities of air pollution began to decrease. The environmental movement of the 1960s raised public awareness and put pressure on the federal government to begin addressing issues of air pollution in a more direct manner. By the 1970s, smoke had become a much smaller issue due to the establishment of the United States Environmental Protection Agency (US EPA) and its power to set air quality standards using the 1970 Clean Air Act legislation.

However, enforcement of this and other national laws have not always applied to East St. Louis. Take for example several years beginning in 1987 when trash service was halted and many people had to resort to burning it in their yards or dumping it elsewhere.[20]

Beyond abnormal mass burnings of garbage due to a bankrupt city government, the focus of the region and nation began shifting to specific industrial fumes and ozone levels from vehicle exhaust.[21]

Ozone is created when the sun and heat interact with by-products from the burning of fossil fuels like gasoline.

The ozone smog season for East St. Louis and the surrounding region is May through September because they are the warmest months of the year. Ozone is known to increase asthma rates in children and irritate the

respiratory system.[22]

The East St. Louis region is continuing an overall decreasing trend in air pollution; however, it is still above the accepted federal standards for ozone and fine particles. Since 1970, the Illinois Environmental Protection Agency (IEPA) has increased air pollution regulations on major industries, and more recently further regulations have been focused on the general population. Vehicles have become the single largest source of air pollution in Illinois. The United States EPA mandates vehicle emission testing in the East St. Louis region and this has resulted in more than a 12 percent reduction in vehicle pollution.[23]

According to data compiled by the East-West Gateway Council of Governments, the St. Louis metropolitan region has a decreasing trend in average days when ozone is at unhealthy levels.[24] In 2008, there were

Industrial plant at Sauget, 2009 Powell Photo

eight days that exceeded this threshold.[25] One of the regional monitoring sites capturing this data is located in East St. Louis, representing the continued concern of high levels of ozone in the city.

The St. Louis Regional Clean Air Partnership and the East West Gateway Council of Governments have led the way in promoting alternative methods of transportation and other steps individuals can follow to lower ozone throughout the region. However, even after decades of improvements to air quality, regional and state organizations need to focus greater attention on the unique air quality issues and their effects on the residents of East St. Louis.

Industrial air pollution, particularly being emitted from Sauget, continues to degrade air quality in East St. Louis. Major active industries located there include Monsanto AG Products, Solutia, Inc., Pfizer, Pharmacia Corporation, Cerro Flow Products, Afton Chemical Corporation, Big River Zinc and Veolia Environmental Services, a hazardous waste incinerator. One recent study found that these companies accounted for one-fifth of the entire metropolitan regions risk to air pollution exposure.[26] The 2008 Toxic Release Inventory conducted by the US EPA shows seven operating facilities in Sauget with toxic air pollution releases totaling 570,379 pounds, three in East St. Louis producing 14,420 pounds, and one in Alorton producing 4,403 pounds.[27]

Sauget continues to be the main source for industrial air pollution with two particularly noteworthy

industries. Afton Chemical Corporation emitted over 400,000 pounds, or nearly three-quarters of the area's airborne toxic waste, and Veolia Environmental Services released 70 different identified toxic wastes in 2008.[28] This heavy concentration of environmental polluters create a much higher risk of airborne exposure to extremely harmful toxic pollutants for residents of East St. Louis when compared to other industrial areas throughout the St. Louis metropolitan region.

Since 2009, over 300 plaintiffs have filed similar class action lawsuits against many of these major industrial operations in Sauget, claiming that they knowingly have been polluting the air with PCBs, dioxins, and furans for more than 70 years.[29] Most of these companies also have a history of violations with the US EPA. The judicial system continues to be the most direct avenue for residents to challenge companies that degrade personal health and property, but not always an affordable option.

Hazardous Waste: Polluting Soil and Water

The benefits of cheap inputs and nearly non-existent environmental or public health regulations fostered an agglomeration, or cluster, of hazardous waste emitting industries in and around East St. Louis that relied on coal and each other's by-products to operate. The interconnectedness of a coal dominated toxic industrial base continued to evolve. Steel mills attracted blast furnaces, metal plating firms and metal fabrication plants, which attracted coke works and acid works. The National Stockyards attracted the coal dependent packing industry, which in turn

attracted by-product industries like tanneries and chemical plants.[30]

According to Craig Colten, "hazardous waste products are not unique by-products of the post-war period," when referring to the common misconception that toxic industrial waste only began entering the environment after World War II.[31] Industries in and adjacent to East St. Louis had already released many toxic substances into the environment prior to 1930:

• Lead and zinc smelters –toxic metals that posed heath risks to employees and damaged surrounding vegetation

• Foundries – also accumulated toxic metals

• Steel mills – acids, phenols, cyanides, and oily liquids.

• Coal and by-products – a variety of hazardous substances including mercury and on site storage led to accumulation of substances

• Gas works – tars and phenolic wastes

• Coke works – similar waste as gas works; tars and toluene became products for ammunition and roofing industries

• Creosote operations – pentachlorphenols (PCPs)

• Leather tanning operations – chromium waste after the 1920s

• Glass works – arsenic and cadmium

• Petroleum refineries – oil, acids, metals, and phenolic wastes.[32]

This industrial waste was often dumped in the closest and most convenient locations. This included improper disposal in "open pits, surface impoundments, vacant land, farmlands, and water bodies".[33] Even though this type of dumping is not desirable anywhere, it became especially harmful for the residents in and around East St. Louis.

Since the city and all other municipalities located in the American Bottom were developed on an alluvial floodplain, they are all above (or at times submerged in) a large source of groundwater from the sand and gravel aquifers that exist in this historic floodplain. When toxic industrial waste was dumped into wetland systems, the pollutants traveled via natural systems into the groundwater supplies. When waste was dumped into streams, it was eventually conveyed into the Mississippi River, but also had the opportunity to enter the groundwater supply through stream banks on its way.

Not surprisingly, these practices have had a long-term affect on local residents. In the late 1990s, East St. Louis and Sauget under the direction of the Illinois EPA both passed ordinances making the use of groundwater extraction for human consumption illegal.[34] Over a century of blatant disregard for not only the citizens but the natural habitat compounded pollutants to such a level in the aquifers that proper treatment is now mandatory before any groundwater may be pumped into the surface water system.

After 1930, large industries continued to grow and smaller firms closed due to market forces and the Great Depression. During World War II, industries that supported the war, including steel mills, munitions, and oil refineries, expanded temporarily. The peak in industrial employees occurred in 1953 in the region.[35] The following years saw a steady decline in most industries, some of which began moving to cheaper labor markets, leaving employees looking for jobs elsewhere.

However, one industry saw rapid growth during this postwar period. The petrochemical industry spurred the creation of many new materials that "quickly won the acceptance among farmers, industrialists, and ordinary household consumers".[36] Because these materials lasted longer against natural processes of decomposition, they became particularly dangerous to people and wildlife. Synthetic chemicals began accumulating in animals when ingested and passed through the food chain in fatty tissues to humans.[37] Synthetic toxic waste was being dumped on land, in water bodies, or incinerated around East St. Louis.

Industries began storing toxic waste on-site or dumping it off-site at secretive locations to circumvent any enforcement from the new air and water quality laws. This created large-scale toxic dumps in and around the city, many of which still require remediation. The Lanson Chemical Company of East St. Louis produced paint and floor wax and provides a typical example of improper waste disposal. From 1962 to 1978 the oils, solvents and PCB laden resins derived from manufacturing were either dumped into neighboring wetlands or stored in drums on site.[38]

South of the city in Sauget an even greater crime against residents and the environment was occurring. During a time span of approximately five decades from the 1930s to the 1970s, manufacturers from the East St Louis region and Missouri were able to dump some of the most toxic waste ever created directly into Dead Creek. Zinc, petroleum, fertilizer, chemical, metal, oil refining, and munitions companies all dumped as the Sauget village president oversaw the operation.[39] Government and industry goals were one and the same and this level of collaborative corruption created the most hazardous dumpsite in the region. Today, the only two hazardous waste sites in the East St. Louis region on the National Priorities List (the nation's most polluted sites) are both located in Sauget and one includes the Dead Creek dumpsite.[40]

The US EPA began cleaning Dead Creek in 1999.[41] Several companies were identified as partially responsible and ordered to conduct the cleanup. High concentrations of metals, volatile organic compounds and PCBs were all found in soil tests. Remarkably, as of January 2010, EPA released a final report indicating that the cleanup of the creek has been successfully completed and that "surface water in Dead Creek was sampled and is safe for wading".[42]

The development of waste treatment facilities by the 1970s provided an alternative for the city to treat sewage and industries to dispose of waste. Polluters that did not already have their own sewer system were now able to dump the same waste in a municipal system that moved it off site and managed some of the pollutants. However, many factories continued illegally

Sauget Village Hall, 2009 Powell Photo

dumping on site, increasing the contamination in these industrial zones. The by-products of the waste treatment facilities themselves were also improperly put into landfills .[43]

In 1976 the Resource Conservation and Recovery Act was the first law to begin control of solid and hazardous waste from creation to disposal at active industrial sites. This signified the beginning of monitoring industries that created toxic wastes. Four years later, the Comprehensive Environmental Response, Compensation, and Liability Act (Superfund) passed in order to develop a source of money that would remediate closed industrial sites that had previously created hazardous

waste. The EPA now has authority to identify parties responsible for cleanup. This law also established the National Priorities List, identifying the most toxic and dangerous hazardous waste sites in the country. Two former illegal dumpsites in Sauget known as Site 1 and 2 are included on this list. There are 15 Superfund sites in East St. Louis and 10 more archived for further action in the future. [44]

In 2002, an update known as the Brownfields Law provided funding to assess and clean toxic waste sites, defined liability protections against businesses, and provided funding to states to clean a broader array of dangerous sites. The US EPA defines brownfields

as "real property, the expansion, redevelopment, or reuse of which may be complicated by the presence or potential of a hazardous substance, pollutant, or contaminant".[45] These sites can include a variety of locations from large industrial facilities to smaller sites like gas stations and dry cleaners.

The Illinois EPA has also supported a number of brownfield site remediation projects in and around East St. Louis for over two decades. Programs that the IEPA operates include:

• Leaking Underground Storage Tanks (LUST) Program – 93 sites have been identified in East St. Louis and 40 have been cleaned.

• Site Remediation Voluntary Cleanup Program – 17 sites in East St. Louis are enrolled to conduct voluntary cleanup activities. 9 have been completed.

• State Response Action Program - for preventative and short-term actions that other programs cannot provide. 11 sites are enrolled in East St. Louis

• Brownfields Program - started in 1998 providing technical and financial support for brownfield redevelopment.

• Municipal Brownfields Redevelopment Grant Program: Grants for investigation and cleanup of brownfields are available to communities. East St. Louis has received $58,666 from this program for 2 sites.

• Targeted Site Assessments – offers site evaluations for municipalities at no cost to identify potential obstacles and costs for cleanup.

• Illinois Removes Illegal Dumps (IRID) - $40,000 spent for solid waste cleanup in the city since 2009.[46]

The Illinois EPA provides many avenues for brownfield cleanup and has staff devoted to a cleaner future for East St. Louis. Approximately $4.2 million have been spent by the US EPA and $1.4 million by the IEPA since 1988.[47] This increased involvement at the state and federal level has created positive changes throughout the community, but often cleanups only occur as monies are granted to the city. The need for increased dedicated funding is necessary in order for more clean up and redevelopment projects to occur

providing residents of East St. Louis with a clean, safer, healthier, and more sustainable quality of life.

Environmental Justice and Public Health

Racism has been present throughout the history of East St. Louis. The same industries that left the city environmentally devastated also fostered generations of racism and hatred. Many freed slaves moved to the city for employment in a city with abundant jobs. Many times individuals would become strikebreakers intentionally hired by these industries in order to show striking labor unions that they could be easily replaced. This served to lessen the power of the unions and spark racial tensions that led to the horrific 1917 race riots. Racial tensions seem to have continued to permeate through generations and personally seem very present today. Drastic demographic differences between East St. Louis and other nearby large Illinois communities, further inhibits broad acceptance of racial and cultural diversity making it even more difficult for many to attempt to understand the unique environmental problems residents in East St. Louis must face every day.

One type of racism, environmental racism, has become more apparent as the city's population has remained almost completely African American for half a century. The definition of environmental racism is "any policy, practice, or directive that differentially affects or disadvantages (whether intended or unintended) individuals, groups, communities based on

race or color."[48] It is difficult to identify historic intentional decisions that contributed to environmental racism due to a number of factors, including laissez faire governmental policies and industries that located facilities primarily based upon transportation options, cheap land availability, and were willing to dump waste on site or next door no matter if the neighborhood was white, black or Hispanic.

Instead, environmental racism has become more apparent over the last several decades in a less direct, more institutionalized manner- at times intentional, at others unintentional. Market factors, continued local government failures, and public policies have all contributed to the increased numbers of African American residents in the city since the 1960s who bear a disproportioned share of environmental injustice. Examples of these issues include:

• the loss of industrial base to cheaper labor markets in the South

• exclusionary zoning codes in other communities

• the federal government's role in developing the interstate system, creating loan policies to encourage single family home ownership, and subsidizing infrastructure expansion all encouraging urban sprawl

• real estate market redlining keeping minority families out of new subdivisions

• the city's mounting budget problems and loss of an industrial tax base

• the increased knowledge of

environmental conditions and their health side effects

• As class and race became more intertwined, public policy decisions, determined what locations environmental laws were enforced and where money was allocated for environmental improvements based mostly upon politically motivated costs and benefits of those decisions.[49]

Sign at Sauget, 2004 Theising Photo

Due to these policies and problems, many white residents began to move to communities on the bluff to escape degraded environmental conditions, for new job opportunities, and for better public services provided by local governments following a stronger social contract than most of the industrial suburbs in the American Bottom. Remaining were African Americans unable to move to other areas and new black residents who were being directed to the city through restrictive real estate polices in other areas because of more affordable housing choices and hopes for

employment in a job market that continued to shrink.

During this time of urban decay and demographic shifts in East St. Louis, Sauget to the south has continued to attract the most toxic industries with open arms.[50] While it is difficult to determine early-intended examples of industries choosing locations due to race, it is important to note that black neighborhoods like Alta Sita in south East St. Louis have always neighbored toxic industries in Sauget.

The history of hazardous waste incineration since the demographic shift further builds the case for environmental racism. In 1972, the US Air Force wanted to burn Agent orange at a Monsanto Incinerator, which was supported by an IEPA Air Pollution division employee but finally denied by the Director of IEPA.[51] In 1979, a new incinerator was constructed and handled waste from private entities and from cleaned Superfund sites. This incinerator was able to operate with no clean air permit and with a record of IEPA violations and fines from 1995 to 2008.[52]

A suit by local groups including the Illinois Sierra Club and the American Bottom Conservancy in 2006 pushed the US EPA to take action. New regulations reduce the amount of particulate matter that may be omitted and regulates the amount of mercury that may be burned.[53] Given the minority population living adjacent to a relatively recent large hazardous waste incinerator facility that has been able to operate with little enforcement for years, one begins to see several variables

coming together that form a very intentional example of environmental racism.

A comparison at the St. Clair County level shows that minorities are 2.4 times as likely to be burdened by the release of toxic chemicals and 1.5 times as likely to be exposed to cancer risks from hazardous air pollutants compared to the white population. On the other hand, whites are .29 times as likely to be burdened by a Superfund site throughout the county, showing that race is the major determining factor but not the only one when considering environmental injustices.[54] Take, for example, Granite City, Illinois, which is 95 percent white, has exposed lead piles, a superfund site, and recently ranked second in the nation as most likely to contract cancer as a result of breathing toxic air.[55] This is why environmental injustice in the region must not be approached only by race but also by class in order to gather a diverse group with a common goal of environmental justice.

The environmental justice movement is based upon the principle that all people regardless of race or income should have the right to a clean and healthy environment, be protected from environmental pollution, and have meaningful involvement in developing, implementing, and regulating environmental policies .[56] The movement is known for beginning in North Carolina in 1982 over a PCB landfill wanting to locate in an African American community. The movement has brought together social justice, civil rights, and environmental groups empowering all economically disadvantaged people affected by pollution, by providing them with a voice in environmental policy decisions.

In 1994, the federal government passed Executive Order 12898, Federal Actions to Address Environmental Justice in Minority Populations and Low-Income Populations. Recently the Illinois EPA passed an Environmental Justice policy in 2008 in order to "promote environmental equity in the administration of its programs," particularly for minority and low income populations.[57] These policies show that the federal and state government recognizes past inequalities as it relates to environmental policy decisions and regulation of laws in low-income and minority communities.

The struggle for environmental justice in East St. Louis has been fought for much longer than the official formation of the environmental justice movement. Since the early 1900s, the main avenue for citizen enforcement of pollution control on companies was the nuisance law. If a company incorporated its own community to exempt itself from nuisance laws, citizens in East St. Louis affected by pollution could still file a lawsuit. Local courts in St. Clair and Madison Counties often supported plaintiffs who sued companies for excessive pollution or workforce related exposure lawsuits, but these decisions were often overturned by appellate or state courts, showing that the local juries and courts were greater advocates for citizen's protection.[58]

Soon a statewide commission formed so that the public could file complaints for excessive water pollution. Illinois created the Rivers and Lakes Commission in 1911 and granted it the power to order operations to stop polluting. A successful example of environmental justice occurred when East St. Louis filed complaints against National Stockyards for dumping into Cahokia creek and the commission required the construction of a sewer system to improve water quality and air quality for residents.[59]

Residents of East St. Louis and surrounding towns in the Bottom were not as successful when filing complaints against cities on the bluff that released sewage into creeks that naturally flowed in the towns in the historic floodplain. Since this was a legal means for government to dispose of sewage at the time, the commission only provided recommendations for the cities.[60] The geography and topography alone have made East St. Louis a case for environmental discrimination as sewage came down streams from the bluff towns. Even when pumping systems were installed to put the waste into the Mississippi River, they did not always work, leading to an extremely unhealthy and unsanitary environment for residents.

The local St. Clair County court cases and policies of Illinois waterways represent a recognition that unjustified harm did occur to residents who neighbored polluting industries and "industrial polluters would not be destroyed by the addition of adequate treatment equipment".[61] This recognition displays an early hunger for environmental justice by all citizens in East St. Louis.

In 1992, a local activist group named Project H.O.P.E. (Helping Other People Emerge) began helping concerned residents in the Alta Sita neighborhood bring attention to the Lanson Chemical facility. The organization found that an unusually high number of residents had medical problems or had died of cancer, while the Illinois Department of Health (IDPH) found the site to pose "no apparent public health hazard." Later that year, the US EPA began an emergency clean up of the site after PCB contaminated resin was released from storage tanks. Residents and Project H.O.P.E. charged the IDPH for insufficient data collection, sharing of information, and failing to consider exposure through other means.[62] Here, a local church-based group advocated for citizens' environmental justice and helped clean a former hazardous waste site. However, a severe lack of trust toward the IDPH was firmly established. The deficiency of early neighborhood involvement and proper analysis of interactions between pollutants, residents and environmental systems appear to be the cause of this distrust.

Since the incorporation of environmental justice policies and education training among state and federal agency employees, some policy improvements have been made. Project H.O.P.E. went on to assist in training a corps of local lead abatement inspectors with the EPA, and opened discussions with major industries and their impacts on the surrounding neighborhoods.[63]

In 1999, the Illinois EPA, US EPA, and Illinois Department of Public Health formed an East St. Louis

Broadway and 17th, East St. Louis, 2009 Powell Photo

City-wide Lead Contamination Task Force (later to become the Metro East Lead Collaborative, including many other local organizations) in order to test lead contamination on previous industrial sites as well test the blood levels of area children. According to the US EPA, "four times as many children were found to have lead poisoning than in the surrounding communities, and the rate of lead poisoning was four times higher than the national average".[64]

The collaboration studied several industrial sites throughout the city and replaced the soil in twenty residential lots around two selected industrial sites with high lead contamination. This project represents a milestone as the "first state of Illinois funded residential cleanup in recent history".[65]

This collaboration and funding

represents an excellent model of positive action in East St. Louis where an unusually high level of lead contamination is directly impacting residents that cannot address this issue alone.

Another partnership between the University of Illinois East St. Louis Action Research Project and the Emerson Park Development Corporation provided outside university resources to help create a neighborhood plan for Emerson Park. Early implementation of the plan consisted of assisting community residents in conducting a major trash cleanup throughout the neighborhood. Additional assistance helped the Emerson Park Development Corporation plan and advocate for a Metrolink stop where the neighborhood organization eventually developed Parsons Place, an affordable transit

oriented housing development on a former brownfield site.[66] The assistance from the University of Illinois has provided technical assistance and empowered a neighborhood organization that continues to lead economic development, education, and community empowerment projects in East St. Louis.

This year the old Buick dealership on State Street was remediated using East St. Louis Housing Authority money from a US EPA stimulus funded brownfield grant. The Unity for a Better Community organization opened a farmers' market on the site in May of 2010. Further plans are to redevelop the structure as an indoor market creating the first step toward a model for sustainable communities in East St. Louis.[67] Still this is a powerful example of the vision and leadership needed in East St. Louis that can continue to empower and provide sustainable redevelopment of former brownfields. But it cannot be done without the broad support of the community's residents seeking a healthier future and willing to collaborate with outside organizations, as well as the need for expanded regional assistance with local community groups. Only when the residents of East St Louis lead these efforts and take a vested interest in change can essential projects like farmers' markets and community gardens, the backbone of sustainable and healthy communities, be successful.[68]

Conclusion

Where the struggle for environmental justice goes from here will determine the environmental history at East St. Louis' bicentennial and beyond. There are numerous organizations and partners within the city and throughout the region that are already doing what they can to assist residents who have historically not had a stable government to rely on. It is time to broaden that partnership and provide assistance directly to the residents through existing community organizations that are ready to develop a clean, healthy environment free of aging toxic waste.

A future environmental justice coalition must be established at a regional level that welcomes residents from all communities suffering from environmental injustices and who lack the political power and financial resources to make a change alone. This will require residents to welcome each other into their neighborhoods with open hearts and open minds. This group must first discuss the many forms of past and present intentional and unintentional forms of environmental racism, and it must be understood and accepted by all as a major component the larger movement. Then, with a common mission and vision, this group from different backgrounds and cultures can organize under a common goal of environmental equal rights for everyone, regardless of race or economic status.

Both former residents and current residents really want to see a revival of the city. I hear people throughout the region asking what can be done to "fix" East St. Louis. The interest is there and it should be realized that in order for the region to prosper, East St. Louis must once again prosper. If you haven't recently, I encourage you to take a drive through the city and visualize the potential. Urban prairies can be remediated and turned into local urban farming plots, creating jobs and a source of healthy local food; other brownfields can be redeveloped into environmentally sustainable mixed use developments with affordable housing; a trail system can provide residents with recreational and educational opportunities; and the list goes on and on. There is a lot more positive action yet to be seen if we all have patience, listen and learn from each other, and choose to work together.

End Notes:

1. Graham Romeyn Taylor, *Satellite Cities. How Industry is Jumping across the Mississippi while Civic and Social Progress follows Slowly* (New York: Survey Associates, 1913), 130

2. Andrew J. Theising, *Made in USA: East St. Louis: The Rise and Fall of an Industrial River Town* (St. Louis: Virginia Publishing, 2003), 67

3. Ibid., 59.

4. Ibid., 59.

5. Craig E. Colten, "From Environmental Justice on the American Bottom: The Legal Response to Pollution, 1900-1950," in *Common Fields* ed. Andrew Hurley (St. Louis: Missouri Historical Society Press, 1997), 166.

6. Theising, *Made in USA*, 42.

7. Ibid., 10

8. Edward English, *The Good Things of East St. Louis* (Mascoutah: Top's Books, 1992), 4.

9. English, *The Good Things of East St. Louis*, 4

10. Theising, *Made in USA*, 97

11. English, *The Good Things of East St. Louis*, 16

12. Ibid., 4-16.

13. Craig E. Colten, *Historical Assessment of Hazardous Waste Management in Madison and St. Clair Counties, Illinois, 1890-1980.* (Springfield: Illinois Department of Energy and Natural Resources, 1988), 13.

14. Andrew Hurley, "From The Environment." In *St. Louis Currents: A Guide to the Region and its Resources* (St. Louis: Missouri Historical Society Press, 1997), 137-138.

15. Joel A. Tarr and Carl Zimring, "From The Struggle for Smoke Control in St. Louis: Achievement and Emulation," In *Common Fields*, ed. Andrew Hurley (St. Louis: Missouri Historical Society Press, 1997), 215

16. Andrew Hurley, "The Environment", 138

17. Graham Romeyn Taylor, Satellite Cities: *A Study of Industrial Suburbs* (New York: Appleton and Company), 130.

18. English, *The Good Things of East St. Louis*, 4.

19. Harper Barnes, *Never Been a Time: The 1917 Race Riots that Sparked the Civil Rights Movement* (New York: Walker & Company, 2008), 86.

20. Jonathan Kozol, *Savage Inequalities* (New York: Crown Publishers, Inc., 1991), 8.

21. Joel A. Tarr and Carl Zimring, From The Struggle for Smoke Control in St. Louis, In Hurley, *Common Fields*, 220.

22. *Quality of Life: It Matters to Us All: Air Quality Issue Statement* (St. Louis: RegionWise, 2002).

23. *Illinois Environmental Protection Agency, Biennial Report 2007-2008, 2009.* Springfield, IL: Illinois Environmental Protection Agency, 40-42.

24. East-West Gateway Council of Governments, "Air Quality History: Air Quality in the St. Louis Area," Air Quality Research Center. http://www.ewgateway.org/environment/aq/AQHistory/aqhistory.htm

25. St. Louis Regional Clean Air Partnership, "St. Louis Then and Now" *Local Air Quality.* http://www.cleanair-stlouis.com/local-air-quality.html

26. Troy Abel, "Skewed Riskscapes and Environmental Injustice: A Case Study of Metropolitan St. Louis," *Environmental Management* 42, no. 2 (2008): 232-248.

27. United States Environmental Protection Agency, *Toxic Release Inventory Explorer: Facility Report*, http://www.epa.gov/triexplorer/facility.htm.

28. Ibid.

29. Kelly Holleran, "95 Plaintiffs file suit over toxic exposure in Sauget," *The Madison St. Clair Record*, December 20, 2009. http://www.madisonrecord.com/news/223768-95-plaintiffs-file-suit-over-toxic-exposure-in-sauget.

30. Craig E. Colten, *Historical Assessment of Hazardous Waste Management in Madison and St. Clair Counties, Illinois, 1890-1980,* 13-15.

31. Ibid., 3.

32. Ibid., 15.

33. R.F. Anderson, "Solid Waste and Public Health" in *Public Health and the Environment,* ed. M.R. Greenberg (New York: Guilford), 182, quoted in Craig E. Colten, *Historical Assessment of Hazardous Waste Management in Madison and St. Clair Counties, Illinois, 1890-1980* (Springfield: Illinois Department of Energy and Natural Resources, 1988), 3.

34. U.S. Army Corps of Engineers, *East St. Louis & Vicinity, Illinois Ecosystem Restoration and Flood Damage Reduction Project, 2003,* Appendix G.

35. Craig E. Colten, *Historical Assessment of Hazardous Waste Management in Madison and St. Clair Counties, Illinois, 1890-1980,* 15-17.

36. Andrew Hurley, "Flood, Rats and Toxic Waste: Allocating Environmental Hazards Since

World War II" in *Common Fields* ed. Andrew Hurley (St. Louis: Missouri Historical Society Press, 1997), 254.

37. Ibid., 254-255.

38. Ibid., 257.

39. Ibid., 257.

40. United States Environmental Protection Agency. *Superfund National Priorities List.* http://www.epa.gov/superfund/sites/npl.

41. United States Environmental Protection Agency. "NPL Site Narrative for Sauget Area 1," National Priorities List, http://www.epa.gov/superfund/sites/npl/nar1654.htm.

42. United States Environmental Protection Agency. *Dead Creek Cleanup Done; EPA Issues Final Report* (Chicago, IL: EPA Region 5 Superfund Division, 2010, 3.

43. Craig E. Colten, *Historical Assessment of Hazardous Waste Management in Madison and St. Clair Counties*, Illinois, 1890-1980, 38.

44. United States Environmental Protection Agency, *Region 5 Superfund*, http://www.epa.gov/region5superfund/hub_state_illinois.html.

45. United States Environmental Protection Agency, *Brownfields*, http://www.epa.gov/brownfields/index.html.

46. Illinois Environmental Protection Agency, *Biennial Report* 2007-2008, 32-37.

47. Tom Miller, e-mail message to author, May 15, 2010.

48. Robert Bullard, *Dumping in Dixie: Race, Class, and Environmental Quality* (Boulder: Westview Press, 2000), 98.

49. Andrew Hurley, "Flood, Rats and Toxic Waste: Allocating

Environmental Hazards Since World War II", 259-261.

50. William Spain, "Tiny Sauget, Illinois, likes Business Misfits" *Wall Street Journal*, October 3, 2006, http://www.post-gazette.com/pg/06276/727066-28.stm.

51. Associated Press "Look Elsewhere For Disposal Area", *The Southeast Missourian*, January 26, 1972. http://news.google.com/newspapers.

52. "Illinois Hazwaste Incinerator Permitted Despite Explosions, Fires" *Environmental News Service*, September 15, 2008. http://www.ens-newswire.com/ens/sep2008/2008-09-15-091.asp.

53. Ibid.

54. Scorecard: The Pollution Information Site, *St. Clair County Environmental Justice Summary Report.* http://www.scorecard.org/community/ej-summary.tcl?fips_county_code=17163&lang=eng#dist.

55. Kim McGuire, "EPA finds air pollution in Granite City poses high cancer risk," *St. Louis Post-Dispatch*, June 25, 2009. http://www.stop158.org/2009/2009-06-25_Post.htm.

56. Illinois Environmental Protection Agency, *Biennial Report 2007-2008*, 12.

57. Ibid., 12

58. Craig Colten, "From Environmental Justice on the American Bottom: The Legal Response to Pollution, 1900-1950," 171-175.

59. Ibid., 170.

60. Ibid., 169.

61. Ibid., 174-175.

62. Agency for Toxic Substances and Disease Registry, Public Health Assessment: Lanson

Chemical Company, http://www.atsdr.cdc.gov/HAC/pha/pha.asp?docid=567&pg=1.

63. Andrew Hurley, "From The Environment." *In St. Louis Currents: A Guide to the Region and its Resources*, 143.

64. United States Environmental Protection Agency, *Environmental Justice Collaborative Model: A Framework to Ensure Local Problem-Solving* (Washington D.C., Office of Environmental Justice, 2002), 31.

65. Illinois Environmental Protection Agency, *East St. Louis Lead Threat Avoided: Soil Accumulations put Children at Risk*, www.epa.state.il.us/environmental-progress/v28/n1/lead-threat.html.

66. Kenneth Reardon, "Riding the Rails" National Housing Institute, http://www.nhi.org/online/issues/128/ridingrails.html.

67. Unity for a Better Community, East St. Louis Farmers Market, http://www.llife.org/farmersmarket.htm.

68. Dr. Gerald Higginbotham, phone conversation, September 3, 2010.

Majestic Theater Detail, Powell Photo

East St. Louis and Its Relationship to the River

Bryan Werner

Metro East Park and Recreation District

Les Sterman

Southwestern Illinois Flood Prevention District Council

While the Mississippi River is a natural boundary between East St. Louis and its neighbors to the west, the political, social and economic divide is far bigger. Over the last two centuries there have been continuing attempts, mostly successful, to control the river, yet the fortunes of the communities along its banks have often defied the best efforts at control by planners and community leaders. An ongoing puzzle for many is how to explain the dramatically different appearance and function of the riverfront in East St. Louis along the east bank of the Mississippi from its counterpart to the west in downtown St. Louis, Missouri. This visual disparity is a symbol of the diverging fortunes of the two communities and a metaphor for the intractable problems faced by East St. Louis.

Skyline at night, 2010   Werner Photo

St. Louis, Missouri has embraced its riverfront, while East St. Louis has all but abandoned it. While St. Louis invested heavily along the west bank of the river first as a commercial asset and in later years as a symbol of community identity, a tourist attraction and regional amenity, East St. Louis' efforts to develop the riverfront have been sporadic and largely futile. Even the Casino Queen, the only commercial investment in years on the East St. Louis riverfront, turns its back to the river. Paradoxically, recent efforts to reimagine the East St. Louis riverfront are led by Missouri-based philanthropists and civic leaders, with little meaningful participation in their efforts by the leadership of East St. Louis. This paper explores the historical, physical, and cultural roots of the starkly different outcomes on the opposing banks of the Mississippi and concludes with some thoughts about an opportunity to bring about positive change.

Each evening blessed with a clear horizon, the residents of East St. Louis have the opportunity to watch the setting sun; one that drops behind the iconic Gateway Arch and its surrounding neighbors in the St. Louis skyline, an image of economic success that casts a long shadow over the far less fortunate city to the east. The only thing that separates this economic and social gulf is the very same river that has these communities together. The Mississippi River was historically the life-blood of both communities. As each city developed, the river and the political boundary that it represents has tragically become a barrier to collaboration and

progress.

As if political challenges weren't enough to overcome, both cities have battled Mother Nature as well. The geography and geology of the area and the unpredictability of the Mississippi have combined to create 174 square miles of floodplain in Illinois known as the American Bottom. The meandering nature of the Mississippi in this stretch has over geologic ages scoured the surface, creating a natural flood plain stretching from around Alton, Illinois on the north to the Kaskaskia River on the south. The elevation of this vast expanse of old riverbeds is merely feet above the Mississippi's normal surface waters. East St. Louis and the other communities located alongside the Mississippi first adapted to periodic flooding in order to survive and then, as modern engineering and construction techniques allowed, built levee systems, dams and other structures, and channelized the river to control its velocity, volume, and elevation. East St. Louis even established a high grade policy in 1875 where the city council ordered all streets to be built above the 1844 high water mark.[1] The City of St. Louis made similar efforts to expand usable and less flood prone space of its own. It wasn't until the construction of the current levee system that the American Bottom area dried out and the frequency of flooding diminished.

The history of the American Bottom is as layered as the river sediment deposited by years of frequent flooding. It is no surprise that some of the earliest inhabitants were known as the Mounds People

or Mississippians. The city of Cahokia, the largest city of Pre-Columbian North America, was a thriving metropolis in the 12th and 13th centuries, made up of numerous man-made/hand-built mounds that stretched from an area near the present day City of Collinsville west to downtown St. Louis. Why mounds? To the Cahokia people these mounds had religious significance, representing hierarchy designation. The mounds also represented a territorial presence, and offered the Cahokians an advantageous perspective for security and protection. Besides fulfilling these important roles, the mounds were also some of the earliest flood protection measures. Perhaps it is no coincidence that there were so many mounds built in the flood plain. After all, one way to keep your community dry is by building mounds that exceed the flood elevation of the river. For numerous reasons, one of which may be the struggles associated with the frequent floods, the community known as Cahokia disappeared in the early 14th century.

For the most part, the land now known as the metropolitan St. Louis region went unsettled for several centuries until it was claimed again, this time by French immigrants. Several towns dotted the map including Cahokia, Prairie du Pont, Fort Chartres, St. Charles, and St. Louis to name just a few. Most significant is the fact that communities began growing in strength and population primarily on the west side of the Mississippi River. The greatest difficulty in settling the area to the west of the Mississippi was simply crossing one of the most powerful and expansive rivers in the world. The great demand to move families and their belongings across the river spawned a new and growing business for anyone that had the know-how and equipment. One such gentleman was James Piggott. Mr. Piggott saw the success of a ferry just south of St. Louis and thought there should be another alternative for those wanting to travel to or through the growing town of St. Louis. He began in 1792 making the necessary improvements to what is now the East St. Louis riverfront in order to provide his new ferry service in 1795. Although he was successful in his venture, James Piggott passed away only years later in 1799. What survived, however, was his ferry service; it grew along with the demand for the service. The Piggott ferry continued to be operated by John McNight and Thomas Brady,[2] only to be purchased by Samuel Wiggins in the early 1820s.[3]

With the new ownership came improvements to the ferries. Man powered vessels were replaced by horse powered paddles, and vessel loads grew as well. These advancements led to increased speed, frequency, and load capacity. With the ever growing population to the west of the Mississippi came an expanding need for supplies and the industries that followed. In short order, Samuel Wiggins grew the company and monopolized ferry service from the East St. Louis riverfront to St. Louis. In addition, the Wiggins Ferry began catering to the railroads and the up-and-coming steamboat industry. Vast amounts of coal were not only transported to and

ferried over from the Wiggins yard but fully loaded rail cars as well. Coal was plentiful on the east side of the river and was used to generate power for St. Louis and other nearby towns as well as for the passing steamboats.

Steam changed river navigation. Prior to steam power most long-haul river transportation flowed in one direction-downstream. Steam made travel up river more feasible and thus became the new standard. As commerce grew, it became vitally important to keep the river channel deep enough and free of obstacles to allow these vessels to navigate unimpeded. Samuel Wiggins, along with other businesses up and down river, began working with the Corps of Engineers in an attempt to begin controlling the unpredictable and ever-changing Mississippi channel. The town of St. Louis and the Wiggins Ferry company were not simply interested in meeting the navigation needs of steam boats, but protecting their growing riverfront investments. The latter required attention to a growing problem; a sand bar turned island just off the East St. Louis riverfront. This island, known as Bloody Island, was growing larger by the year and the Mississippi waters were increasingly being diverted to the eastern channel between the island and the shore. Left unchecked, the Mississippi River would have meandered to the east, as it had in earlier geologic ages, and found a new home further inland on the east side, thus cutting off the existing and established riverfront improvements in St. Louis. Wing dams, dikes, and numerous other methods were used to combat the river's eastward shifts. Ultimately

these efforts proved successful, the Mississippi channel east of Bloody Island slowly filled in and the island became a contiguous extension of the east bank, forming what we now know as the East St. Louis riverfront.

East St. Louis was incorporated in 1861. Railroads were prosperous and plentiful and the town was thriving, courtesy of the expanding economy of the City of St. Louis across the river. Unfortunately, this success was halted, often interrupted by frequent flooding. These conditions led to the high grade policy adopted by East St. Louis. Analogous to the early efforts of the Mounds People, East St. Louis began elevating their community to a hopeful height above the Mississippi's flood stage. Ironically, it was reported that some of the old Pre-Columbian mounds that remained were leveled and used for fill material in elevating the ground. This effort proved mostly successful but only for a small area since the American Bottom area is vast, taking in around 174 square miles.

In 1908 the East Side Levee and Sanitary District was formed to tackle the problem of flood protection in a more organized and concerted fashion. A series of canals were created to channel runoff from the bluffs to the river and the fill was used to build the area's first levees along the east bank of the Mississippi ("mainline" levees), along with additional "flank" levees further connecting to the bluffs. For the first time in the area efforts were made to regionalize flood protection in the American Bottom region. Local efforts to control flooding on a regional scale were soon followed by federal action. The 1936 Flood Control Act was the first federal commitment to flood protection in the Upper Mississippi Valley and it officially authorized the East St. Louis, Illinois project. Early construction by the U.S. Army Corps of Engineers was to a levee grade of 45.5 feet on the St. Louis gage. By comparison, the flood of record in St. Louis reached 49.58 feet on the St. Louis gage on August 1, 1993. The current St. Louis floodwall would be overtopped at 52 feet. Flooding in 1943 and 1944 led to federal authorization to increase the levee grade to 49 feet and in 1954, based on new design studies, the authorized grade was increased to about 54 feet, the grade now often referenced as the "500-year flood."

The Corps of Engineers was at first a reluctant participant in flood protection efforts, preferring to confine its activities to navigation measures. The Corps was particularly averse to involvement in continuing maintenance of a vast system of levees and related facilities. Maintaining the rebuilt levees, pump stations, gates and other structures became the responsibility of the East Side Levee and Sanitary District, a local political subdivision that crossed the boundary between St. Clair and Madison counties. The shared governance of the District is itself a politically contentious and colorful story and would consume too much space to be told here.

Suffice it to say, however, that the job taken on by the District is massive, involving the ongoing maintenance and daily operation of 28.6 miles of levee, 27 closure structures (such as floodgates), 40 gravity drains (to drain water from behind the levees into the river during low water), 340 relief wells to control water pressure under the levees, 3.1 miles of floodwall, and a series of pump stations, each with a capacity of pumping up to 1.2 million gallons of water per minute. This is a system that is all but invisible to the public when it works as it should. When it fails, which hasn't happened in any significant way since the modern system was finished in the 1950s, the outcome would be nothing less than catastrophic, swamping

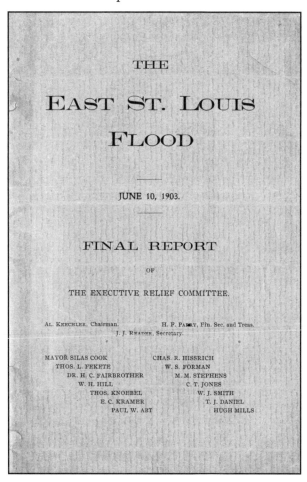

Flood Committee Report, 1903   Bowen Archives, SIUE

some 155,000 inhabitants, 86,000 acres and several billion dollars in property assets.

With these modern flood protection improvements came the confidence of the people who lived and worked in the American Bottom. Population and industry boomed and East St. Louis flourished. In addition, roadways began to crisscross the area and new bridges like the Eads Bridge (completed in 1874) spanned the Mississippi. Ferry service, like that provided by the Wiggins Ferry company, was no longer necessary to cross the river. The advent of the Interstate Highway system in the 1950s and 1960s further shifted the focus from a system of river-based industrial commerce to one more closely related to auto and truck access but perhaps the most significant legacy of the Interstate era for East

St. Louis was the almost complete isolation of its downtown from the riverfront. The construction of the I-70 bridge and its many approaches and ramps (sometimes referred to as the "spaghetti bowl") now create an imposing, sometimes forbidding barrier on the landward side of the riverfront. East St. Louis and the Mississippi River have now become economically and physically disconnected.

The danger of flooding is still ever-present in East St. Louis. More than 100 years after the need for serious attention to flood protection was first recognized, that system continues to be tested by the unruly Mississippi River. In 1993 the Mississippi River crested at over 49 feet in St. Louis, the record high water mark (suggested to be a 350-year flood). The urban levee system

in East St. Louis and surrounding communities successfully held back the river, although not without significant attention to some weak areas that became evident by the appearance of sand boils (water and sand tunneling under the levees due to high water pressure from the river). Yet, the flood of 1993 was a graphic reminder of the largely invisible yet vitally important 70 year old earthen mounds that make up the primary defense against flooding. The devastation of New Orleans from Hurricane Katrina is an even more timely reminder of the consequences of failure to adequately maintain flood control systems. The metro-east St. Louis region is in fact the second largest population center in a floodplain along the Mississippi River. Never has it been more important to keep East St. Louis and the American

Poplar Street Bridge approaches, 2010   Powell Photo

Bottoms area free from the river's unforgiving ways. Although the city itself has fallen on rough times, the region that surrounds it has grown into an economic powerhouse. Warehousing, manufacturing, retail, and a growing population base exist in the American Bottoms area and would endure a catastrophe if the area's levee system failed. The American Bottom has become the industrial heartland of the St. Louis region, housing at least 56,000 jobs, including many in large manufacturing industries like refining, chemicals and steel. These are industries that need river, rail and road access, so the American Bottom has become a strategically important area. There are few other locations in the St. Louis area where such large industries can locate. Curiously, much of this industry has left East St. Louis, leaving a city nearly bereft of economic assets.

Whether it was the 1993 flood or Hurricane Katrina, or numerous instances of serious flooding around the nation, the Federal Emergency Management Agency has turned increased attention to identifying flood hazard areas. In 2007, FEMA announced its intentions to declare the American Bottom a flood hazard area because of deficiencies in the now 70 year old design of the flood protection system. This announcement was a devastating economic blow to the region, since it would require every property owner to buy costly flood insurance and virtually prohibit any development built at any elevation under the height of 100-year flood. In cities like East St. Louis, that could mean a building elevation of 15-20 feet (harkening

back to the original flood protection strategy adopted by East St. Louis in 1875!). Cities like East St. Louis, already suffering from a dearth of economic assets, would have little chance to attract new business, and much of the already low-income populace would be in no position to afford flood insurance premiums.

In 2008, the Illinois General Assembly provided authority for the three counties in the American Bottom to impose a new quarter-cent sales tax to pay for improvements to the area levee systems. The Southwestern Illinois Flood Prevention District Council was established as a rare partnership between the three counties to receive the sales tax money and oversee the restoration of the flood protection system in Madison, Monroe, and St. Clair counties. East St. Louis and all the other communities west of the high bluffs that span the eastern edge of the American Bottom hope the levee improvements will continue to keep the water out and restore sufficient confidence to encourage new investment in the area.

Over the past half-century, East St. Louis has struggled to retain and recruit commercial and residential development and its population has drastically and steadily diminished. Much of that population is impoverished and the vast majority is African-American. Yet, the East St. Louis riverfront transects one of the most heavily traveled corridors in the state and the region, a portal to the city, the region and the state. Sadly, however, the riverfront is mostly uninhabited, and the majority of the land and property is abandoned, neglected,

in disrepair, or rendered unusable from a legacy of toxic chemicals left by years of industrial use. So this arguably prime real estate simply lies fallow. With a couple of notable and incongruous exceptions, the East St. Louis riverfront remains undeveloped and very little evidence of the old river days still exist. One such exception is the Casino Queen. The casino and hotel combination are a much-needed source of jobs for the area and a significant component of the city's desperately needed revenue stream. This casino is situated just south of the Eads Bridge and north of an industrial property, the Cargill granary. The granary stands tall and it's apparent that it was built not for its looks, but as an efficient facility to store grain and move it from truck and rail onto barges. The structure is the de facto Illinois counterpart to the Gateway Arch -- it is simply the most visible structure (leaving aside the rear of the casino) on the east bank of the Mississippi across from downtown St. Louis. The granary, its barge loading facilities, and a series of well-used railroad tracks are a legacy of the industrial past of East St. Louis and a constant reminder that river transportation and industry remain viable economic assets.

Just south of Cargill is a parcel of land that has drastically changed in appearance over the past couple of years and it too has a fascinating history. This property, known as Malcolm W. Martin Memorial Park, is named after a visionary St. Louis attorney who took it upon himself to carry out Eero Saarinen's original vision to extend the Jefferson National Expansion Memorial to the East

St. Louis riverfront. The Illinois extension of the Memorial was eventually dropped from the Saarinen plan in creating the national park, but it was not forgotten by Mr. Martin, who stubbornly and persistently worked for decades to protect and promote the expansion of the national park in Illinois. Mr. Martin founded the Gateway Center of Metropolitan St. Louis, a non-profit organization located in St. Louis that is dedicated to the development of the park on the east bank of the river, and he raised the funds to purchase just over 30 acres in order to carry out his vision. Malcolm Martin loved East St. Louis and its riverfront and in 1995 he completed some of the first park improvements made to the site. The most visible and compelling feature was the Gateway Geyser, a soaring water fountain (second highest in the world) capable of propelling water 630-feet into the air, a height equivalent to the Gateway Arch.

Until his death in 2004 at the age of 91, Mr. Martin and the Gateway Center continued to lobby locally and nationally on behalf of the park in an attempt to cause it become an extension of the National Park.[4]

Sadly, Malcolm Martin died prior to witnessing the outcome of his dogged persistence and hard work. He gifted a majority of his estate to the Gateway Center, which in 2005, donated the Gateway Geyser and the park land to the Metro East Park and Recreation District (MEPRD) as a means to manage and sustain the park and to assist with its further development. In 2009, MEPRD and the Gateway Center opened the park to the public. The new park includes a dramatic Mississippi River Overlook, a 40-foot tall viewing platform that rises above the Mississippi River levee and offers some of the most spectacular views of the Gateway Arch and downtown St. Louis

skyline, as well as a terrific vantage point to view the geyser. Other features of the park include a new administrative facility, pavilions, public restrooms, and an extensive network of walkways, with additional future improvements planned. Most impressive is the fact that the development and continued operation of the park has been and continues to be fully financed by the private donations from the park's benefactors, Malcolm Martin and the Gateway Center, solely for the benefit and enjoyment of the public.

Malcolm Martin's dream and Eero Saarinen's vision to include the Illinois riverfront in the national park may yet be realized. In 2009, the National Park Service (NPS) began a design competition ("Framing a Modern Masterpiece") to "invigorate the park and city areas surrounding one of the world's most iconic monuments, the Gateway Arch in St. Louis." Competing design

Mississippi River Overlook 2010 Werner Photo

teams were instructed to improve connections between the Jefferson National park and downtown St. Louis, improve the park's connection to the Mississippi River, and, most important, to East St. Louis, to consider expanding the national park up to 100 acres in Illinois across the river from the Arch. [5] The design competition requires that all new features be noticeably complete by October 2015. This design competition is giving the St. Louis region's leadership an opportunity to reimagine the Gateway Arch grounds and reinvent the East St. Louis riverfront. Malcolm Martin's isolated but highly visible park is in no small way a catalyst for perhaps the last, best opportunity to make something great from the East St. Louis, Illinois riverfront.

As this discussion has only partially illustrated, there are a variety of conditions, some natural, some man-made, that have conspired to prevent East St. Louis from realizing the value of its most prized physical asset – its frontage on the Mississippi River.

The historical threat of flooding combined with the imposing levees that block the view of the river.

A system of unsightly highways and railroads that encircle the riverfront, divide it from downtown East St. Louis and from the river itself. Access to the riverfront is limited and problematic.

A city government that has not generally been a reliable partner for those who are likely to develop the riverfront or surrounding governments who are likely to provide support.

Unscrupulous developers who have taken advantage of a city desperate for revenues, leading to serial scandals that have all but extinguished legitimate interest in development.

The City itself is impoverished, without the resources to create a safe environment and infrastructure to create opportunities for development.

The legacy of an industrial past that has left the riverfront tainted by hazardous and toxic waste.

The last vestiges of riverine industries that continue to occupy the riverfront but whose presence is inconsistent with the vision of the river as an amenity and attraction for people.

Despite these imposing barriers and past mistakes, hope remains that East St. Louis can reclaim the dream of riverfront development. Perhaps the last, best hope to do so rest, ironically, with the plan to rework the Arch grounds on the west bank of the river in Missouri. The design competition has fortuitously rekindled Eero Saarinen's vision of a river developed on both of its opposing banks as a monument to westward expansion. The vision is big enough that it will require a deep reservoir of support on both sides of the river. This is an opportunity that should be recognized, shaped and vigorously embraced by leadership in East St. Louis and surrounding communities. If not, East St. Louis will pass its uneasy relationship with the Mississippi River on to yet another generation.

End Notes:

1. Bond, J.W. *The East St. Louis, Illinois, Waterfront : Historical Background.* Washington, D.C.: National Park Service, 1969:11.

2. English, Edward. *The Good Things of East St. Louis.* Mascoutah, IL: Tops Books, 1992: Chapter 1.

3. Hier, Marshall D. "Kindred Civic Spirits – Luther Ely Smith and Malcolm Woods Martin - Part II." *The St. Louis Bar Journal,* 2009-Fall: 50.

4. Prost, Charlene. "National Park Service signs off on design competition plan for the Gateway Arch," *St. Louis Beacon.* November 23, 2009.

5. Reavis, L.V. "East St. Louis : Its Past History-Growth-Present Status and Future Prospects." *The Future Great City of the World.* St. Louis: C.R. Barnes, 1876. 51-53.

Chapter 2

The Question of Race & Culture

Limits to Black Political Empowerment: The Historical Significance of Pre-1950 East St. Louis as a Foreshadow to Post-2008 Black Political Dilemmas

Charles L. Lumpkins, Ph.D.

Department of Labor Studies and Employment Relations,
The Pennsylvania State University

On November 5, 2008, American voters did what many thought was the unthinkable: they created a most historic moment by electing Barack Obama, a black American, President of the United States of America, a majority white nation with a deep history of racial divisions.1 Elated with Obama in the White House, his supporters expected him to start to solve the nation's deeply rooted social divisions and economic problems. By 2010, in the President's second year, many Americans, including black Americans, were less euphoric and questioned if Obama could initiate substantive changes favorable to working people of all colors, from ending the worst economic downturn since the Great Depression (1929-1940) to restoring civility in the political culture.

THE MASSACRE OF EAST ST. LOUIS.

Riot victim with bloodied face, 1917   Bowen Archives, SIUE

Influential black critics increasingly have found fault with the Commander-in-Chief for lacking empathy for black Americans and not leading the nation to overcome racial inequality. These commentators should know that even under the most favorable circumstances, African American politicians, including big city mayors and members of Congress, have been ineffective in implementing thoroughgoing policies and programs to end racial inequities that adversely affect black Americans, particularly those in the lower income brackets. Such critics, and Americans generally, need to remember from history that without major changes in the nation's political, economic, and social relations, black political leaders, including Obama, cannot bring about the level of empowerment needed to meet the needs of African Americans.[2]

The history of East St. Louis, Illinois, from 1917 to 1950 reveals the difficulties of achieving black political empowerment of African Americans advancing their ethnic interests to eradicate inequality rooted in racialized hierarchies. The city had been the terrain where black people contested the local manifestations of broad national issues in American history, from battling against racial segregation and discrimination to advancing civil rights and black economic interests. While black East St. Louisans engaged in the formal political arena, such as voting and seeking office, they struggled to end their exclusion from decision-making authority and power sharing in governance.[3] East St. Louis' political culture allowed black residents to demand, protest, and mobilize to attain needed services and black politicians to seek appointive and elective

office while local white political and business elites prevented the attainment of black political empowerment.[4]

From 1917 to 1950, black residents confronted the white factions that commanded the political culture and aggressively used the East St. Louis race riots of 1917 as an opportunity to throttle the black quest for political power sharing over the next several decades.

The city's elites fomented the riots as politically inspired attacks to destroy a racial or ethnic community—a veritable pogrom, a Russian word meaning destruction, rather a riot, which is a spontaneous, disorganized outbreak of mass social violence.

Similar to the anti-Jewish pogroms in Czarist Russia of the nineteenth and early twentieth centuries, the East St. Louis race riots were

Smoke from the riot as seen from St. Louis, 1917   Bowen Archives, SIUE

pogroms in that officially tolerated organized elements launched assaults with the intent to cleanse the city of black people. Even Jewish immigrants and Jewish Americans of Russian background labeled the July riot a pogrom. Henceforth, this essay employs the term pogrom, not riot, to reveal the key reason for the racial violence was to terminate black East St. Louisans' efforts to achieve equality and power sharing. This narrative ends in 1950 when black residents successfully desegregated the city's public school system, signaling that they overcame the legacy of fear of pogroms via demonstrations and court proceedings, not through the formal political arena.[5]

The East St. Louis pogroms of 1917 were two separate episodes of mass anti-black violence. The first erupted on May 28. Leaders of the East St. Louis Central Trades and Labor Union (CTLU), an association of local labor unions, held a public meeting to discuss with Mayor Fred Mollman and city council members ways to prevent black southerners from migrating to East St. Louis to fill job vacancies caused by labor shortages during the First World War (1914-1918). Union leaders realized that the several thousand black migrants who settled in the city after 1915 were part of the Great Migration (1915-1929), a movement that expanded to hundreds of thousands of African Americans leaving the South for employment and a better way of life in northern industrial cities. CTLU officials accused industrialists of recruiting black migrants to break strikes, including the bitter strike that started in mid-April at the huge Aluminum Ore Company facility on the edge of town, and to undermine the drive to unionize the mainly white industrial workforce. The CTLU called upon Mollman to prohibit migrants from settling in the city, but attorney Alexander Flannigan of neighboring Belleville, and other non-union persons hijacked the meeting and exhorted the audience to assault black people. As if on cue, a number of men, some of whom were not East St. Louisans, responded to the call

Ruins of the Broadway Opera House, 1917   Bowen Archives, SIUE

to attack. The pogrom ended on Tuesday, May 29, when the Illinois National Guard under the command of Lieutenant Colonel E.P. Clayton suppressed the assailants. By then the police had arrested dozens; hundreds of black and white individuals had received injuries; and arsonists had torched a few buildings. Fortunately, the pogromists had not killed a single person.[6]

The second East St. Louis pogrom exploded on July 2, making the May event look small and benign in comparison, and forgotten. Between May 29 and July 2, former patrol officer Gus Masserang and other white terrorists drove through black neighborhoods at night, shooting out windows of residences in hopes of sparking racial confrontations. They failed to ignite trouble as long as the National Guard remained in town to deter outbreaks of racial violence. The terrorists saw their chance to create chaos improve when the troops left the city on June 27. These terrorists got the excuse they wanted in the early hours of July 2, when they heard the news of a black armed self-defense group who suspected plainclothes police detectives Samuel Coppedge and Frank Wadley as drive-by terrorists, and shot and killed the two men. By noon, small gangs of armed white men began attacking black men, women, and children in the downtown district, in the predominantly white neighborhoods adjacent to downtown, and along the city boundary next to National City, the small town that housed the facilities of the meatpacking giants Armour & Company, Swift & Company, and Nelson Morris. Unlike the May pogrom, white assailants decided to drive all African Americans from the city in order to turn East St. Louis into an all-white sundown town. At least seven thousand black men, women, and children sought refuge across the Mississippi River in St. Louis, Missouri, and perhaps many hundreds escaped to neighboring Illinois towns. Unlike the May pogrom, some white police officers, outraged about the deaths of Coppedge and Wadley, killed isolated African Americans. Unlike the May violence, the July explosion claimed lives. After National Guard units returned to restore order, officials counted nine white men and 39 black men, women, and children slain. Many black and white townspeople, however, estimated more white people killed and a much higher number of black people murdered.[7]

Observers and commentators in 1917, and many scholars

Searching for bodies in the ashes, 1917   Bowen Archives, SIUE

since then, put forth several reasons for the occurrence of the pogroms, particularly the one in the July, and the failure to turn East St. Louis into a sundown town. Although they have agreed that the reasons are not mutually exclusive, most cite interracial competition for jobs as the primary reason for the racial violence. No doubt, Michael Whalen, Harry Kerr, Earl Jimerson, and other CTLU officials and organizers vociferously denounced black southern migrant laborers as threats to white workers' interests and unionization. Union leaders often joined Thomas Canavan, George Locke Tartlon, and other real estate politician-businessmen in criticizing black migrants for creating a housing shortage for white working people. Although profiting from a racially restricted housing market that forced black

residents to pay higher rents or mortgages for substandard homes, the real estate men speculated that too many black residents would deter white homebuyers from settling in East St. Louis.

White politicians, business owners, trade unionists, and civic leaders accused black southern migrants for the heightened crime wave and immorality as additional reasons that moved white East St. Louisans to commit mass anti-black violence. Attorney Maurice V. Joyce led white residents in claiming that black southerners brought their guns and criminal behavior with them. Baptist minister George Allison and other white community leaders who considered themselves civic progressive reformers asserted that black migrants exacerbated widespread problems of social immorality such as prostitution. Allison and other reformers not

only damned political machine bosses for continually plunging the city deeper into debt and for deriving some of their wealth from saloons, prostitution, and gambling operations, but also for keeping black voters dependent on clientage politics as well as on saloons and prostitution.[8]

Townspeople and observers knew that interracial competition for jobs and housing, crime, and public immorality proved baseless. Everyone knew that far more white people than black people engaged in strikebreaking, consumed alcoholic beverages to excess, lived off prostitution, and did other things deemed socially undesirable. For example, concerning job competition and anti-unionism, CTLU officials knew that black workers had joined and led strikes, including the July 1916 meatpacking strike and that black workers were no

Mineola McGee, arm lost to gunfire, 1917   Bowen Archives, SIUE

more or less interested in unions than white workers were. Despite CTLU's denunciations of black southern migrants taking jobs from white workers, the dentist LeRoy Bundy, physician Lyman Bluitt, and other black political leaders met with CTLU people to discuss unionizing black workers en masse. Indeed, in 1919, some 300 black packinghouse workers, with much support from their clergy, met in East St. Louis City Hall auditorium and pledged to unionize. More importantly, since the competition for jobs and housing, crime waves, gambling, and prostitution existed for decades before (and after) the pogroms, another factor--politics----had to spark and sustain the pogroms.[9]

Politics, not issues relating to labor disputes, laid the foundation that made the pogroms possible and in turn crushed attempts by black citizens to exercise political independence or even to have equal access or entitlements

to city services and resources. Industrialists wanted African Americans for their labor power and heavily armed black residents on the city's south side were key reasons for East St. Louis not becoming a sundown town. Political bosses curried the favors of industrialists, and to keep the loyalty of their black constituents, in June Mayor Mollman ordered the police department to return the guns it confiscated from black residents. In addition, machine politicians rewarded, for example, the ex-slave and community politician Captain John Robinson, bondsman and saloonkeeper William "Buddy" Bell, prostitution ring boss and political operative "Kid" Amos, and other black individuals and their friends for working within the framework of white-dominated clientage politics. They knew that black voters, mindful of their racially restricted position in the local economy, saw patronage as resource distribution and disapproved progressive reform

candidates who sought to end such patronage.

Political machine bosses tolerated black residents selling their votes and engaging in swing and bloc voting when they cast ballots for those city and county Democratic or Republican Party political machine candidates who rewarded them with patronage in exchange for their loyalty.[10] In April 1917, the nascent black political machine of independent-minded Republican and Democratic politicians and operatives led by Bundy demanded its rewards from the Tartlton-Canavan machine whose candidate, Fred Mollman, won reelection as mayor on the strength of the black voter turnout. The black machine never collected its rewards. It lost its direction with the May pogrom, and it was shattered by the July pogrom. Parden, Bundy, those associated with the black machine, and other community activists were arrested on charges of scheming to massacre white

Narcis Gurley, age 70, showing severe burns, 1917   Bowen Archives, SIUE

townspeople, and some, including Bundy, were imprisoned for a few years.[11]

The pogroms marked a watershed in East St. Louis' history and allowed white factions to reconstruct city governance that thwarted the black quest for equality and power sharing over the next few decades in East St. Louis. With support from the Illinois and federal governments, Allison, Superintendent of Missouri Malleable Iron Company John P. Pero, former Mayor John M. Chamberlin, and other progressive-minded reformers seized the opportunity to impose white tutelage over politically "irresponsible" black townspeople and to dethrone the political bosses. Through the ad hoc Committee of One Hundred, comprised of leading business and civic citizens and other organizations, reformers reconstructed city governance on the commission form of municipal government model because it redistributed power from the mayor to several commissioners responsible for different functions of city government. At the same time, reformers and members of the Real Estate Exchange agreed to a strict adherence of residential segregation. They and white neighborhood improvement associations imposed rigid housing segregation through various means without resorting to violence of the likes that occurred in Chicago where terrorists bombed residences that black homebuyers purchased in white areas.

Reformers failed to dismantle the political machines whose bosses adapted to the commission form of government, but they succeeded in deemphasizing the importance of the black vote because, unlike the city council with its ward-based elections, the new government rested upon citywide elections of commissioners. As a result, boss politicians no longer competed strenuously for the black vote, reformers gained an efficient form of governance, and black townspeople had their political strength diminished significantly and had to reside in certain districts rather than live anywhere in the city as they did before. More ominously, in the years after 1917, various white sources occasionally reminded black townspeople not to challenge, let alone overturn, the new political reality or risk provoking a new round of anti-black violence.[12]

In the decades following 1917, various events had the makings of erupting into mass racial violence, but such possibilities never materialized, further dramatizing the political nature of the pogroms in that various factions decided when to unleash violence. Periodically, black East St. Louisans heard that the city avoided a "race riot" because the authorities arrested troublemakers or because African Americans moderated their behavior that would otherwise move white people to anger. For example, toward the end of the

nationwide meatpacking strike of 1921-1922 for higher wages and union recognition, black and white packinghouse workers in East St. Louis remained united despite the fact that some white strikers shot and killed two black strikebreakers while ignoring the white strikebreakers, an action that never occurred among strikers in 1917. The authorities, however, took swift action against the shooters and others, using the opportunity to protect strikebreakers (and management interests) and to end the strike. For another example, when unemployment rose in East St. Louis in 1924, CTLU leaders and the East St. Louis Overseer of the Poor did not want black laborers coming to seek jobs in the city. They pressured Mayor Melburn Stevens to inform Clarence J. McLinn, Bessie King, and other officials of the East St. Louis chapter of the National Association for the Advancement of Colored People (NAACP), formed earlier that year, to tell black southern migrants to stay away or risk the possibility of mass violence similar to the pogroms of 1917.

Whether or not the NAACP succeeded in decreasing the number of new black arrivals to the city, its actions showed a desire to defuse the possibility of anti-black violence. Black townspeople heard a similar warning of a probability of mass violence in 1943 when labor representative Fred Olds told Lincoln High School principal O. V. Quinn that black East St. Louisans were asking for trouble if they did not "leave things alone as they now are." Olds was reacting to Quinn's statements that city leaders must include black residents in discussions on planning the future of East St. Louis.[13]

Black East St. Louisans confronted a reconstructed political culture that allowed them to operate freely within the parameters of segregation and white oversight, minus the right to forge an independent path to empowerment for their community. They had neither the numbers to elect black candidates in citywide elections nor the breadth of territory to influence many white politicians. Instead, black residents found themselves tightly bound to Fred Gerold and other machine politicians who treated African American neighborhoods as their fiefdoms. Black residents also encountered George Alison, John Pero, and other progressive reformers using the local chapter of the National Urban League to aid low-income African Americans, especially the new arrivals from the South, on acclimating to life in a white-dominated industrial city. Lincoln High School administrator John W. Hughes, the Reverend G.H. Haines, and other black chapter members who espoused black middle-class racial uplift virtues such as sobriety, thrift, and punctuality to the black poor found that their ideas converged with those of the reformers. In 1920, Reverend John DeShields and other black members who disliked white oversight left the Urban League chapter and joined with concerned black townspeople to form the politically active social welfare-type organizations like the Colored Welfare Association. These persons wanted their groups to have some degree of autonomy from white East St. Louisans who had no desire to challenge, let alone dismantle, the white-dominated social hierarchy.[14]

Since African Americans in post-pogrom East St. Louis wanted a better way of life, they had no choice but to forge ways to achieve political empowerment. Increasing numbers of African Americans entered industrial employment during the 1920s and after. Many, however, occupied menial and unskilled positions, mainly in meatpacking, steel manufacturing, and other labor-intensive mass production industries. Having little or no workplace seniority, most black workers remained vulnerable to both downturns in the economic cycle and employment discrimination. With few prospects for opportunities at the workplace, black East St. Louisans fashioned different strategies, some concurrently, to advance themselves as they found ways to circumvent the limits that boss politicians, progressive reformers, and employers and labor unionists imposed on them. Although the choices of actions spanned the spectrum, most black political activism manifested itself in separatist and community-based approaches, the latter involving leftist and mainstream associations, clubs, and political parties.[15]

A minority of black residents pursued separatist politics associated with organizations like the international mass-based Universal Negro Improvement Association (UNIA) in the 1920s or the miniscule pro-Japanese

Pacific Movement of the Eastern World (PMEW), the latter based in East St. Louis, in the 1930s and early 1940s. Such separatist-oriented organizations envisioned black empowerment through all-black jurisdictions, be they towns or nation-states, or black-owned institutions. For instance, in 1939 and 1940, against the opposition of integration-oriented physicians, Dr. Nathaniel Hagler built and opened a fifteen-bed hospital for black maternity patients on the notion that black people must have their own medical facility rather than rely on white-owned city hospitals that delivered segregated, often inadequate, services to black patients. Separatist approaches were short-lived, failed to reach the objectives they sought, and did not spark movements toward social and economic advancement. Local adherents of the UNIA gravitated to other groups, including the PMEW, when the national UNIA faded after the federal government imprisoned its charismatic founder and leader Marcus Garvey of mail fraud and later deported him to Jamaica. Within weeks after the Japanese bombardment at Pearl Harbor, Hawaii, on December 7, 1941, the pro-Japanese PMEW met its demise when the Federal Bureau of Investigation arrested David Erwin and other PMEW leaders in East St. Louis and forced the organization to disband.[16]

Most Black East St. Louisans overlapped their participation in informal politics-protests, demonstrations, boycotts, labor movement activities, and other actions--with their desire to work within the formal political arena. They often used such actions to pressure the authorities to make concessions. In the 1930s and 1940s, for example, some residents worked with socialist or communist groups mainly to mobilize working class residents and industrial workers around issues pertaining to wage earners such as unemployment relief, union protection, and collective bargaining rights. Black and white members and supporters of leftist groups found themselves victims of police harassment and arrest because the authorities despised socialist and communist groups and any racially integrated leftist movement.[17]

African American industrial workers entered the labor movement in the 1930s and 1940s to win collective bargaining rights and to end discrimination at the workplace. Even in labor unions with pro-civil rights officials, black workers ran into barriers that white unionists and employers constructed to end the erosion of white entitlements to resources.[18] Most black townspeople, however, agitated through the local NAACP chapter and other community-based groups to win, among other things, better schools, streets, city services, healthcare facilities, and housing. What concessions they won proved short-term and limited in scope, forcing them to engage in another cycle of protests.[19]

From the 1920s, black East St.

Louisans searched for ways to empower themselves as a community. Of course, William "Buddy" Bell, Joseph Chunn, and Harvey T. Bowman, and other black Republican and Democratic operatives continued the clientage system for their personal needs. On the other hand, mortician Charles Nash, laborer Walter Nichols, and others ran unsuccessfully as candidates for various offices, including East St. Louis representative to the Illinois General Assembly. These community-oriented politicians joined with others to continue the decades-long tradition of forming men's and women's political clubs to educate and mobilize African American voters to support the Democratic or Republican Party candidates. Political club members worked within the precinct committee system as precinct committeemen and committeewomen who formed the backbone of the

local party structure in their neighborhoods. Democratic Party operative Eliza Hart and her Republican counterpart Nevada Hamilton who, in 1928, became the first black women as precinct committee leaders, and other committee persons made their highest priority the effort to get voters to the polls on election day, particularly when black candidates ran for office. Nonetheless, African Americans in East St. Louis knew that the precinct system served at the pleasure of the political party, which rarely worked to meet the special needs of the black community.[20]

Black East St. Louisans knew that both mainstream parties lacked the will to overturn the status quo of racial segregation and discrimination. With the exception of individuals working with socialist or communist groups that demanded an immediate end to segregation,

Congressional investigators at City Hall, 1918   Bowen Archives, SIUE

most black activists and politicians took the pragmatic approach to improve black East St. Louisans' lives within the parameters of segregation. Some community activists, however, saw the pragmatic approach of accommodating to segregation as a temporary tactical maneuver until the black community developed the muscle to dismantle racial barriers. Toward that goal, Horace Adams, Charles Nash, and other activist politicians, disgusted with the local Republican Party taking black voters for granted, founded in 1926 the Paramount Democratic Organization (PDO), an all-black political machine closely allied with the Democratic Party. The founders made the PDO indispensible to Democratic Party leaders by making the organization a powerhouse in mobilizing black voters for the party not only in East St. Louis, but also across southern Illinois. Paramount Democratic Organization leaders channeled resources like appointive political offices and patronage jobs from the party and city hall to the black community.

PDO officials welded a black constituency loyal to the Democratic Party. Before the PDO, black East St. Louisans often voted for Democratic candidates for local office, but not for national level candidates because they identified the national Democratic Party as the chief architect and bulwark of legalized segregation in the southern states. In 1928, when a majority of black voters in several urban locales switched from the Republican Party to the Democratic Party in the presidential election, the PDO led a similar effort

among black East St. Louisans. The organization convinced a majority of black voters that the national Republicans under Herbert Hoover ignored black people's needs while Democratic presidential candidate Alfred Smith, a Roman Catholic, promised hope for African Americans having a greater role in national politics.

PDO's success foreshadowed the completion of the historical switch of party allegiance from the Republican to the Democratic Party in the presidential election of 1936 when the majority of black Americans nationwide (71 percent, up from 23 percent in 1932) voted for President Franklin Delano Roosevelt and joined the Democratic Party-New Deal coalition. The PDO's most significant victory occurred in 1934 when its candidate, dentist Aubrey Smith, won the seat as representative of East St. Louis in the Illinois General Assembly. Smith won the plurality of the vote because black residents organized as a voting bloc while the white vote split among several candidates. Smith held his position for one term because white political factions, not thrilled that a black man was the city's representative in state government, succeeded in disciplining themselves to lead the effort to vote Smith out of office.[21]

PDO founders and their successors maintained an effective organization in mainstream politics by not acting independently of the white political machines and learning to stay within well-defined limits after boss politicians had harassed, beaten, and framed Adams on charges of corruption in 1929

and sent him to Leavenworth Prison in Kansas for one year.[22] PDO leaders reaped rewards for the black community for its loyalty to white political machines, but it could not make certain breakthroughs such as electing African Americans to key offices like the mayor, police commissioner, or the director of the levee board. The PDO could not assert African American issues such as total desegregation in housing and education without undermining its effectiveness to win patronage and other resources for the black community. More importantly, the PDO was part of the Democratic Party's New Deal coalition, and from 1933 to 1940, the New Deal provided much needed work relief and new federally built housing.

Black East St. Louisans, however, criticized the New Deal for entrenching racial discrimination with segregated jobs programs (for example, both the Works Progress Administration and the National Youth Administration)

and segregated federal housing (the John Robinson Homes for black residents and the Samuel Gompers Homes for white residents). Like African Americans and other victims of racial, ethnic, and religious discrimination across the United States, black East St. Louisans applauded the existence of the Fair Employment Practices Committee (FEPC), established in 1941 by President Franklin Delano Roosevelt and the pro-civil rights wing of the Democratic Party to nudge employers with federal contracts to end discrimination. Although African Americans knew that the FEPC lacked muscle to enforce antidiscrimination, they enlisted the committee in their many fights against workplace discrimination. In general, PDO members had to agitate through community organizations outside of the formal political arena and the Democratic Party to seek racial equality and promote the expanding civil rights movement.[23]

Like African Americans elsewhere, black East St. Louisans built and sustained a mass-based civil disobedience phase of the Civil Rights Movement to battle for racial equality beyond what the Democratic and Republican parties were willing to grant. In 1949, they began their assault on the segregated public school system, dating to the 1870s, that violated Illinois civil rights laws. Attorney Louis Orr and other black members of the NAACP chapter started the school desegregation campaign of demonstrations and court litigation that ended in victory in 1950 when the school board agreed to end segregation. Black residents expanded their civil rights struggle into the 1950s and 1960s with actions to end segregation in public accommodations and residential districts.[24]

African Americans in East St. Louis, especially after the Second World War, expected their lives to improve as they dismantled segregation and discrimination.

If LeRoy Bundy and his cohorts had succeeded in establishing an independent black political machine that held the promise of power politics and reshaping political dynamics, then black residents would have had the chance for both substantive racial equality and power sharing.

When the pogroms and the reconstruction of East St. Louis smashed the promise of black empowerment through such a political machine, black residents had no choice but to continue their involvement in patronage and clientage politics under the decision-making authority of white machine boss politicians and politician-businessmen. Black East St. Louisans increased their numbers and percentage in the urban industrial economy dramatically during and after World War I and more so during and after World War II. Unfortunately, most black families arrived during and after the early 1920s when East St. Louis reached its apogee in the rate of industrial growth.[25] Some black East St. Louisans saw improvements in their lives, but most reached the point where patronage and clientage politics and community-based mobilization had their limits and proved ineffective.

The majority of residents did not have the chance to build a solid foundation of intergenerational

wealth between the 1920s and the 1960s when, in the latter decade, the city deindustrialized.

When black townspeople began to take advantage of the opportunities that the Civil Rights Movement had brought in the mid and late 1960s, they had a city that experienced complete deindustrialization, a political culture in shambles, and a drain of wealth when white residents moved from the city to the suburbs.

African Americans in East St. Louis saw that their city's survival depended on the largesse and dictates of county, state, and federal governments.[26]

As one has scholar noted, numerous African Americans now know that clientage politics as practiced by the Democratic and Republican parties failed to deliver the necessary level of resources to prevent the urban black community from sinking further into economic despair and political isolation. They question if President Obama has the tools to direct his party toward sharing power with black America. Some black urbanites, however, have turned to various forms of political activism that are about power politics. Their aims somewhat echoed the voices of a short-lived black political machine in East St. Louis in 1917.[27]

End Notes:

1. For examples of recent publications documenting Barack Obama's journey to the White House and/or Obama in context of the Civil Rights and Black Power movements or generally in context of American culture, including the reactions of anti-Obama Americans, see, John Amato and David Neiwart, *Over the Cliff: How Obama's Election Drove the American Right Insane* (Sausalito, California: PoliPointPress, 2010); Gwen Ifill, *The Breakthrough: Politics and Race in the Age of Obama* (New York: Doubleday, 2009); Peniel E. Joseph, *Dark Days, Bright Nights: From Black Power to Barack Obama* (New York: BasicCivitas Books, 2010); David Remnick, *The Bridge: The Life and Rise of Barack Obama* (New York: Knopf 2010); T. Denean Sharpley-Whiting, *The Speech: Race and Barack Obama's "A More Perfect Union"* (New York: Bloomsbury, 2009); John Kenneth White, *Barack Obama's America: How New Conceptions of Race, Family, and Religion Ended the Reagan Era* (Ann Arbor: University of Michigan Press, 2009); Tim Wise, *Between Barack and a Hard Place: Racism and White Denial in the Age of Obama* (San Francisco: City Lights Publishers, 2009).

2. Radio and television talk show host and commentator Tavis Smiley and political left radical philosopher and activist Cornel West are among the leading critics of Obama in the African American community. See, for example, Smiley in Irv Randolph, "Aiding Black Agenda without Political Suicide," *Philadelphia Tribune*, March 16, 2010, 11A; see West in "Cornel and Tavis," *Sentinel* (Los Angeles), March 10, 2010, A7. For examples of recent publications that criticize Obama for not aggressively pursuing an open debate about whether or not America is "post-racial" see Jon Jeter and Robert E. Pierre, *A Day Late and a Dollar Short: High Hopes and Deferred Dreams in Obama's "Post-Racial" America* (Hoboken, New Jersey: John Wiley & Sons, 2010). A discussion about the pressures black mayors endured negotiating the fulfillment of economic civil rights and pleasing the white business and political communities in numerous cities see J. Phillip Thompson, *Double Trouble: Black Mayors, Black Communities, and the Call for a Deep Democracy* (New York: Oxford University Press, 2006). The essay's foundational principle of complex, interactions of economics and politics is drawn from Paul Kantor, *The Dependent City Revisited: The Political Economy of Urban Development and Social Policy* (Boulder, Colorado: Westview Press, 1995), 5-7.

3. This essay agrees with scholars who argue for the need to study and evaluate segregation as a cultural and political construct, not as an analytical and descriptive category of de facto and de jure segregation. For example, see Matthew D. Lassiter, "De Jure/De Facto Segregation: The Long Shadow of a National Myth," *The Myth of Southern Exceptionalism*, edited by Matthew D. Lassiter and Joseph Crespino (New York: Oxford University Press, 2010), 27-28. The local level where people expend much of their energy to win their rights and achieve equality through demands, protests, electoral mobilization, and other tactics and strategies is discussed generally in Rufus P. Browning, Dale Rogers Marshall, and David H. Tabb, eds., *Racial Politics in American Cities*, 3rd ed. (New York: Longman, 2003). Examples of works that show how white American working people use ethnicity or race to advance their class or economic interests, see David R. Roediger, *The Wages of Whiteness: Race and the Making of the American Working Class* (London: Verso, 1991); Ira Katznelson, *When Affirmative Action Was White: An Untold History of Racial Inequality in Twentieth-Century America* (New York: Norton, 2005).

4. On East St. Louis political culture generally, see Andrew J. Theising, *Made in USA: East St. Louis: The Rise and Fall of an Industrial River Town* (St. Louis: Virginia Publishing, 2003); On history of black East St. Louisans and their relationship to the city's political culture before 1945, see Charles L. Lumpkins, *American Pogrom: The East St. Louis Race Riot and Black Politics* (Athens: Ohio University Press, 2008).

5. Jewish European immigrants and Jewish Americans referred to the East St. Louis race riots as pogroms. See Lumpkins, *American Pogrom*, 127. On riots and pogroms, see, for example, John D. Klier and Shlomo Lambroza, eds., *Pogroms: Anti-Jewish Violence in Modern Russian History* (New York: Cambridge University Press, 1992); Paul R. Brass, ed., *Riots and Pogroms* (New York: New York University Press, 1996).

6. For description of the May 1917 riot, see Elliott M. Rudwick, *Race Riot at East St. Louis, July 2, 1917* (Carbondale: Southern Illinois University Press, 1964); Malcolm McLaughlin, *Power, Community, and Racial Killing in East St. Louis* (New York: Palgrave Macmillan, 2005); Lumpkins, *American Pogrom*.

7. For a description of the July 1917 riot, see Rudwick, *Race Riot at East St. Louis*; McLaughlin, *Power, Community, and Racial Killing in East St. Louis*; Lumpkins, *American Pogrom*. On sundown towns, see, for example, James W. Loewen, *Sundown Towns: A Hidden Dimension of American Racism* (New York: New Press, 2005).

8. For examples of historians arguing that white workers' fears of black competition constituted the primary reason for triggering both episodes of mass violence of May and July 1917, see Rudwick, *Race Riot at East St. Louis*; Malcolm McLaughlin, *Power, Community, and Racial Killing in East St. Louis*; for politics as the primary reason, see chapters three and four in Lumpkins, *American Pogrom*. On clientage politics in East St. Louis, see Roger Biles, "Black Mayors: A Historical Assessment," *Journal of Negro History*, 77 (Summer 1992), 111. East St. Louis also attracted white migrant laborers. Research is necessary to determine the percentage of white East St. Louisans of southern origins between 1900 and 1920. Circumstantial evidence suggests that white southerners or white East St. Louisans of southern origins formed a measurable percentage of the city's white population. On migrations of white southerners to the North and West, see James N. Gregory, *The Southern Diaspora: How the Great Migrations of Black and White Southerners Transformed America* (Chapel Hill: University of North Carolina Press, 2005). The presence of over 300 saloons in early 1917 and the rampant prostitution were two of many examples of East St. Louis as a dependent city. East St. Louis was an economically dependent municipality when it became a city in 1861, and became increasingly dependent as the city attracted industrial corporations in search of tax breaks and pro-growth policies. On the creation of economically dependent cities, see, for example, Kantor, *The Dependent City Revisited*, 45-46, 75. On East St. Louis as a dependent city, see Theising, *Made in USA*, 59-93; Lumpkins, *American Pogrom*, chapter one generally.

9. Lumpkins, *American Pogrom*, 103-104, 158.

10. Lumpkins, *American Pogrom*, parts of chapters three and four. On an extended discussion of black armed self-defense in East St. Louis, see McLaughlin, *Power, Community, and Racial Killing in East St. Louis*. In national elections prior to 1928, black East St. Louisans generally voted Republican, the "party of Lincoln," but in local elections, black voters voted for Democratic Party candidates as often as they voted Republican, much depending on which party promised to deliver patronage.

11. Lumpkins, *American Pogrom*, 44-73. Interestingly, the authorities and pogromists did not harass, let alone harm, Captain John Robinson, William Bell, and other African Americans who white boss politicians and other city leaders approved.

12. Lumpkins, *American Pogrom*, 132-134, 139-140.

13. Lumpkins, *American Pogrom*, 160-161, 202-203. Some black residents established an NAACP chapter in 1915. Members disbanded the chapter in 1919 in anger or disappointment when the NAACP National Office refused to give Bundy unquestioned support for his legal defense in the trials that sent him to prison; see Lumpkins, *American Pogrom*, 138.

14. Lumpkins, *American Pogrom*, 161-165, 170.

15. Ibid, 151-154.

16. Ibid, 146, 182-183, 197.

17. Ibid, 187-189.

18. Ibid, 190-191.

19. Ibid, 179-187.

20. Ibid, 166-170.

21. Ibid, 171-172, 192-193.

22. Ibid, 172, 193. Chances were that Adams conflicted with Republican Party bosses who hated the PDO making inroads in the traditionally Republican-oriented black community.

23. Ibid, 177-179, 183-187, 193-194, 196, 199-201.

24. Ibid, 36-37, 177; Elliott M. Rudwick, "Fifty Years of Race Relations in East St. Louis: The Breaking Down of White Supremacy," *Midcontinent American Studies Journal* 6, no. 1 (Spring 1965): 3-15.

25. Lumpkins, *American Pogrom*, 148, 206.

26. On black empowerment as political activism when black voters, activists, and politicians no longer want to be clients but participants and decision makers in American pluralist politics, see James Jennings, *The Politics of Black Empowerment: The Transformation of Black Activism in Urban America* (Detroit: Wayne State University Press, 1992). On the social and political impact of deindustrialization on East St. Louis, see Theising, *Made in USA*, 19-48.

27. On factions of politicized African Americans deemphasizing clientage politics and turning toward the power politics, see Jennings, *The Politics of Black Empowerment*.

A University Without Walls: Katherine Dunham's Performing Arts Training Center and Public Humanities, 1967-1977

Kim Curtis, Ph.D.

Department of Social and Behavioral Sciences
Harris-Stowe State University

What do we teach our young ones?
What do they think?
What would they tell us if we would let them,
if they were, as articulate as they should be?
Should we start with the truth about ourselves
who we are, where we live? Let us start with...The Young Adult.[1]

During many programs of the Performing Arts Training Center Company, directed by Katherine Dunham, "The Lesson" preceded the company's signature act "Ode to Taylor Jones." This poetic meditation embodied the philosophy and activism of the center, which was established in East St. Louis in December 1967. The center was designed to provide the disadvantaged youth in this predominately African American, inner-city community opportunities to pursue higher education that were otherwise unavailable to them. Giving voice to the inarticulate through movement, music, and theatrical performance, the center taught African Americans "the truth about [them]selves"—their heritage, history, and culture, and the value of multidisciplinary training in the arts and humanities for underprivileged urban minority youth.[2]

The Katherine Dunham Center for the Arts and Humanities, in the opulent
Maurice V. Joyce manse, 2010   Powell Photo

The Performing Arts Training Center (PATC) is more complex with more significant contributions than previously recognized. It has been identified as a participant in the Black Arts Movement and, indeed, heavily emphasized raising black consciousness in East St. Louis through African-American and African history and art. On the other hand, however, the PATC also offered cultural and educational experiences that celebrated additional ethnicities and nationalities. The philosophy behind its inception also has yet to be discussed in much detail, obscuring the center's complexity and uniqueness. Rather than being a simple educational or community center, this essay argues that the PATC in theory and practice served as a non-traditional "university without walls," which frustrates efforts to categorize it. During the years in which Dunham served as its director, especially during its first decade of operation, the center existed in an unusual space where it simultaneously affirmed and challenged the Black Arts Movement and was associated with institutions of higher education at the same time that it sought to revolutionize them.

Within and outside the PATC's intellectual and artistic boundaries, the creative and performing arts, black consciousness, the humanities, Western and non-Western cultures, psychology, and intellect collided. Bringing the ivory tower to the gritty urban environment of East St. Louis and breaking down that tower's walls, the PATC disseminated knowledge of multiple cultures to the city's community. In addition, it showed a racial group with no collective memory of its own African and African American culture, while simultaneously exposing that group to the languages, music, and movement of other cultures. Ultimately, it was part of general efforts to raise consciousness about the type of education—multidisciplinary arts and humanities training—best suited for urban populations. The center brought the cultures of the world to East St. Louis, instilled pride among its residents, and changed definitions of community and higher education.

"Miss Dunham": A Brief Biography

Born June 22, 1909, in Glen Ellyn, Illinois, Dunham began her career in dance as a teenager. She studied ballet and anthropology at the University of Chicago where she earned her bachelor's, master's, and doctoral degrees, and developed skills as artist, anthropologist, public intellectual, and "interpreter of African traditions."[3] During her many visits to the Caribbean to study its nations' cultures, Dunham matured as a choreographer and dance anthropologist who fused her studies with an appreciation for Caribbean countries' unique styles of movement. Inspired by these travels, she created the Dunham technique, a "fusion of the Afro-Caribbean dance with ballet and modern movement" that combined African and European cultures.[4] From the late 1940s to 1967, she taught at the Dunham School of Dance and Theatre, did research and traveled abroad, and toured with her history-making African American dance company before settling in East St. Louis. She resided there (in addition to Haiti and New York) for most of the rest of her life. With a career spanning almost seventy years, Dunham left an iconic legacy of art, international activism, scholarship, and "myriad accomplishments" that span multiple disciplines and make her as complex and extraordinary as the institutions she created.[5] She appeared in films, on television, and performed in venues as diverse as nightclubs and opera houses; choreographed and staged countless television and theatre productions; gave lectures, taught at the university level, and wrote scholarly and creative works; was a poet, painter, and musical composer; and received numerous awards and eighteen honorary doctorates.

The Performing Arts Training Center

Dunham's PATC existed within the context of life in city communities during an era of urban renewal, suburbanization, and increasing poverty. By 1960 the majority of African Americans resided in northern cities in which they encountered the obstacles of decaying industrial infrastructures, racial and spatial segregation, job discrimination, poverty, and white flight to suburban areas.[6] East St. Louis was an example of these trends. In 1960, East St. Louis received recognition from *Look Magazine* as "an All America City" due to its social welfare institutions, the development of its built environment, and societal reforms. As Andrew Theising explains, however, this recognition belied the persistence of economic problems and social ills in the city.[7] During the mid-1950s, there was a domino effect of one industry after another losing profits and cutting thousands of jobs, beginning with the city's main industry, Aluminum Ore Company. In the decade following these losses of profits and jobs in East St. Louis, even more companies began to close their doors or lay off significant numbers of workers. The city did not experience the effects of the nation's booming economy after 1945, instead maintaining a 21 percent unemployment rate. For African Americans the situation was bleaker, with unemployment reaching 33 percent by the early 1970s and no opportunities to work union jobs.

Amidst these economic and social problems during the 1960s and most of the 1970s, many African Americans transitioned from participating in the integrationist Civil Rights Movement to affiliating with militant movements for black nationalism and Black Power. Although they had acquired unprecedented social and political rights, African Americans remained economically and culturally impoverished, relatively estranged from their African heritage, and unsure about their cultural and racial identity. Inspired by the philosophies articulated by Malcolm X, Marcus Garvey, and other black nationalists, many African Americans wanted to feel a rejuvenated respect for and pride in blackness. The Black Power and Black Arts movements created a social, cultural, and intellectual milieu in which these collective desires were fulfilled. Raising black consciousness, or creating a worldview grounded in African

and African American history and culture, became a significant part of black nationalist ideology and the artistic expressions of Black Power. Intellectual, psychological, and spiritual freedoms were thus posited as critical precursors to maximize the benefits of recently-obtained political freedoms.

In this environment, Katherine Dunham founded the Performing Arts Training Center in East St. Louis, Illinois, funded by a grant from the Equal Opportunity Commission and in partnership with Southern Illinois University-Edwardsville (SIUE). Dunham came to East St. Louis three years earlier to choreograph "Faust," an opera produced by Southern Illinois University Carbondale. After a trip to Senegal to which she was invited by its president to have her *Ballet Negre* perform in a black arts festival, she returned to serve as artist in residence and cultural affairs consultant for SIUE. During this time, she created an arts education program, which became the Performing Arts Training Center. Eugene Redmond, poet, scholar, senior consultant to the PATC, and member of the center's Performing Company, describes Dunham's arrival in East St. Louis as "a catalyst for . . . 'revolutions' in cultural arts, social/political thought, and community service."[8] Indeed, in East St. Louis in the 1960s and 1970s, Dunham's presence awakened minds, liberated bodies, tempered aggression, and lent a cosmopolitan flair to a poverty-stricken, insular urban community.

The PATC was part of Southern

Illinois University's Experiment in Higher Education, and began offering associate of arts degrees in 1969. Located next to one of the campuses of the university, the center's classes, performances, and activities were held at 616 North 10th Street and its affiliated Dynamic Museum was located at 532 North 10th Street. Both were located on the same street on which Dunham lived. Teaching "cross cultural communication" and being "oriented, at least initially, to the environmental demands of the Afro-American experience," the PATC prepared students to perform art as a profession or teach the performing and creative arts.[9] Each quarter, it served approximately one thousand people of all ages—from preschoolers to senior citizens—through credit and non-credit classes, public seminars, workshops, and activities. The center's mission was to provide quality, easily accessible education, encourage its students to participate in community service, and sponsor a performing company.

Continuing the philosophy of the Dunham School, which Dunham created in New York in 1943, the PATC's main goal was to develop the intellectual interests and improve the psychological health of disadvantaged youth who otherwise would not pursue higher education.[10] As Dunham described it, the PATC was "a unique effort to motivate and stimulate the unchallenged young people of the East St. Louis area through the use of an alternative value system and point of view that the arts provide."[11] She believed that students should be educated as people and humanists who are aware of the present and can change society.

The PATC primarily was an educational center. Its academic program included college-level courses and a community services program. Character and personalities were shaped as well as minds. The program was rigorous, as instructors made use of a variety of scholarly texts and distributed lecture notes prior to class as required reading. The academic program offered by the center consisted of two years or eight quarters. Instructors from cities throughout the United States and countries as far away as Senegal, France, and Japan taught the curriculum, which combined the humanities and the performing arts through four main areas of study: music, dance, theatre, and applied skills. The center's community services program offered non-credit classes in the performing arts and arts instruction to residents of East St. Louis and its surrounding communities, and Illinois high schools, churches, and elementary schools.

In addition to its formal academic program, the PATC educated the public through its Dynamic Museum and Performing Company. The museum educated students and the public, blacks and whites, about African and African American visual art. It served as a cultural center that housed art from Africa, the West Indies, and the Caribbean, memorabilia from the Dunham Company's travels, and Dunham's personal art collection. Inverting the traditional priorities of museums, the Dynamic Museum focused on educating whites and blacks in African American

culture and then devoting its attention to acquiring art. Composed of students, teacher-trainees, and instructors, the Performing Company served institutions in the metropolitan area, cities across the nation, and other countries. It did so by presenting African, African American, West Indian, South American, and European poetry, music, dance, and folk cultures to black and white audiences in America and abroad.

From its inception, the PATC struggled to have adequate facilities, personnel, and financial support. For example, Dunham brought lighting, flooring, plumbing, and washroom fixtures to East St. Louis from the Dunham School in New York City, but there initially was no money to have them installed. Due to limited space, the Actor's Studio had to serve many purposes in these early years, being used for everything from after-school snacks to putting on plays. In addition, Dunham was working so much for the center, serving as both its director and entire administrative staff, that the publication of her book *Island Possessed* was delayed by five years.[12] Moreover, although some were funded by institutions such as the Danforth and Rockefeller Foundations, many of the grant proposals Dunham submitted to various foundations for financial support were denied. Under Dunham's direction, however, the center thrived at its original location until 1977, when it was renamed the Katherine Dunham Center and relocated to 1005 Pennsylvania Avenue in East St. Louis. There, it evolved into the Katherine Dunham Centers for Arts and Humanities,

which presently serves the city's community. During its first ten years, the PATC participated in the Black Arts Movement while simultaneously celebrating West Indian, South American, and Asian cultures. It also established itself as an innovative attempt to meet the educational and psychological needs of the inner-city communities.

An Emphasis on Black Culture: The PATC and the Black Arts Movement

As part of the Black Arts Movement in America, the PATC taught and performed the revolutionary ideologies of Black Power and black nationalism for audiences across the United States and the inner-city African American community of East St. Louis. Like many African American activists, scholars, and artists of her time, Dunham believed in encouraging African Americans to mentally and psychologically embrace their identity, heritage, and culture. The center's degree program, for example, was intended to "answer current Afro-American identity questions" and to reflect "the African and Afro-American aesthetic."[13] The PATC, in the words of Joyce Ashcenbrenner, was "the ultimate fulfillment of [Dunham's] view of 'art for life's sake.'"[14] The center caused a "cultural awakening" for its students through the teaching and performing of African history, songs, dances, and drumming and African American history, songs, and dances.[15] As Oleya Cruz Banks argues, it also provided "decolonizing dance education."[16] It challenged the oppression and suppression of African American bodies caused by racism and

Eurocentric ideologies.[17]

Spanning the years 1965 to 1975, the Black Arts Movement (BAM) was a multidisciplinary movement in African American culture. The BAM consisted of cohorts of radically political poets, essayists, musicians, visual artists, dancers, and dramatists in cities across America. They created art that expressed the political ideologies of the era. Rejecting Western and European institutions, canons, and traditions, BAM artists used a range of styles, media, and techniques to make African Americans' history and African ancestry relevant to contemporary issues and experiences. Described as the "spiritual sister" of the Black Power movement by artist, scholar, and BAM co-founder Larry Neal, the BAM had an

aesthetic that privileged functional art over art for art's sake.[18] The movement's art was created for the purpose of raising consciousness, or teaching African Americans about their history and ancestry, and non-western spiritual beliefs.

The PATC's curriculum achieved the goal of the Black Arts Movement to raise consciousness among the masses of African Americans about traditional African culture, African American history, and black art. Most required courses taught students about non-white art and cultures. Primarily, the non-white cultures to which they were exposed were that of Africans and African Americans. To graduate, students had to take Traditional African Music, Traditional Negro Music, Afro-American History, African

Nations of Today, Contemporary African Language, and African American Oral and Written Drama. These courses were intended to teach students about African American participation in the theatre from slavery to the 1960s, the languages spoken by millions of Africans, the traditional songs sung in Africa and Haiti, and African American styles of music such as jazz, gospel, and spirituals. They also sought to teach students the history of African Americans and their experiences of oppression in the United States.

The curriculum was not the only way the center participated in the BAM. The repertoire of the PATC Company, performed by former members of the Dunham Company and PATC

Trendley Avenue by the Gateway Geyser, 2010   Powell Photo

students, teacher-trainees, and instructors, served as BAM art that encouraged psychological and intellectual liberation. Although they did not always perform at black culture events, all performances in some way paid homage to the BAM. African drumming, jazz, militant poems, and a Congolese mass were among the ways the company illustrated the Afri- and Afro-centric focuses of the BAM. The programs the company performed in the St. Louis metropolitan area and across the nation raised African Americans' consciousness of black activism, Black Power ideology, and African and African American music and dance.

At the Kansas City Black Arts Festival in 1968, the Performing Company's songs, plays, and poems increased their own and their audience's pride in being black, knowledge of their African heritage, and appreciation for radical African American activists in the late 1960s. Two elements of the company's program were African songs and percussion sequences. As a parallel to the impetus to create a black nation in America that was often expressed in BAM art, the company also performed scenes of the story of Chaka, a South African folk hero. Chaka reunited the Zulu tribes and created a Zulu empire. "Libertad," a song written by Katherine Dunham and PATC Music Director Bernie Dunlap, was also sung at the festival by all company members. It addressed black revolutionaries' experiences with a refrain that defined "libertad" as liberty or freedom, a sentiment that spread across the United States from East St. Louis to Watts, California.

Poetry also was performed at the festival, such as the militant works "Ditties," "To a Honky Cat," and "Ballad." The narrator of "Ditties" speaks of being "tired of the token bed" and being unwilling to accept "the crumb" handed out by white America.[19] The poem concludes with the stanza "If this is power, black or not/ Then brother it's devine [sic]/ To be from sentiment re[l]eased/ and know my soul is mine."[20] Even more radical, "To a Honky Cat," boldly states to white Americans that they have "neuroses, complexes, crocodile/ Tears," and that African Americans did not want to be a part of their culture "for all the tea in/ China."[21] "Ballad" celebrates blackness by stating "the great good earth/ Is black./ There is no white, Unless it be/ The searing sand of desert waste."[22] The festival's program concluded with "Ode to Taylor Jones," a tribute to an African American activist from East St. Louis that included music, movement, and poetry.

"Ode to Taylor Jones," a standard piece in the performance company's programs, also included elements critical to the Black Arts and Black Power movements. It was a choreographed (and at times improvised) musical and theatrical tribute to Dunham's friend Taylor Jones from East St. Louis. Jones fought for social justice as chairman of the Mid-Eastern Region of the Congress of Racial Equality (CORE). Killed along with his wife on October 13, 1967, on his way to a National Action Committee meeting of CORE, he was a lecturer and leader of workshops on Black Power philosophy. Dunham's tribute to him was written to explain the

experiences and issues facing African American men in the late 1960s.

Dunham's ode included a chorus who occasionally shouted black militant phrases. It also included the song "Libertad," which paid tribute to black nationalists and Black Power heroes Marcus Garvey and Malcolm X, and Black Panther Party Leader Huey Newton. Various militant poems were performed next, such as "To a Honky Cat," and the chorus danced to the song "New Borns" while "revolutionary phrases" were shouted.[23] In some performances, a poem called "Laugh" then was recited. It decried the "evil" of white power and warned white Americans that hundreds of thousands more would take the place of Jones in the burgeoning Black Power movement:

Ol' white power's given out
While Black has just begun. And there's
No way to compensate
For the evil you have done
To a hundred million Thousand and one.[24]

During "Taylor Jones Song," which concluded the ode, Black Power signs were made.

Through the inclusion of these symbols, gestures, words, and songs, the ode immersed its performers and audience in the ideology and aesthetic of the BAM.

In the rest of their repertoire in general, the performance company continued to participate in the Black Arts Movement. In 1973, the company's programs began to be more cohesive and chronological in character. The performers took audiences through black history beginning with plantations and continuing into the turn of the twentieth century and the 1920s. They finished with an acknowledgement of the then-current fascination with Africa by doing a Senegalese welcome dance and African rain forest dance.

Beyond the Black Arts Movement: Bringing the World to East St. Louis

In addition to portraying the aesthetic and ideology of the BAM, the Performing Company's programs also presented to audiences the sights and sounds of parts of the world beyond Africa and the United States Although the PATC company's program for the Kansas City Black Arts Festival included ostensible references to black American culture, it also served as an example of the center's appreciation for the art of many different cultures. The company's performance began with "Choros I and IV," described in the program as "variations on a sixteenth century Brazilian quadrille."[25] Four couples danced this slow, formal, originally French square dance to Brazilian music composed by Heitor Villa-Lobo. The dance's inclusion in the program was significant. For several moments, it took the performers and the audience away from the BAM's emphasis upon African and African American art and culture and toward an appreciation for the dance and music of Europe and South America.

Within some of the acts themselves that the company

performed, there was an intent to immerse audiences in Cuban and West Indian culture alongside black nationalist and Black Power ideologies. One version of "Ode to Taylor Jones" included a dance ritual called "Shango," which honored the Yoruba god of thunder. Choreographed by Dunham, the dance combined West African culture with aspects of cults from Trinidad and Haiti. The religion Santeria, as practiced in Cuba, also was inspiration for the dance. West Indian culture also was included in the ode through a dance called "Papa Gede." In Haiti, Papa Gede was a figure who represented death. The inclusion of this dance commemorated Jones's death as was done in Haiti.

The PATC's curriculum mirrored the Performing Company's artistic expressions of Western and South American history and culture. As much as required courses offered at the PATC were intended to develop African Americans' self-awareness and familiarity with black culture, they also sought to develop well-rounded students who could place particular issues and cultures into a global context. Stylized forms of the martial arts were taught to students who specialized in dance to improve their grace, posture, physique, and agility. Beyond their practical purposes, these courses introduced students to Asian culture and movement in ways that enhanced their simultaneous training in the dances of other cultures. Conversational French also was taught to students. The course provided them with a temporary immersion in European culture. Another course, Comparative Cultures,

examined the African tribe the Watusi, Kwaikutl Indians, Negritos in Southeast Asia, and the Kikuyu in Kenya. Its premise was to study human behavior and compare the similarities and differences among cultures around the world.[26] This multicultural curriculum thus took students beyond the confines of African American and African history and art into the realms of Eastern, Western, and other parts of the world.

"New Horizons of Thinking"– The PATC as an Example of Innovative Urban Education

Beyond encouraging African Americans to both remain within and transgress the cultural boundaries of the BAM, the PATC raised a collective consciousness of the power of interdisciplinary arts education to help urban youth. The center provided unemployed, under-educated young people in East St. Louis a place to grow mentally, culturally, and emotionally. Arts and humanities education thus had the power to develop the intellect and behavior of inner-city populations, heighten their self-awareness, and encourage them to serve their community. Dunham envisioned the center as an example of innovative education and, indeed, educational institutions often sent representatives to the PATC to observe the center's programs firsthand. The staff of Kansas City's Turner House, for example, visited the center in January 1973 to learn about its pedagogy and to apply its methods and philosophy of teaching their own curricula and teaching practices.

The philosophy behind the PATC's multicultural curriculum, Performing Company, and

Dynamic Museum evinced a commitment to new methods of educating non-traditional, disadvantaged populations in higher education. Each of the center's components emphasized community service and community education; creating public intellectuals who could, at the completion of the program, provide their communities with the same type of education they had been given. The goal was to "improv[e] the individual's self awareness and personal identification" and "uplif[t] the community's view of itself," thereby "breaking the poverty cycle."[27] Through the visual arts, theatre, music, dance, and public performance, the PATC aimed to give poor people coping skills, a feeling of belonging in society, and a better outlook on life.[28]

As a result of its relationship with communities outside of academia, the PATC communicated between the "unlike worlds" of the university and the "urban ghetto" of East St. Louis.[29] Dunham's center served as a university without walls; a "'bridge' organization" between institutions of higher education and society at large.[30] In Dunham's words,

The ivory towers of apartheid colleges and universities, restricting staff and matriculates to the edicts of guidelines and textbooks are beginning to crumble. In their place have arisen new horizons of thinking, of universities without walls, of new and innovative methods and programs . . .[31]

Dunham recognized that most Americans in the 1960s and 1970s did not fit into the category of students who attend elite universities. Urban areas had high drop-out rates and low rates of attendance at institutions of higher education, mainly due to young adults' academic deficiencies.

There was a need to serve disadvantaged student populations through creative and methods of education based upon the philosophy that communities should progress as some of their members participated in higher education. Traditional methods of education often did not develop the potential of these students, Dunham believed. New methods, consequently, were needed to best use the talents of underprivileged students. Education in the creative and performing arts could give them a feeling of being totally

Artwork at the East St. Louis Higher Education Center, 2010   Powell Photo

involved in the world, provide alternatives to violence, and humanize and socialize them.

Ultimately, the Performing Arts Training Center counters both the reality and perception of East St. Louis as an example of a failed, formerly industrial city. Amidst the urban blight, political corruption, and economic strife the city's residents experienced in the post-World War II era, Katherine Dunham's center stood as a testament to the existence of cultural activity in 1960s and 1970s East St. Louis. As much as it resists easily being categorized as a result of its simultaneous participation in and challenge to both the Black Arts Movement and traditional higher education, the PATC prevents East St. Louis from being disregarded as a cultureless, hopeless case of urban decay. The center—an institution that evolved into the Katherine Dunham Centers for Arts and Humanities that today continue to bring the arts and cultures of the world to the city—shows that physical, educational, economic, and racial boundaries are never absolute. Arts and humanities education, when made public, has the potential to sharpen minds, uplift spirits, and provide self-awareness and an appreciation for other cultures regardless of how racially segregated, forgotten, or economically challenged a city may be.

End Notes:

1. Observations, East St. Louis, Illiinois, 1968, Katherine Dunham Papers, Missouri History Museum Archives, St. Louis.

2. Ibid.

3. Joyce Aschenbrenner, *Katherine Dunham: Dancing a Life* (Chicago: University of Illinois Press, 2002), 17.

4. Ojeya Cruz Banks, "Katherine Dunham: Decolonizing Dance Education," in ed. Noel Anderson, *Education as Freedom: African American Educational Thought and Activism* (Lanham, MD: Lexington Books, 2009), 124.

5. "Introduction" in *Kaiso!: Writings by and about Katherine Dunham*, (Madison: The University of Wisconsin Press, 2005), 3.

6. Thomas J. Sugrue, *The Origins of the Urban Crisis: Race and Inequality in Postwar Detroit* (Princeton: Princeton University Press, 1996), 7.

7. Andrew J. Theising, *Made in USA: East St. Louis The Rise and Fall of an Industrial River Town* (St. Louis: Virginia Publishing, 2003), 193.

8. Eugene Redmond, "A Note on the Origin of the Kwansaba," *Drumvoices Revue*, vol. 12, nos. 1 and 2 (Spring-Summer-Fall 2004), 15.

9. "Resume of the Performing Arts Training Center, Southern Illinois University, East St. Louis, Illinois," Katherine Dunham Papers, Missouri History Museum Archives, St. Louis.

10. "Performing Arts Training Center and Dynamic Museum," Katherine Dunham Papers, Missouri History Museum Archives, St. Louis.

11. Katherine Dunham Papers, Missouri History Museum Archives, St. Louis.

12. Narration,, Katherine Dunham Papers, Missouri History Museum Archives, St. Louis.

13. Resume of the Performing Arts Training Center, Southern Illinois University, East St. Louis, Illinois, 17 September 1970, Katherine Dunham Papers, Missouri History Museum Archives, St. Louis. To this end, many of its consultants were people supportive of the Black Arts and Black Power movements and helped shape the center's mission, activities, and performances.

14. Aschenbrenner, *Katherine Dunham*, 185.

15. P.A.T.C. as a Focal Point for a New and Unique College or School, 1970, Missouri History Museum Archives, St. Louis.

16. Banks, "Katherine Dunham," 122.

17. Ibid., 123.

18. Larry Neal, "The Black Arts Movement," *Drama Review* 12 (Summer 1968): 29.

19. Ditty, Katherine Dunham Papers, Missouri History Museum Archives, St. Louis.

20. Ibid.

21. To a Honky Cat, Katherine Dunham Papers, Missouri History Museum Archives, St. Louis.

22. Ballad,, Katherine Dunham Papers, Missouri History Museum Archives, St. Louis.

23. Ode to Taylor Jones Script, Notes, Etc, Katherine Dunham Papers, Missouri History Museum Archives, St. Louis.

24. Laugh, Katherine Dunham Papers, Missouri History Museum Archives, St. Louis.

25. Program for the Kansas City Black Arts Festival, 15 October, 1969, Missouri History Museum Archives, St. Louis.

26. Curriculum, Katherine Dunham Papers, Missouri History Museum Archives, St. Louis.

27. Performing Arts Training Center and Dynamic Museum, Katherine Dunham Papers, Missouri History Museum Archives, St. Louis

28. Ibid.

29. PATC and the University,.

30. Ibid.

31. Katherine Dunham, "Performing Arts Training Center as a Focal Point for a New and Unique College or School" in *Kaiso!* 556.

Personal Reflections on East St. Louis through the Years

Lillian Parks, Ph.D.

Retired Superintendent,
East St. Louis Public School District 189

In the early 1900s, East St. Louis was on the brink of economic disaster despite the fact that the city was an economic engine to many industries. East St. Louis ranked #1 in the sale of horses and mules and was the world's largest aluminum processing center; second largest railroad center; and led the country in manufacturing of roofing material, baking powder, and paint. East St. Louis' advantageous location on the Mississippi River across from a major city, its relationship with industry and the railroads that connected the city to other major industrial sites belied the fact that East St. Louis had extremely limited tax support. The larger industries located outside the city limits and several of these industries eventually created their own cities that included Sauget, National City, and Alorton. Employment at these major industrial sites was a primary impetus for racial discord. Secondarily, racial discontent mounted because the Republican Party "imported" Blacks from the South in a failed attempt to increase the Republican vote in the 1916 Presidential election. This labor unrest coupled with the importation of Blacks from the South fomented deadly aggression.

The second Lincoln School, 1911 Bowen Archives, SIUE

Succeeding In Spite of Negative Words and Actions

If there were a theme to this essay, it would reflect the lack of opportunity that African-Americans failed to receive from the beginning. A contributing factor for this lack of opportunity could be traced back to the days of slavery when it was a crime to teach slaves to read. The result was that African Americans, even freed slaves, epitomized the "mis-education of the Negro" because their masters and others controlled the slave's mind. The controlling of the mind translated to some extent in East St. Louis as part of the schools, churches, employment, politics, housing and everyday life. In reviewing and evaluating the All-American city, it is good to keep Carter G. Woodson's statement in mind as we reflect on the condition of East St. Louis:

"When you control a man's thinking you do not have to worry about his actions. You do not have to tell him to stand here or to go yonder. He will find his 'proper' place and will stay in it. You do not need to send him to the back door. He will go without being told. In fact, if there is no back door, he will cut one for his special benefit. His education makes it necessary."

"History shows that it does not matter who is in power…those who have not learned to do for themselves and have to depend solely on others never obtain any more rights or privileges in the end than they did in the beginning."[1]

Corporations, factories, stockyards, aluminum production, glass manufacturing, and steel mills existed and jobs were plentiful in and around East St. Louis in the early 1900s. The city became a mecca for Blacks who were migrating from the South in search of opportunity. Many came directly to East St. Louis while others continued north to Chicago and Detroit. It was during this time that several catastrophes occurred. In spite of the catastrophic events, East St. Louisans were able to survive. These catastrophes included the tornado of 1896 and the flood of 1903. Government was also impacted with the debate and conflict between the low graders and high graders who were in favor of raising the principal streets of East St. Louis out of the flood plains. The "High Graders" were industrialists and land speculators. The "Low Graders" argued that the city charter did not allow the city council to authorize debits in excess of $100,000. Both sides had their reasons to work diligently to implement their position. The "High Graders" held a special election and won; the "Low Graders" were left to question the legitimacy of the election. The inability of the two sides to compromise led to the establishment of two police forces, two city councils and two mayors. The city's history of corruption has often become the subtext when East St. Louis is the focus of discussion. Pat Gauen of the *St. Louis Post Dispatch* wrote these words as part of his column on April 23, 2009.

"Assigned by this paper about 20 years ago to write a short history of the city, I figured I'd finally discovered the truth behind conflicting stories that early crooks either blew up the City Hall to cover insider crimes or burned it down. Silly me, it wasn't one or the other, it was both.

Well, sure. Anything was possible in a place where the state-charters and city-chartered police forces once decided with a deadly gunfight just who would use the station. Where railroads sent private detectives to probe boxcar thefts and found they had been arrested by local cops and put to work patching potholes. Where emotions on the board of education once ran so high that one unpaid member was convicted of trying to have another murdered.

But the city's history has not all been about crime and corruption.

East St. Louis delivered jobs, products, prosperity and quality life to generations. The city also delivered Jackie Joyner Kersee, said by some to be the best female athlete ever; Donald McHenry, former U.S. Ambassador to the United Nations; and jazz great Miles Davis. Even international dance queen Katherine Dunham selected East St. Louis as home after her retirement from active dance. East St. Louis High School's Flyers football team often dominates and has been the recipient of several state championships. The high school's chess team consistently cleaned up the boards."[2]

Before and After the Riots

There were other events that occurred in East St. Louis that were devastating to the city and helped to negate the business atmosphere growing in East St. Louis. The most horrendous event was the 1917 race riot. Many persons attributed the riot to Blacks coming to East St. Louis for jobs, thereby taking jobs from Whites. The July race riot, actually an American pogrom, marked the salvo in a broad battle by many white Northerners who sought to maintain a rigid racial hierarchy through violence, if necessary. The dynamics of Black politics forced certain white elements either to access the possibility of equality for African Americans or to respond with violence against them to maintain White domination. Real estate man and political boss Thomas Caravan, for one, stated his awareness of the political dimension when he said, "Something has got to be done, or the damned niggers will take over the town. "Another real estate man, Locke Tarlton said, "This is going to be a white man's town hereafter; the blacks will be run out of here and we'll have a white man's town".[3]

Fortunately, this tone of superiority by Whites and the idea of getting rid of Negroes continued to prevail on a limited basis. Most progressives, like many White Americans influenced by scientific and cultural racism, thought black people contributed greatly to social disorder. Even racial egalitarians generally regarded black people as predisposed to corruption, squalor, gambling, prostitution, vice and criminal violence. Racism ran rampant in East St. Louis and throughout the country. Some Black citizens of all ages "knew their places and stayed in their place"[4]. Even though there were Blacks who gained some middle class status enough to begin thinking for themselves, especially those who worked in St. Louis. There were also those Blacks who did not "learn to do for themselves and had to depend solely on others and never obtain any more rights or privileges in the end than they did in the beginning. "Although there were Blacks in East St. Louis who sought to improve their status, Whites reminded them constantly by word or deed to stay in their places, especially in sundown towns like Red Bud, Illinois and Granite City, Illinois, although Blacks were later allowed to work at Granite City Steel. "sundown" places and segregated neighborhoods constantly reminded families of the evils of racism. Even children knew their places but also knew that the "n" word was particularly offensive.

Horace A. Adams, about the time of his death in 1935. He was an early civil rights leader in East St. Louis, community activist, and founder of the Paramount Democratic Organization

Organizations

In spite of negative conditions and obstacles in the path of Black citizens, they persevered. They realized that working together in an organized manner, could be beneficial. Therefore groups were organized for various purposes. Some groups were political; others were organized for community improvement and some for social purposes. Some groups that were established by East St. Louis Black citizens included:

1910: National Association of Colored Women's Clubs

1917: Zeta Phi Beta

1925: Treble Clef Club

1930: Paramount Democratic Organization

1932: Scotia Calhoun School of Beauty

1934: Tuesday Guild

1941: Sigma Gamma Rho

1942: Delta Sigma Theta

1945: Las Amigas

1946: Alpha Kappa Alpha

1946: Universal Business College

1947: Alpha Phi Alpha

1954: Venus Temple #1042

1955: Omega Psi Phi

1955: Kappa Alpha Psi

1956: Kimball School of Music

1957: Crusader Kids Picnic

1963: Lincoln Park Tennis

1964: Beauticians Local 175

1965: Jack and Jill

1985: Top Ladies of Distinction

1986: Gateway Chapter of Links

1988: Women Organized for Community Survival

2005: East St. Louis Lions Club

These organizations had purpose and goals. It is important to know that every organization did not emerge for good: the Ku Klux Klan in the East St. Louis district rose with the fortunes of the national Klan; its membership totaled 4,000 in 1922 and peaked at 8,000 in 1925. There were several civil rights organizations whose purposes were obvious. The NAACP came to East St. Louis in 1915 and CORE, Committee Organized for Racial Equality, came in the 1960s.

"Black East St. Louisans responded to such antiblack terrorism through organizations determined to oppose the rising violence. Following the Wyatt lynching in 1903, they established the Imperial Social Club to reassure city authorities to enforce equal protection laws. They also organized local chapters of existing national associations. For instance, in 1915 a group of black East St. Louisans, including veterinarian Fred Halsey, R.M.C. Green, and others, formed a local branch of the National Association for the Advancement of Colored People (NAACP)". [5]

Businesses

Some of these organizations encouraged business to be established in East St. Louis. Businesses in East St. Louis are owned by a variety of races including Armenians, Ukrainians, Jews, Vietnamese and Arabs. There have been many businesses through the years; however, there are some that have operated in East St. Louis longer than 50 years. These business owners were generally encouraged to be as independent as possible.

Several businesses stand out because of their long term commitment to East St. Louis. For over one hundred years First Illinois Bank, Paul Mirring Florist and Illini Digital Printing have served the city. For over fifty-years Nash Funeral Home, Officer Funeral Home, New York Cleaners, LeAnn furs, Switzer's Wholesale, Daisy Florist, London Shoe Shop, Schwartz Hardware, Sieron Reality, The Monitor Newspaper, Conrad Fish Market and cosmetologists Lee Annie Bonner, Myrtle Allen, and Cornelia Armstrong have served the city.

Churches

Churches have historically played a major role in meeting the needs of groups and individuals. In many cases, it gave Blacks a voice, and thereby heeding the advice of Carter G. Woodson, who stated that we should not let others "control our thinking". In addition to organizations, East St. Louis citizens had a need to feel that a higher being was present to give them hope, assistance, and guidance. Coming together to worship and praise God at church was important for citizens. Churches have played a major role in East St. Louis beginning in 1863 when Macedonia Church was organized. St. Luke A.M.E. is the second oldest church in the city and still "follows the mission stated" in 1880, that of serving the present age through spiritual, social, educational and recreational development. Truelight Baptist Church was organized in 1910 under the leadership and ministry of Reverend James Alfred Lampley. New Hope Baptist Church was organized in 1914 under the leadership of Rev. J.L. McBride. Wesley and Bethel churches combined into one congregation on January 24, 1965. Since that time, Wesley-Bethel Church consolidated three Methodist churches to become Trinity Methodist Church in 2005.

Education

Blacks recognized that if real progress was to be made, education was needed. East St. Louis realized that in spite of segregated schools and old books being sent to Black schools from White schools, learning could still occur. The first public school was built at 700 Bond, by Captain John Trendley. The first school built for Blacks in East St. Louis was the Lincoln School located at Sixth and St. Louis Avenue opened in 1886. It served as an elementary and secondary school until 1909, when it was converted into the Board of Education.

At these early schools, the curriculum included reading, arithmetic, language arts, including handwriting and spelling, some arts, coloring, music, and a little history. Of course , history for or about Blacks was not included on a regular basis within the city school district until Vivian Adams became Administrative Assistant in Charge of Elementary Education. In addition, in the secondary

schools, ongoing change came when the wave of industrial education became prevalent in education. For a generation, including within East St. Louis' District 189, the quarrel as to whether the Black should be given a classical or a practical education was the dominant topic in Black schools and churches throughout the United States. W.E.B. DuBois a noted cultural and educational leader, was a proponent of classical academics and preparing bright Black students (whom he called the talented 10th) for college. On the other hand, Booker T. Washington espoused industrial education. These opposite views promoted the poem, "Booker T and W.E.B." wherein the theme is repeated throughout the poem: "It seems to me", said Booker T; "I don't agree", said W.E.B.

To some educators, practical education counted in reaching that end of preparing students for the world of work. A few real industrial schools actually equipped themselves for this work and turned out a number of graduates with such preparation. The secondary schools in District 189 prescribed to this training. Even a school built in 1916 had signage which prescribed the entire curriculum-the Monroe Manual Training School.

Unfortunately, the classical curriculum and the popular approach developed with a battle of words, the majority of Negroes preferred industrial training. District 189 tried to adhere to a three phase approach to education practical, vocational, and industrial. Vocational training was encouraged in District 189. Vocational education remains important to the District as it is

currently constructing a multi-million dollar facility on the campus of East St. Louis Senior High School.

There is a great emphasis in the curriculum on test scores since they are the measure of academic competence. When standardized tests were introduced, it was discovered that District 189 students did not always measure up. They were not at the bottom of the schools in the Metro East area, but improvement was needed. In evaluating and assessing the various test items, the cultural differences between the races resulted in Black students performing poorly. To assist students language arts training was increased and additional support came with the introduction of Title I in 1965. Language arts training resulted from the observation of children's use of non-standard patterns called Ebonics or Black English. In District 189, there were those teachers who wanted students to speak "correctly" using Standard English. District 189 introduced a new Title I program to bridge the language gap-"Project Speak", an oral language program for the disadvantaged with a goal to give students another mode of expression, standard language.

Some students after graduating high school attended the local community college that helped East St. Louis students to prepare for careers and further training.

In spite of the negative comments made about District 189, especially on money management, students were generally successful academically, most assuredly in the arts. For example, Lincoln High School often placed first or second on the state level in choir and band. Through the years from the 1920s to the 1990s, Lincoln High School Choir directors produced award winning choirs. Band director, Elwood Buchanan, who directed jazz great, Miles Davis, and many other talented youth, won state contests on a continuous basis. In 2008, the boys' and girls' track teams won state trophies. Perhaps what is most astounding is that East St. Louis schools have produced chess team champions on the elementary and secondary levels.

Integration of District 189 schools began on February 1, 1949 Mr. Perry Storman, a storeowner from "The Goose Hill" neighborhood of East St. Louis, and Attorney Billy Jones were the leaders of the plan, along with the NAACP president David Owens and Board member Norvell Hickman. After four non-productive days, the children were withdrawn from the school and Attorney Billy Jones filed one of the first lawsuits in the country to integrate public schools. A year later the Court of Appeals smiled in favor of the children and in January 31, 1950, one hundred black students were admitted to six schools that had previously been attended by White students only; 14 at Canady Elementary, 17 at Rock Junior High, 21 at East St. Louis Senior High, 28 at Webster Elementary, 15 at Alta Sita Elementary, and 5 at Monroe Elementary School. At Franklin, which had been all Black, two White students enrolled. All schools ultimately developed an integrated staff.

All of the Black students who integrated East St. Louis Senior High School performed admirably in and out of the classroom. Some of the first East St. Louis Black high school students included:

Delores Storman Ray, Maxwell Brooks, Richard Taylor, Ronald Mitchell, Dennis Perry, Gus Doss, Thomas Little, Louis Williams, Valleta Smith House, Mary Granger Sims and Doris Robinson Ellington.

In addition to the integration of schools. East St. Louis' Blacks felt that business should be integrated to provide Black citizens with opportunities like any other citizen. There were many methods used to integrate businesses and service delivery. Three methods were used in integrating banks-sit-ins, lay-ins and boycotts. Ben Phillips and Homer Randolph were leaders in the sit-in method. When the Jones Park swimming pool was integrated, much planning was included. Jeanne Allen Falconer and Joan Armistead took the plunge that day for the benefit of all African American city residents. Helping

Washington (Public) School. East St. Louis, Ill.

Washington School, c. 1910   Bowen Archives, SIUE

to direct the youth in activities were Elmo Bush, Vivian Adams, and Jeanne Falconer who all served as NAACP sponsors at different times.

Boycotting was a very successful technique. In the 1960s, some nightclub and tavern owners had been complaining about Falstaff and Budweiser having no Black truck drivers. After contacting the companies, and patiently waiting for openings for drivers, the tavern owners decided that they would boycott Falstaff and Budweiser products. Led by Bestine Tourijigian, the owner of the very popular neighborhood lounge "Pudgey's" and the owner of "The Matador" a local lounge, Lafayette McIntosh, the liquor selling establishments did not sell any Falstaff or Budweiser products. After only two days, the companies miraculously needed and found Black truck drivers. East St. Louis played a major role in employment activities for drivers.

There was a great desire to inform the public about the good events that were occurring in East St. Louis but the local media was not receptive. In the 1980s, several news worthy achievements were taking place at East St. Louis Senior High School. The superintendent called the local daily newspaper, the *Belleville News Democrat* about covering the assembly where the athletic teams and academic teams were to be honored. The superintendent was informed that the assembly was not news. The superintendent

responded that if she could stage a news worthy fight among students on the front lawn of the school, that would certainly be covered and the reporter could cover the assembly when the fight concluded. The paper's staff member laughed and sent a reporter without a fight being staged.

Media are important because it affects how some opinions are shaped. Most people agree that drugs, guns, and domestic violence are the real problems, and the leadership continues to work on erasing those problems.

The present mayor, Alvin Parks Jr., has adopted the theme of "Life More Abundantly" from John 10:10. He has set goals and is working towards them. To help meet the goal of cleaning up the city, he has organized a cleaning team of citizens who go to various parts of the city to clean. He has received a broad range of assistance from as far away as Indiana. As the chief elected official, the Mayor is often blamed for everything, but continues to work diligently to address the problems of the city.

Confidence and hope are being restored in East St. Louis and the desire is to build hope among the citizens of the city. The hope is that the "man in the mirror" will play a major role. That reference draws from a popular Michael Jackson song.[6]

Mayor Parks has set goals that are being met. Several projects that have been completed through the

persistance of local non-profit and business organizations include:

1) more houses: several new groups of houses have already been built, including Rush's Senior Building; villas sponsored by Mount Sinai, and the Willie Nelson Homes. Several downtown projects are being discussed including the renovation of the Broadview Hotel;

2) economic development: over 200 businesses are now operating in East St. Louis;

3) Construction of a new 200 acre port facility will begin in 2011;

4) the Comprehensive Behavioral Health Center of St. Clair County Inc. has developed a multi-million dollar building to improve service delivery; and

5) the crime rate is still too high, however, with the assistance of state and federal law enforcement professionals, several crimes are being investigated and solved much faster[7].

As confidence, hope, and achievements increase and accomplishments are present, we need to let citizens in East St. Louis and throughout the country know that we are "knowing and growing." East St. Louis still has some good people who care about their city. They realize that it did not get this way overnight and the problems will not magically disappear. With hard work, hope, conscientious effort, and positive attitude, East St. Louis can again become "An All America City".

End Notes:

1. Carter G. Woodson, *The Mis-Education of the Negro.* Trenton: African World Press, 1932

2. Gauen, Pat. 23 April 2009. *St. Louis Post Dispatch.* St. Louis: St. Louis Post Dispatch.

3. Charles, Lumpkins, *American Pogrom.* Athens: Ohio University Press, 2008.

4. Woodson, op.cit.

5. Ibid, *American Pogrom.*

6. Michael Jackson, *"The Man in the mirror"* Bad (Epic Records, 1988).

7. Editor's Note: The Mt. Sinai Village project created 30 single family lease-purchase housing units while the Rush Senior Gardens Apartments development added 54 units of senior housing to East St. Louis' housing stock. The Comprehensive Behavioral Center's new complex was a $12.7 million project constructed to provide intensive in-patient alcohol and substance abuse treatment and out-patient mental health services.

East St. Louis Is My Career and My Life

Billie Gloria Turner

East St. Louis Action Research Project
University of Illinois Urbana-Champaign

My name is Billie Gloria Turner and I have lived in East St. Louis my entire life. But East St. Louis has been more than my home. It has been my job as well. I have the privilege of writing this essay from the perspective of someone who works for the East St. Louis Action Research Project (an agency sponsored by the University of Illinois at Urbana-Champaign) and explaining how my growing up in East St. Louis has had such a tremendous impact on my career. My job is literally living, breathing, and serving my home, my family, my friends, and our community every day. I have had such a fantastic experience coming of age in this city that I want everyone now living in East St. Louis to have the same experience—or better—than I have had.

Catalpa trees in bloom at Lincoln Park, 2010   Powell Photo

My neighborhood had it all, but I am getting ahead of myself. I see things in East St. Louis that others do not see. When I look at a vacant lot, I think of what used to be there instead of what is actually there now. Of course, there are bad memories too. I remember being in the sixth grade at Alta Sita Elementary School and having to fight to attend George Rogers Clark Junior High School, which was a school that was attended by predominantly white students. I remember being a sickly child with migraine headaches during all of my years of schooling in East St. Louis and college. But on the whole, my life in East St. Louis has been amazing. I have been truly blessed by the people who have been in my life. It seems that the people who have surrounded me have been so very supportive that

they have more than made up for the ones who have not been.

As I evolved as a person, I knew that I had to give back to this community. Each job I have had has been a stepping stone for my present work here in East St. Louis. Somewhere down the road, as a result of my previous job experiences and my life experiences as a whole, I have emerged as an enthusiastic advocate for East St. Louis. I love East St. Louis and want it to be again the kind of place where I grew up. Working for the East St. Louis Action Research Project (ESLARP) is not merely my job. It is my passion. The children of today do not know the East. St. Louis that I knew and with which I fell in love. I feel guilty that our children do not get to see downtown Collinsville Ave.

as it was when it was lined with businesses. It is my mission to help to improve East St. Louis so that everyone will once again experience East St. Louis as a truly special place.

What Made East St. Louis So Special

The older residents in East St. Louis played a large role in trying to make East St. Louis special and trying to keep it that way. Our older family members and older neighbors instilled pride in us, and they reinforced our parents' teachings. For one thing, they had witnessed hard times and they did not take anything for granted. If you saw trash, you picked it up, even if you had not put it there. You had to respect these older adults or you would get in big trouble.

The Mary Brown Center, Lincoln Park, 2010   Powell Photo

We had valuable interaction with the senior citizens who shared all kinds of stories about coming up north only to be able to live in certain sections of town. Nonetheless, East St. Louis was the "land of milk and honey" to these older residents and was a real community where people really cared for one another. You had people like Mary E. Brown, who was concerned about the children living in her neighborhood. She lived in the South End and she was worried about the children not having someplace safe to play. Ms. Brown made this her special project. She was one lady with a vision. She was constantly talking to others and was able to sell this dream and concern to the community. As she became a voice for the children, she was able to form a choir of voices who were on the same page with her. Eventually, what is now the Mary E. Brown Community Center was built in Lincoln Park, and it stands out even today as a physical structure. Buckminster Fuller designed this Center and left his trademark on this building—its very unique copper dome that is now blue. (The Center was closed for several years and recently reopened in 2006.) This Center was a full service community center, which had a small library, offered GED and craft classes, and of course, there were programs for the children.

While this older generation of East St. Louisans like Mary Brown created many of the institutions which are still vital today, their real value for "younger" people like me was how they taught us our values and our history as well as how they showered us with love. Not having had a chance

at a real education coming from the South, they encouraged us in every way that they could to stay in school and stay on track. But maybe more than anything else, they showed us with their very lives what it meant to live in a community. Every day their lives were a statement that a neighborhood was more than a collection of buildings. It was a network of people caring for one another.

Working in East St. Louis

East St. Louis was the place to come if you needed a job— especially if you were African American. You had the National Stockyards, Steel industry, Obear-Nestor Glass Co., the meat packing companies, etc. My maternal family was no exception. As my grandmother watched her siblings do well in the North, and as her husband had problems with adjusting to "the southern ways", East St. Louis looked better and better. My grandfather, Tang Crawford, moved to East St. Louis around 1941 or 1942 to look for employment, and his two oldest sons came with him. His wife, Uneeda, and six other children stayed in the South until Tang told them it was time to move to East St. Louis. The East St. Louis he moved to had plenty of businesses and he was able to get hired at the old Aluminum Ore and his sons were able to find jobs too.

The Crawford family moved to East St. Louis during one of the periods of United States History when African Americans were migrating from the South to the North. Uneeda had siblings with their families already living in East St. Louis who appeared to be doing quite well. Her half

sister, Nevida Hamilton Gates, was the first African American Republican, precinct committee woman in East St. Louis.[1] This family developed a great sense of gratitude, loyalty and love for a city called East St. Louis.

Growing Up in East St. Louis

As this family grew, Uneeda enjoyed taking her grandchildren to downtown East St. Louis. She would load her car up with as many grandchildren as she could and we were off to the city. By this time, my grandparents were living on a farm, so we loved going to the city with our Grandmother. Most of our parents were working, but grandma's job was to take care of her grandchildren. She would go to the Sears and Roebuck Store on 10th & State, and then proceed on to Collinsville Avenue, which was in downtown East St. Louis. You had Zerweck's Jewelry Store, Woolworth's, the old Majestic Movie House, and several other stores. I loved to go to the five and dime stores with grandma. We always got snacks at Kresge's or Woolworth's. There was a bakery at 1400 State St. Also, there was a house on Louisiana Boulevard which sold donuts out of the basement. I want to say this house was located in the 3100 block. Sometimes we had to stop at Rodman's Farm Supply store in National City to get something for the pigs, cows, etc. There were car dealerships such as Bundy Oldsmobile, Haas Chevrolet, as well as a Buick and a Lincoln/Mercury dealership. As you can tell, we had a booming East St. Louis.

There were two neighborhoods that allowed African Americans to live in them when they migrated to East St. Louis, and they were Goose Hill, which was located near the National Stockyards and the South End. Lincoln Park was located in the South End and it was considered the African American Park while Jones Park—on the other side of town—was the White Park. The South End was a city within a city. There were barber shops, grocery and drug stores, shoe repair shops, restaurants, and quite a few churches. There were night clubs located in this section as well, and one such night club was the Cosmo on 17th & Bond, I have been told that quite a few of the famous musicians performed there such as Chuck Berry, Miles Davis, Ike and Tina Turner—just to name a few.

The South End was a cultural mecca and everyone knew everyone else. I have been told stories about some of the Park Police. It has been said that they knew the people who lived in the neighborhood so well that when a child violated the age curfew, they knew whose family that child belonged to and whether or not that child was too young to still be in the park. My mother has shared a story about Lincoln Park that I so enjoy hearing. She said that at school the children would make plans to meet at Lincoln Park during the weekend. Best friends would meet there, girlfriends would meet boyfriends there—in short, it was the place "to see and be seen." One Sunday when she was living with her aunt and name sake, Nevida Hamilton Gates, she came skipping down the steps to the door and her aunt "Auntie" as she was so fondly called, asked her where she was going and she said, "Lincoln Park". Auntie asked her if she had gone to church that day and they both knew the answer was no, which meant that she could not do anything the rest of the week, but attend school. She said that the following Sunday, she made sure she arrived at church before anyone else so that she could go to Lincoln Park on that day.

But the park was not just for young children and teenagers; it was where the adults of the community would congregate as well. As a small child, I saw Lincoln Park as the place where my father played baseball with the East St. Louis Giants as a Third Baseman. There were other teams that played at Lincoln Park. Some of those players were able to play against people who later became major league baseball players.

The current Alta Sita School, 2010   Powell Photo

One of the people my father played with was Mr. Sam Taylor who later played for the Kansas City Monarchs who were part of the old Negro Baseball League. In addition to baseball, Lincoln Park was where the adults of the community would go for picnics and church socials.

The Challenge of Racism

As you can tell, East St. Louis has had its ups. Many people feel that there have been more downs than ups. In many ways, though, I feel that those downs have made me and my community stronger and have led me to the career I now have.

What has always made East St. Louis so special for me is how the people of the neighborhood always cared for one another. As a child, I grew up in the Alta Sita neighborhood and attended Alta Sita Elementary School. Our neighborhood had a few family members living in it. Mom had at least one and sometimes two siblings who lived in the neighborhood with their families. Also, she had some cousins who lived in the same block. My father's brother and his family lived next door. The odd thing was everyone in the neighborhood treated each other as family even if they were not. It was as if the whole neighborhood was one big family. For example, there was a young couple in the neighborhood where the wife made the mistake one day of jumping double Dutch rope with the girls in our block. We would often knock on her door and ask her husband if she could come out and play. We thought of her as one of us—a child. East St. Louis was just that kind of place.

Of course, some things during this time were not so nice. When I was in the sixth grade in Alta Sita Elementary School and getting ready for junior high school, the school board informed my parents that I would be attending Hughes Quinn Junior High School. This is when I learned about the pervasiveness of racism in our society—even in my neighborhood. My parents felt that my fellow students and I were being sent to Quinn Junior High just because it had a predominately African American student body. Where they wanted us to attend was George Rogers Clark Junior High School, whose student and staff population was predominantly white. Having a strong PTA, the Alta Sita parents organized and mounted a protest against the school board. Throughout the summer after my sixth grade, my parents or a designee picked us up and took us to the School Board Administrative building off 6th & St. Louis Avenue. We carried signs that said "we shall overcome" and we sang this song as we picketed the school board. This happened around 1965/1966. By the fall of seventh grade, we attended Clark Jr. High School.

Taking Charge of My Life

Although this experience made me aware of racism in America, it showed me the power of community and how things could be accomplished in a non-violent way. My family always told me to do my very best and if I applied myself, good things would happen. They instilled within me the belief that in spite of racism, I had the power to shape my life. Even though I did not know exactly what she meant, my

grandmother would tell me even when I was a little girl that I was going to attend college someday. She would tell me over and over that I was going to get a good job like her son, Ralph, who attended Lincoln University in Jefferson City, Mo.

But before I could take on the world, I had to take on changing myself. Growing up, I was tremendously shy. I knew if I was going to make it in the world, I needed to overcome my shyness and have confidence in myself. Again, my community came to the rescue. A lady from church, Mrs. Patricia Kelly Redds, gave me a book which literally saved my life. It was *Positive Thinking* by Norman Vincent Peale. I read it during the summer before I started at Southern Illinois University at Edwardsville (SIUE). When I got to SIUE, I spent the first two weeks hiding in the girls' restroom. But after that I was a real "socialite." I started talking to all kinds of people—both students and adults—and before long my Norman Vincent Peale philosophy started to kick in. I took speech that first semester and for the first time, I really felt confident that I had something to say. Now able to reach out and connect with people I did not know, I was able to make much of the SIUE community an integral part of the support network that had shaped me in East St. Louis. While at SIUE, I had some wonderful mentors like Dr. Richard Millett and Prof. Wilbur McAfee, who encouraged me and looked out for me from the very beginning. They were my heroes. But with my newfound confidence, my community and my world kept expanding. As I pursued my major in history, professors like Dr. Shirley Carlson Portwood, Dr. Patrick Riddleberger, and my many other History Professors, showed me a whole, new, awesome world.

However, my days at SIUE also showed me that this outside world was not always so supportive. Once I was walking on campus and I heard a student remark out loud about another student he saw walking on campus, "oh, she must be from EAST St. Louis". He said it so negatively, it hurt so much that when he turned and looked at me, he realized that I too was from East St. Louis.

Even though this comment caused me severe pain, this boy's remark had a profound impact on my life. I realized then that I needed to take charge to bring about change in the world. His remark made me think of something in the Bible where Someone says something to the effect, "can anything good come out of Nazareth?" I have since heard some people say, can anything good come out of EAST St. Louis? Like Jesus, I know the answer is yes. But I do not want our babies or my fellow residents to feel like they have to defend themselves or their hometown. I made a silent promise that day to myself that if someone said that I was from East St. Louis, it would be spoken with respect as if my actions and demeanor were something that was expected from people of our fine city.

Discovering My Calling

My dream at SIUE was always to eventually work at a college and maybe teach History. However, when I graduated with my BA,

there was a freeze on jobs and my plans to go back to school were put on hold. After two years of looking, I was hired by River Bluffs Girl Scout Council in Edwardsville, and they assigned me to East St. Louis, Alorton, Centreville, Fairmont City, and Brooklyn (Lovejoy). While it took me away from what I thought was my intended career, this job helped me understand the joys of working in your home community. Each job that I have had since has brought me closer and closer back to my community.

As I worked for the Girl Scouts, I realized that I knew many of the people I served. They may have gone to some of the same schools I did or they attended the same church or we knew each other's family members. It was not the type of job that you could turn off at the end of the day, because you were always getting asked a question that was job related even when you were off. I came to realize that because I worked in my community, working for the Girl Scouts was not just a job- it was my life. The people that I served were more than clients, they were my neighbors. As someone who works in your home community, you are one of them.

I had not been working for the Girl Scouts for very long when I saw a principal from one of the schools that we served at a Martin Luther King, Jr. observance. He saw me walking with my Mom to our seats, and he pointed at me and said something like "I should have known that you were one of them". I asked my Mom what he meant by that and she explained that he and one of her brothers had attended school together. Although he was obviously

making a reference to my mother's family, what he was really saying, "I should have known that you were one of us." In effect, he was welcoming me home as an adult—a full fledged member of the community. As a field director with the Girl Scouts, I worked with the girls and adults, school personnel, church people—all community people. Already being a part of the community afforded me a great foundation.

My Career Takes a New Direction

When I was working in the community for the Girl Scouts, I kept hearing about this NTAC (Neighborhood Technical Assistance Center) program which was sponsored by University of Illinois at Urbana-Champaign. I knew that students came down from the University (Champaign) and worked in the community, but I did not know exactly what they did. One day I needed a particular map and I called the NTAC office to see if they had a copy. I did not know that this map quest would map out a whole new direction for my career. While talking to one of the NTAC staffers, I found out there was a job opening for which she thought I would be a good fit. As it turned out, I applied for the job and was certainly blessed to get it.

My main initial responsibility with NTAC was to work intensively with eight non-profit boards of directors for five months and help them build their capacity. I would conduct workshops that were tailored around their individual board needs. The funding for my position came from a two year grant that the University of Illinois received from HUD. In addition to supporting my position, the grant also allowed me to bring in U of I professors and other professionals to provide training.

As I became more familiar with my duties, and as I became familiar with the agencies, I started to help them in other areas besides building up their boards. As I worked with these agencies, I learned about the whole gamut of social service agencies in East St. Louis and their missions. The organizations I worked with did everything from being neighborhood organizations, to serving male, homeless veterans, to giving shelter to victims of domestic violence. Just as with working for the Girl Scouts, NTAC became more than a job for me. I became attached to the organizations that I served because they served my community.

NTAC was the baby of the East St. Louis Action Research Project (ESLARP). Working with NTAC, I got to know more about ESLARP and its relationship with the University. I also got to know about all the partnerships that they had in the community. Over time, those partnerships became my network of partnerships as well. Of course, when I developed a relationship with someone or an agency, my Mom would also start a relationship with them and the next thing I would know, I would get a family member, sorority sister, church member or friend involved in a project.

Although my main focus was on board trainings, I started to get involved in the community outreach work that many of the agencies undertook. Because much of this outreach work took place on weekends, this is when I got a chance to meet and work alongside a lot of the students and professors. This really helped me to better understand my role with the University and with the community and how these roles were tied with each other. I started talking to students who were bright, energetic, compassionate, and eager to work in East St. Louis on various projects. Many of these students fell in love with some of our projects and/or community partners.

Over time, I discovered, that the students and the residents formed a real emotional bond with one another. Although most of the students that I worked with when I was with NTAC came from much more affluent backgrounds than the residents with whom they served and who came to East St. Louis initially to satisfy some course requirement or another, they usually discovered that they got much more out of the experience than the residents. For many of them, being in our community was a life changing experience. There was one student who quickly comes to mind. One semester this particular student was assigned to SENDO, the neighborhood organization located in the South End. After the semester was over, he shared with me a story about his relationship with the president at the time. Apparently during one break around Christmas or New Year's, this student was talking to the president on the phone at home and as he was hanging up, he said "I love you". Well, his mother heard him saying this and she wanted to know who he was talking to, and he told her and explained that that was how SENDO's president always ended her conversations and he felt he should do the same. But when he recounted the story to me, he said that when his mother overheard him saying "I love you" to the SENDO president, it was not just words. He really did mean it. He had been so moved by his experience with SENDO and East St. Louis that he actually was in love.

The East St. Louis Bug

This student—just like countless other ones over the years—had gotten what I call "the East St. Louis bug". The "EAST St. Louis bug" occurs when a student, staff person or professor cannot stay away from working in East St. Louis even when a project is completed. That person will take another class, or teach another class which deals with East St. Louis just so he or she can come back to East St. Louis.

ESLARP reminds me of a television show I used to watch as a child and as a young adult. I do not remember the name of this show, but it focused on young law students or young lawyers fresh out of law school. These students or young lawyers would roll up their sleeves and get practical experience by working with regular people who lived in neighborhoods where they were victimized or exploited. Or they worked with people who had jobs that were dangerous or did not pay them a decent wage. Although they were helping the people who they were serving, it was these law students and young lawyers who were the real beneficiaries. Their lives were changed in ways that they could never have imagined before they literally became "addicted" to making a positive difference in people's lives.

To make a long story short, I became addicted too. Working in NTAC, I got the ESLARP "bug." I simply could not get enough of helping people in my community, of truly making a difference. After working in NTAC on "soft" money, I became a permanent member of the ESLARP staff, serving as ESLARP's Community Liaison. My job is searching out community partners and finding ways that our professors, and staff can assist them.

Sometimes I feel like Santa Claus. Sometimes people come into the office totally unexpected and ask for help working on a specific project. In some cases, it might be something as simple as help with a neighborhood clean up. It may not seem like much, but if I am able to get a few students to help them, it puts such a big smile on their faces. This is why this job is so addictive. It is such an amazing feeling when you see a finished product and realize how important the project was to the people involved.

Sometimes the projects are not quite so small and the feeling is even more incredible. One of our professors has been continuously working on KaBOOM applications for some time. KaBOOM is a company that designs and makes playground equipment. They have a grant program where they provide playground equipment to community organizations. Although our applications had been turned down for several years, KaBOOM sent us a letter in 2009 congratulating us on the state of one of the parks owned by the East St. Louis Park District and that they were going to provide new playground equipment for one of the parks for which we had applied. Moreover, the letter notified us that KaBOOM had found an additional corporate sponsor that would assist us in securing even more equipment.

As a result, we were able to get new playground equipment for a small neighborhood park where a local fraternity is a community partner.

Of course, the playground equipment was nice. But that was only part of the gift's impact. The real payoff came when it brought the neighborhood closer together. There was a lady in the

View along 10th Street, 2010   Powell Photo

neighborhood who had sort of adopted one of the parks. For years, she had worked hard to keep the park and the area around it safe and clean. As it turned out, that lady attends the same church that I do and two of her daughters and I belong to the same sorority, one of whom was one of my high school classmates. During a class reunion meeting, an announcement was made about the 'build day" when the equipment would be installed. Not only did some of those classmates show up, other members of the church came, sorority sisters of the lady's daughters came—even a co-worker and two best friends came. They all pitched in, shoveling mulch, planting plants, and working on new signs for the park to make that lady's dream a reality. It was a nice feeling knowing that I had helped improve the park. But what made the experience so special and something that I will never forget is the look on that lady's face after a long day of working as one to make that park as beautiful as we could possibly make it. It might not seem like such a big deal, but that day changed my life. Almost every Sunday now I drive past the park after church because it is an important part of me with which I have to stay connected.

Taking Back Our City

The thing about ESLARP is that it has taught me that community is not just about personal face-to-face relations. Community is about being tied to people through a common sense of place whether you know that person or not. It also means being tied to people who are no longer with us, but who are tied to us through a

common heritage. I love talking to Mayor Park's mother because we can both reminisce about my "Auntie," Nevida Hamilton Gates. By sharing stories about her, we forge bonds between each other and the place we share. The stories about my aunt become our stories cementing us to this place that we call East St. Louis. Similarly, even though I never spent a lot of time at Lincoln Park, my father did when he played with the East St. Louis Giants Baseball team. Consequently, every time I go by the park, I not only feel connected to my father, but to the community which we have both shared.

It is this sense of community which drives me to help restore East St. Louis. I feel that I have an obligation to try to do whatever I can not just for the people who live in the city now, but for all those who lived here once. It is as if all of the fantastic teachers I had and all of the residents who sacrificed so much before me are calling for me to try to help. I have met some residents who have sacrificed so much just to make things better and in comparison to them, I have not done anything. They inspire me to make a difference. When I go to the Alta Sita neighborhood, I start to remember my dad playing baseball with the children in the neighborhood or the school secretary—who lived around just around the corner from our house—who always knew who to call to pick you up if you got sick because she was genuinely concerned. That is the kind of place I want East St. Louis to become again. I want it to feel like home because it is my home.

As a child walking the streets of

downtown East St. Louis with my late grandmother or leaving my first job as a sales clerk at Zerweck's Jewelry Store with my Mom, I saw how busy Collinsville Avenue was. There was no such thing as a vacant lot or an abandoned building located in downtown East St. Louis. Of course, now in 2010, if you walk down Collinsville Avenue, there are vacant lots and abandoned buildings. I can only imagine that for some people it is impossible to conceive of East St. Louis ever being named an "All America City."[2] But I believe in East St. Louis, because I have seen where it has come from and know its rich culture and history. The city should reflect this legacy once again. Since I experienced it in the 1960s and the early 1970s, I know what a nice place it could be to work and live in. It might not ever be what it was, but I firmly believe it can stand on its own again if the right resources and assets come together and if the wonderful people who still live in East St. Louis refuse to leave.

The way we can take back our city is by realizing that we are a community and have always been a community. I remember once looking at postcards that had photographs of the flower beds in Jones Park and being amazed how beautiful they were. What can make East St. Louis beautiful again is if we realize that we are still a community. If just a few of us can work together on projects to help our city, we can not only help to make it a safer, more attractive place to live. We can experience again what it means to be a community where the residents are connected and care for each other.

There Is No Place Like Home

One of my high school classmates recently commented that she wished every member of our class would move back to an East St. Louis neighborhood and just take back our city. After all, we believe that many—if not—most of our class is made up of people who have not forgotten where they came from—that they still think of East St. Louis as home. Undoubtedly, many of the alumni of Lincoln, Assumption, and St. Theresa feel the same way. That East St. Louis is more than just the bad things that are talked about night after night on the news. It is where they grew up.

Home to me feels like a hug you get from Mom when you have had a bad day and Mom's hug just lets you know that everything will be all right. At ESLARP we have not given up on the dream. We still believe that East St. Louis can and is home. There is a saying "How do you eat an elephant?" And the answer is, "one bite at a time." ESLARP believes that the residents of East St. Louis can make the city a home again "one bite at a time." We feel if we all do one little something that will improve East St. Louis, then it will become contagious. Even a simple thing like painting the benches in a park can make a huge difference in a neighborhood. Once you transform one neighborhood it has a snowball effect. Other neighborhoods are turned around and eventually you start to see a difference in the whole city.

East St. Louisans are hard workers and they want to make their streets and homes look better and be safer. They want to reverse the reputation that our city presently has. My job is to show them that they have the power to transform the city if they will only believe that East St. Louis is not just a place to live, it is home. More than just having neighbors who care, they live in a place steeped in tradition as a family. If I can find a way to help East St. Louisans tap into this power, then my mission is accomplished. If they can begin believing that East St. Louis is "one of the places to live" because of its amazing sense of community, then all of our sacrifices and work at ESLARP have not been in vain. If I can do one thing to make a positive difference for the City that has given me so very much, then both my career and my life will have been a success. East St. Louis is in my heart and I love it. There is no place like home.

End Notes:

1. Charles Lumpkins, *American Pogrom: The East St. Louis Race Riot and Black Politics (Law Society & Politics in the Midwest)*, (Athens, Ohio: Ohio University Press, 2008), 167-168.

2. Andrew Theising, *Made in USA: East St. Louis—the Rise and Fall of an Industrial River Town*, (St. Louis, Missouri: Virginia Publishing Company, 2003), 193.

Murphy Building Detail Powell Photo

Chapter 3

Facing the Challenges of De-Industrialization

One Size Does Not Necessarily Fit All:
Harland Bartholomew and the 1920 East St. Louis Comprehensive Plan

Mark Abbott, Ph.D.

Department of Social and Behavioral Sciences
Harris-Stowe State University

East St. Louis may be the most planned city in the country—maybe the world. Faced with enormous challenges in the last half century, East St. Louis has produced plan after plan that have dealt with urban renewal, riverfront development, neighborhood stabilization, and economic rejuvenation[1]. But of all the various East St. Louis planning studies, undoubtedly the most important and influential was the very first one—the 1920 *A Comprehensive City Plan for East St. Louis, Illinois* prepared for the War Civics Committee by Harland Bartholomew.[2] The 1920 comprehensive plan or master plan laid a vision for East St. Louis that still influences public policy in the city. As one of the first comprehensive plans prepared by Harland Bartholomew—who literally came to define what constituted a comprehensive plan—the East St. Louis plan has served as a "template" for comprehensive planning around the world for the last century.

Concept for a public buildings group, 1920 Bowen Archives, SIUE

Ironically, Bartholomew's plan had very little impact on the city. Like the legions of planners who followed him, Bartholomew tried to remake East St. Louis into something that it was not. But what did Bartholomew envision for East St. Louis, and how did it shape not only subsequent plans but the way the city looks today?

Why did the 1920 Plan Even Happen?

Cities undertake comprehensive plans for a variety of reasons. Sometimes they need to get a handle on runaway growth. Other times, they want to come up with a strategic vision for economic development. Occasionally, it has been because they see themselves in competition with other cities or regions.

None of this was the situation with East St. Louis. The federal government mandated that the city develop a plan as part of a program meant to address the issues that had led to the horrific race riot in 1917 that Charles Lumpkins so masterfully describes in this volume.[3] It was not so much that the War Department was concerned about race relations in East St. Louis as such, but that worsening racial tensions had the potential of disrupting the war effort and production now that the United States was an active participant in World War I. Chicago may have had more rail activity because of the volume of production which took place there, but East St. Louis was the central transfer point for goods traveling across the country.[4] As a result, the War Department simply could not afford to have East St. Louis embroiled in another race riot that could shut

down the movement of war goods throughout the United States.

So after a year of probing into the situation, the War Department decided that affairs in East St. Louis could not be resolved internally and therefore decided to take matters into its own hands. On September 16, 1918—a little over a year after the riot had taken place— Secretary of War Newton Baker appointed a "War Civics Committee" that would be responsible for crafting a program to address the race question in East St. Louis. Although the committee and its executive board would be comprised of East St. Louis citizens and interests, it would be under the direct supervision of the War Department itself and be in operation for three years. Clearly, the federal government was not happy with the city.

Although World War I came to a rather abrupt end less than two months after the creation of the War Civics Committee, the War Department proceeded with its mandate. The War Department had already decreed that the industries in the city would foot the bill, so the plan was already funded. For the most part, East St. Louis companies were more than willing to do so. The meat packing industry quickly came up with $100,000 (a little over a million dollars in today's money), and with the notable exception of the railroads (which did not contribute anything), another 42 companies—which read as a "Who's Who in East St. Louis Business"—chipped in another $200,000.[5] With its funding in place, the Committee produced within a year an outline of its program entitled "Building East

St. Louis for Tomorrow" that detailed its strategy for bringing about the social, civic, and physical improvement of East St. Louis, which included the promotion of a city plan.[6]

The Bartholomew Plan

The committee did not look far in deciding who they wanted to produce the plan. Although Michael Allen adroitly points out earlier in this volume that East St. Louis was desperate to create its own architectural identity apart from its mighty neighbor across the river, the Committee chose a rapidly rising young star in the planning profession from St. Louis-Harland Bartholomew.

Only thirty years old, Bartholomew had already made a name for himself by 1919. He had been an important contributor in the 1913 Newark, New Jersey plan—one of the first comprehensive plans in the country—and as a result was made that city's first planning director, a post which he held for three years until 1916 when the newly formed St. Louis Planning Commission offered him the same position in St. Louis. By the time the War Civics Committee offered him a contract to prepare a comprehensive plan for East St. Louis, Bartholomew had already drafted a master plan for St. Louis (1917), a comprehensive street plan (1918), and the second major zoning plan in the country (1918).[7]

While Bartholomew would earn national recognition for his work as St. Louis' planning director, a post which he held until 1953, it was his two other "careers" that he started in 1919 that made him one of the major figures in American urban planning. The first of these was Bartholomew's life as a professor in Urban Planning at the University of Illinois. As a scholar and researcher, Bartholomew wrote several books and hundreds of articles.[8] But it was Bartholomew's third career as a planning consultant in which he established himself as one of the leading lights in the planning profession in the twentieth century in the United States and around the world. His St. Louis firm, Harland Bartholomew and Associates (HBA), produced more than 600 comprehensive plans worldwide before it was sold in 1985.[9]

Of these 600 plus comprehensive plans, perhaps none were more important than the three plans that Bartholomew started in 1919 in Omaha, Nebraska; Hamilton, Ohio; and East St. Louis. While Bartholomew had already written three master plans before 1919 (besides Newark and St. Louis, he had also prepared one for Belleville, New Jersey in 1916), it was during 1919 and 1920 and his work on these three plans that Bartholomew's ideas concerning the structure of a comprehensive plan solidified into the format that HBA would come to use in all of its plans. Because of how extensively it has been used, this "template" is still the dominant paradigm that planners continue to use to draft new comprehensive plans today.

At the heart of the Bartholomew paradigm was the assumption that all cities operated as integrated systems. Unlike the first comprehensive planners— men like Daniel Burnham who wrote the 1909 Chicago Plan and

George Kessler who was part of the team that wrote the 1907 St. Louis plan—Bartholomew did not view planning as primarily an aesthetic exercise. For him, the point to planning was to make the city function more efficiently.   What differentiated Bartholomew from the earlier aesthetic or "City Beautiful" planners was that he believed that the proper approach was to view it as a scientific exercise rather than an artistic one. In his mind, while all cities were different in terms of topography, demographics, culture, and the like, all cities had the same essential structure and could, therefore, all be approached the same way. The job of the planner, whether the city in question was New York or East St. Louis, was to apply universal laws or principles to facilitate the pieces of the city to work together as a harmonious whole.

From this perspective, East St. Louis was a disaster. Although Bartholomew never directly refers to the race riot (or even race, for that matter) in the plan, it is clear that he thought the city was unraveling. In his Letter of Transmittal addressed to the War Civics Committee, Bartholomew implicitly made the argument that the chaos of 1917 was the result of the fact that the city had grown too fast, making it disjointed and dysfunctional. Consequently, according to Bartholomew, the city desperately needed a plan. "The extremely difficult problems of today," Bartholomew told the Committee, "are but an indication of the urgency and wisdom of anticipating the needs of tomorrow."[10]

However, all was not lost. "Certainly few cities have ever

been confronted with more difficult physical problems," Bartholomew noted, "yet," he went on to say, "the present opportunity of planning for the greater and *inevitable* [italics mine] future development should appeal to all citizens as a measure of good business and sound economy." So, while the city's growth was tearing the city apart—like a runaway cancer—Bartholomew assured the Committee that "through planning, we may direct that growth into proper channels."[11]

It was not going to be easy. While East St. Louis had constructed one of the most impressive levee systems in the country just after the turn of the century and had major comparative advantages as an industrial center, Bartholomew made it clear in the plan's introduction that the city faced major challenges.   In Bartholomew's mind, nothing about the physical character of the city made sense. With its central location, abundant coal supplies, and amazing rail facilities East St. Louis should have been on the cusp of becoming "one of the greatest industrial cities in America"; but according to Bartholomew, the city was almost deliberately trying to fail with its "tendency toward haphazard development so glaringly evident wherever one turns, not merely within the confines of the city but throughout the whole district."[12] Bartholomew's list of the city's failings was almost endless: "Railroads have spread at random throughout the city's area; industries have been built where principal streets should be extended…[and] subdivisions have been laid out, pavements laid, and utilities constructed beyond what should have been the natural limits of the city's growth," Bartholomew almost bellowed to his readers. In short, Bartholomew informed East St. Louisans, "there has been scarcely any public action that can be pointed to as evidence of or regard for the development of a great metropolis."[13]

But the purpose of Bartholomew's harangue was not to reprimand, but to educate. As he told the Committee, "these shortcomings are commonly known and are not here stated as mere criticisms. We learn by our mistakes, and those of East St. Louis are recounted in order to show the lack of vision and civic spirit that has attended the vast growth of the city."[14] It was almost as if Bartholomew was saying that East St. Louis had grown and prospered in spite of itself. Yet time was of the essence. Growth was already taking place beyond the city's borders and needed to be controlled and shaped. After the listing the city's challenges in the introduction, the rest of the body of the plan was Bartholomew's scheme for pulling the city back together. For Bartholomew, the job of the planner was to order the physical components of city in such a fashion so that the social, economic, and political facets could operate in as harmonious a way as possible. Although there would be slight modifications to the formula over the next half-century, Bartholomew and HBA divided the comprehensive plan into eight design element components: streets, transportation, transit, public recreation, zoning, housing, public infrastructure, and civic art/city appearance. The last chapter of a Bartholomew comprehensive plan was always

devoted to implementation tactics that involved legal, legislative, and financial strategies. The 1920 East St. Louis plan was a perfect manifestation of the Bartholomew approach.

Streets, Transit, and Transportation

Although the order of the components would change from plan to plan,[15] Bartholomew opened the East St. Louis plan with the street system because he generally viewed it as the most important component and because he obviously saw it [or actually the lack of it] as the city's biggest hurdle. As Bartholomew would articulate later in the 1920 Memphis plan, "the street system is the fundamental element of the city plan. It is the skeleton or framework of the city structure."[16] In Bartholomew's mind, everything about how a city functioned depended upon its streets.

According to Bartholomew, East St. Louis' streets were a total mess. The main problem was that the street system was not a system. For Bartholomew, there were essentially three kinds of streets: main arterial thoroughfares that ran from one end of the city to the other, secondary feeder or cross-town thoroughfares, and minor residential streets. Each type of street had a specific function that required certain specific dimensions. For example, major thoroughfares needed to be at least 100 feet wide or greater, secondary thoroughfares 80-100 feet wide, and residential streets, because they were only supposed to serve local traffic, were only supposed to be 50 feet wide with 26-foot-wide roadways (that is, the section of the street that actually

carried cars or other vehicles).[17] East St. Louis had wide streets where there were supposed to be narrow ones, narrow ones where there were supposed to be wide ones, and none of the streets served as continuous thoroughfares. As Bartholomew noted, "an examination of the city map indicates quite clearly the different subdivisions of property, which, though following the usual rectangular plan, have failed to produce anything even resembling a uniform system of wide, direct, and properly connected main streets."[18]

On the other hand, he exclaimed, "in some portions of the city an excess of street width was the rule, other large sections of the city have been subdivided without a single wide street!"[19]

Why this had happened, Bartholomew explained, was pretty obvious. While East St. Louis was an industrial suburb, it was first and foremost a railroad suburb. As a result, "the existence of railroads seems to have been one of the principal determining factors in locating the majority of the city's streets." But this is where the planner and the plan came in. As Bartholomew told the citizens of East St. Louis, "numerous widening, extensions, openings, if made as indicated upon the map accompanying this report, entitled, 'Proposed Major Street Plan' (No.1), will make possible a complete and satisfactory system."[20]

Although Bartholomew had just started HBA, he was enough of a businessman to know that if East St. Louis residents and companies were hearing of this for the first time all they would be seeing would be dollar signs.

Moreover, they would want to know why an outsider was telling them to spend millions of their dollars. But Bartholomew took great pains to tell them that he had already received "consideration and criticism" to an earlier "preliminary report" including "numerous valuable suggestions by individuals and organizations." However, the main point Bartholomew wanted to make was that while the street improvements were going to be expensive, they would save East St. Louis in the long run. "Such important projects…at first may appear to be almost impossible, and yet experience in cities where such work has been done indicates that improvements of this character, made at a time when property values are low and before numerous costly improvements interfere, will pay for themselves through increases in property values." But time was money. The longer they waited and the more development occurred, the more expensive and difficult it would be to make modifications. "To delay longer the improvements mentioned, together with others in the more closely built up districts," Bartholomew argued, "is virtually to throttle development before it is fairly started."[21]

Bartholomew discussed over two dozen major street projects which he divided into two different categories: radial street connections and the rectangular system. While both were important for Bartholomew, his radial street connections were clearly paramount. In this group, he had four recommendations. On the north side he proposed a new road to Granite City that would veer to the northwest from the intersection of Collinsville Avenue and Ninth Street. Another was to use Mississippi Avenue to join the industrial development to the south and east with the central business district by connecting it to Tenth Street at Piggott Avenue and widening the length of the new street to 100 feet.

But Bartholomew's primary recommendations concerned Collinsville Avenue and State Street. In terms of the former, Bartholomew wanted to open up a direct link with Collinsville Road to the north and to the Eads and Municipal bridges to the south via Tenth Street. In Bartholomew's mind, there was "no more important or far-reaching improvement…before the City of East St. Louis." Having said that, it was clear that Bartholomew saw his proposed State Street/Old Rock Road improvement as equally important. Perceiving

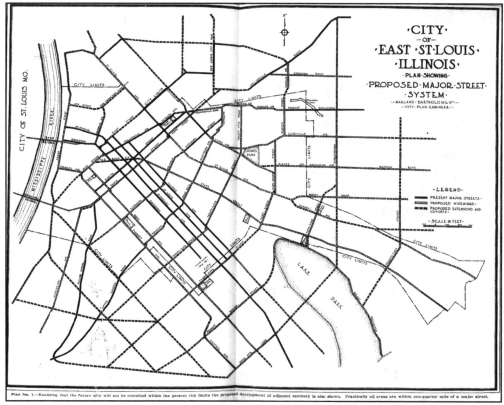

Bartholomew's concept street plan, 1920   Bowen Archives, SIUE

that State Street was the only major thoroughfare that ran virtually the length of the city east to west and that it did not go all the way to the heart of the central business district, Bartholomew's idea was to reopen Rock Road with a 100-foot roadway to Broadway at Fifth. Not only would such a connection provide a continuous arterial from the eastern end of the city to the Eads Bridge, it would relieve much of the congestion on Collinsville Avenue.

Although not as ambitious as the radial connections, Bartholomew's proposed widening and opening of the existing grid system had the same intent. The idea was to take the disjointed street system and superimpose a network of major thoroughfares that would remake East St. Louis into an integrated whole. The metaphor that Bartholomew used to describe the street system was that it was the city's skeleton; however, in keeping with his notion that the city operated as a natural organism, it also acted as its circulatory system. It allowed the lifeblood of goods, services, and people to be transported from one end of the city to another.

Although the chapters on Transit and Transportation did not immediately follow the chapter on Streets in the 1920 plan (though they would in later HBA comprehensive plans), they were closely tied to Bartholomew's street plan in both design and tactics. In Bartholomew's approach, transit dealt with streetcars, motorbuses, and in larger cities, rapid or heavy rail systems. Transportation, on the

other hand, involved the railroads (both passenger and freight), water/harbor facilities, and later, public and private air terminals.

From Bartholomew's viewpoint, the main problem of East St. Louis' transit system was the same problem that plagued the city's streets—it was not really a system. Some areas of the city had great access while others like the city's south side (which just happened to be where the concentration of African-Americans was located), did not. As a result, Bartholomew's recommendations for the streets and the transit system went hand-in-hand. By creating a street system which evenly accessed all points of the city, a transit system could be superimposed on it which would also be accessible to all parts of the city, reinforcing the integration of all its components.

Bartholomew's transit plan had three main recommendations: construction of cross town lines, relief of Collinsville Avenue through the opening and use of the Old Rock Road, and a new Mississippi River crossing to ease congestion on the Eads Bridge.[22] The first was needed because the transit system was too oriented to taking people to St. Louis rather than responding to its own internal needs. Bartholomew basically proposed three north-south lines that would cut across the existing ones feeding into St. Louis. The first two were actually one line that would emanate from the northwestern corner of the city by the stockyards, head south on the western edge of the city via St. Clair, Tenth Street, and Piggott Avenue to "the large colored district in the southern part of the city."[23] At that point, it would

double back north via 25th and 26th streets to Lincoln Park thereby forming another cross town route in the middle of city. "Eventually," Bartholomew said, "a third crosstown [sic] line will probably be needed, at which time it would be possible to make a distinct line operating between the Stock Yards and the southern part of the city making virtually a separate Belt Line."[24]

Bartholomew's second transit proposal involved availing the transit system of the opening of Old Rock Road from State Street to the central business district. As with automotive traffic, this would not only reduce congestion on Collinsville Avenue, Bartholomew said, but "would afford at once opportunities for more direct and quicker service for all lines from the eastern part of the city to the business district of East St. Louis or the business district of the City of St. Louis across the river."[25] The most radical of Bartholomew's three transit recommendations was building a new bridge across the Mississippi. Although he said it was more of a "suggestion rather than a recommendation," the "utter insufficiency of a single highway bridge across the Mississippi" was clear to him even from "casual observation." While the new Municipal Bridge to the south did have a highway deck, it was too far south and too far removed from most residential areas. What was needed, according to Bartholomew, was a new bridge roughly mid-way between the Municipal Bridge and the Eads Bridge that would take vehicular and streetcar traffic from "Trendley Avenue and Main Street in East St. Louis to Fourth and Market Streets in St. Louis, which would provide a highly desirable highway connection between the two cities."[26]

While Bartholomew felt that his transit recommendations were crucial to the long-term health of East St. Louis, he was even more adamant that restructuring the relationship between the railroads and the city was a matter of life and death for the community. From Bartholomew's perspective, the railroads were choking the city. They had so entangled the city there was literally no room to grow. "To the north, south, and west," Bartholomew noted, "it is practically impossible for the city to expand. Railroad lines and yards act as barriers to the extension of streets or transit facilities in these three directions. This is not a healthy condition for the city or the railroads."[27]

Nothing better illustrates the manner in which Bartholomew viewed what city planning was all about was this conflict between the railroads and East St. Louis. "The railroads," Bartholomew told East St. Louisans, "have undoubtedly helped to create the present city and in so doing have enjoyed almost unlimited privileges." "But," he continued, "the time has now come when they must recognize the desirability, wisdom, and necessity of co-operating with the city in solving its problems." Because the city was a unified whole, there was only one common set of interests. "The city's problem is also the railroads' problem," Bartholomew argued, "and through co-operation in solving this common problem the railroads can best help themselves." Ignoring the fact that the majority of their trade was national in scope and not

local, Bartholomew concluded that the railroads would prosper if the rest of the city prospered. As Bartholomew put it, "increased growth, means new industries, and more business, and consequently more traffic and business for the railroads."[28]

The main obstacles keeping East St. Louis and the railroads from realizing this common prosperity were, in Bartholomew's mind, the hundreds of at-grade street and rail intersections. "It is doubtful," Bartholomew explained, "if any city in the United States is confronted with a more serious railroad problem than is East St. Louis." From Bartholomew's perspective, the disruption of traffic flow at the grade crossings was paralyzing the city. The problem was not one railroad or one part of the city, either. It was, according to Bartholomew, the entire relationship of the railroads to the city. "The great need" he said, "is for a comprehensive plan of railroad and terminal arrangement, with elevation and grade crossing elimination."[29]

In essence, Bartholomew was calling for a wholesale rebuilding of the rail system in East St. Louis. While he tried to comfort the Committee—and the railroads— by arguing that "**it would be possible to avoid any necessity for grade crossing elimination at about two-thirds of the points shown on the plan if the grade crossing removals could be accomplished on the major streets** [bold Bartholomew's],"[30] he knew he was suggesting a massive undertaking. Although he presented a map indicating where he thought it was particularly important to eliminate grade crossings, Bartholomew knew that

his recommendations were bound to cause a firestorm and called for a commission to be created for "more extensive study," the East Side Railroad Commission.[31] Realizing that railroad support was essential for significant changes in railroad placement and grade crossings, Bartholomew suggested that his proposed Commission be comprised of two engineers appointed by the city, two engineers appointed by the railroads, and a "fifth member to be appointed by mutual agreement."[32] Bartholomew wanted the Commission also to examine "the possibility of constructing new classification yards east of the city for the major lines and building a new union station as well as assessing the feasibility of terminal facilities on the riverfront."[33]

Public Recreation, Housing, and Zoning

Throughout his career, Bartholomew saw himself first and foremost as an engineer; He saw city planning as merely a type of engineering. As a consequence, he believed that the only legitimate activities of planners were the physical ordering of the city and the legal means of bringing it about. Nonetheless, Bartholomew recognized that the city was not just a collection of streets and buildings. It was an environment for people and as such, had a tremendous impact on how the people of the city interacted with one another.

Though Bartholomew was loath to address social issues in his plans, the chapters on public recreation and housing come the closest to talking about social problems facing the city. Although the plan was the direct result of the 1917 race riot, Bartholomew did not mention it once. However, it was clear that he believed that the racial turmoil that had just boiled to the surface was a result of "adverse living conditions in East St. Louis," and that the way of "creating an environment more favorable to the successful production of war materials" was eliminating those "adverse living conditions" for both races.[34]

For Bartholomew, housing was the worst social problem that East St. Louis faced. There was not enough housing, and the housing that was available was of poor quality. The first problem was a matter of economics. Now that the war was over, industry was growing faster than the ability of the construction field to keep up. Consequently, the price of materials and labor made house-building prohibitively expensive.

"In the past six months," Bartholomew told his readers, "only ninety-eight permits have been issued for new houses." This was just not enough. "The normal increase in population for a city the size of East St. Louis," Bartholomew pointed out, "would indicate the necessity of building at least five hundred homes per year."[35] Even though he did not elaborate, Bartholomew remarked in passing that "in order to meet this situation, a housing company has been organized and an initial group of twenty-five houses will be built within the next few months."[36] While this just a pittance of what was needed, the mere proposal of creating such a company outside of normal market forces made Bartholomew one of the most innovative thinkers in terms of housing as a component of planning.

However, what really interested

Bartholomew in terms of housing was maintaining and improving the existing housing stock in the city. While the city was fortunate not to have large tenements and did not have excessive density, the quality of housing in the city was, according to Bartholomew, deplorable: "a satisfactory type of workingman's home has never been developed." Most homes of the working classes were "shot gun" houses that "are of a one-story frame construction, having only the bare necessities of a good home." The most glaring lack in most East St. Louis housing units was indoor plumbing. Bartholomew pointed to a recent report by the Illinois Health Department that revealed that "there are over 7,700 outdoor privy vaults, compared with a little over 5,000 indoor toilets in the city" (As a point of comparison, St. Louis probably had less than half of its housing units served

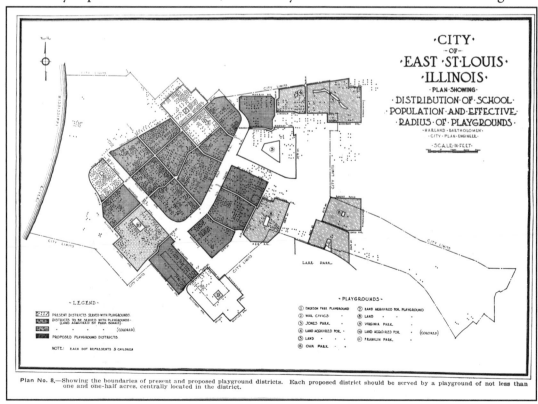

Bartholomew's playground analysis, 1920   Bowen Archives, SIUE

by outdoor privy vaults). In addition, "more than 1,200 of these latter were found to be in bad condition and approximately one-half of the privy vaults were maintained in violation of city ordinance section 734, providing that no privy vaults shall be maintained on a lot adjacent to a sewer." Moreover, Bartholomew observed, "little or no effort had previously been made to collect and dispose of household waste . . . [and] . . . there had been almost no collection of ashes and refuse."[37] It had only been since the creation of the War Civics Committee that the city had actually contracted for the collection and disposal of garbage. But, as Bartholomew pointed out, "no provision was made with respect to the frequency of collection."[38]

For Bartholomew, who always prided himself on being a good businessman, allowing these housing conditions to exist was just bad business, arguing that "good housing is essential to good business in any city and the present housing problems of East St. Louis should receive the attention of the business interests." For him, the bottom line was "unless measures are taken to prevent the spread of these evils a considerable increase in contagious and infectious diseases will be inevitable."[39] The answer, according to Bartholomew, was to have stringent enforcement of health and building codes that were already on the books, as well as new codes that were needed to ensure that new housing complied with new standards and expectations.

While Bartholomew and planners of his generation have often been criticized for believing that "good toilets made good citizens," they sincerely believed that poor living conditions not only led to bad health consequences and social frustrations that led to conflict (i.e., rioting). While the job of the planner was not just to remove or improve those conditions that led to social conflict, Bartholomew thought the planner had the ability and the responsibility to design environments to fuse the people of the city into a cohesive whole.

One suspects that this is why Bartholomew placed the chapter on Public Recreation second in the East St. Louis plan (before housing) even though this was not usually where he placed it in most other comprehensive plans. While today the term "public recreation" usually refers only to the venues where people together come to relax and exercise, the term meant much more to Bartholomew. As with all components of the city, public recreation was a system where different facilities served different functions. In his scheme, there were five types of public recreation facilities: community centers, playgrounds for young children, neighborhood parks with athletic amenities such as sports fields and swimming pools, large parks that served the entire city, and boulevards. Of the five, Bartholomew believed that community centers were the most important. Concentrations of public and private buildings, community centers acted as focal points where the lives of the citizens converged. "The community center is an integral and essential part of any well-organized system of recreation," Bartholomew explained. "It

serves as the only practical means by which the recreational and educational authorities can co-operate directly with the people for the purpose of improving the social welfare and unifying the common interests of a community."[40]

But here was the rub. Even though Bartholomew believed that the city was a system, different components needed to keep their integrity not only to operate efficiently themselves, but in order not to undermine the function of the other elements. While all parts of the city were crucial, some parts of the city were not compatible when mixed together. This was what Bartholomew was really trying to say in the Transportation chapter. He wanted to reconfigure the rail system so that he could separate commercial uses from industrial ones and to separate both from residential areas.

Bartholomew's logic, however, extended not just to railroads, factories, and houses. It extended to people as well. Again, Bartholomew never directly talked about the riot or the question of race. Yet it was a constant theme nevertheless. Bartholomew's unspoken message was that the riot occurred not just because of poor living conditions among workers of both races but because their neighborhoods were no longer clearly defined. Bartholomew's stated purpose for the map showing "Housing Areas, Railroads, and Proposed Major Streets" was to illustrate how the railroads had broken up the continuity of the residential areas. However, by differentiating in the legend between those areas "now occupied by white people" and those "now occupied by colored people," [41] Bartholomew wanted to illustrate how undirected growth had led to a blurring of racial boundaries.

In short, while Bartholomew had clearly implied that community centers could bring the people of East St. Louis together, he also illustrated how public recreation facilities could be used to separate people as well. Though Bartholomew did not say a word about race in the narrative, he knew—like his readers knew—that by designating certain proposed sites for "colored" playgrounds that this would reinforce the racial character of the neighborhoods, just as he knew that the placement of boulevards in certain parts of the city would act as hard borders dividing the city along both racial and class lines. [42]

Although boulevards and parks as well as street, transportation, and transit systems could divide the city into its functional components, Bartholomew believed that a much more effective instrument was a zoning ordinance or a "scheme for regulating the height, area, and use of buildings within the city." [43] By 1920, Bartholomew had already established himself as an authority on zoning or districting in the country, having produced the second zoning or districting plan for a major American city. [44] His 1918 St. Louis zoning plan divided the city into five zones or districts: one for upper end residences based on property values, a second for all other residential uses including multistory apartment buildings, a third which provided for commercial and institutional uses such as

police and fire stations, a fourth that allowed light industry, and a fifth which was unrestricted for the most obnoxious or least compatible land uses.

Bartholomew wanted a similar scheme for East St. Louis. However, as he explained, circumstances in Illinois made it premature to propose one. When the plan was first authorized in 1918, Illinois did not have enabling legislation that permitted zoning. While it had since passed enabling legislation in 1919, Bartholomew thought it was seriously flawed and would soon be revised in the next session. If that was indeed the case, "East St. Louis may then with advantage undertake the preparation of a zoning scheme." Moreover, Bartholomew remarked, "the present comprehensive plan will serve as an excellent guide for such a zoning study and plan, practically all the necessary study maps having been made for this report, excepting only those of building heights and area and of land values." [45]

Bartholomew's zoning or districting paradigm had clear social ramifications. By having multiple residential categories, a zoning plan would not only segregate non-conforming architectural styles and building types from one another. It would also segregate the residents of those structures as well. Almost by definition, neighborhoods of single family houses would have middle-class or affluent residents and neighborhoods comprised of multi-family buildings would have lower or working class inhabitants. But in a bi-racial city like East St. Louis, zoning

would also have obvious racial ramifications. Even the most prosperous African Americans generally had much lower incomes than whites, so zoning could be used effectively to foster both economic and racial apartheid. In recent years, Bartholomew has come under scathing criticism for his zoning approach—and rightfully so. Scholars today such as Colin Gordon have convincingly demonstrated that zoning ordinances in America have been used primarily as devices to promote racial and class segregation. [46] While Bartholomew tried to stay away from the issues of class and race as much as possible throughout his career, he probably would argue if he were alive today that segregation was a good thing. Although today we see such perspectives as both morally appalling and sociologically naïve, Bartholomew undoubtedly felt that the riot had occurred at least in part because the understood racial borders had become blurred and two non-compatible cultures collided. Of course, a century of quasi-apartheidism in America has shown that racial separation only breeds contempt and mistrust, but Bartholomew believed that for different groups to function harmoniously for the good of the whole they needed to be separated just as factories needed to be separated from residential and commercial districts. But writing only a handful of years after several cities, St. Louis among them, had attempted to legislate racial segregation by ordinance, Bartholomew's stance in 1920 was not all that surprising and it was not surprising that he was pushing East St. Louis to adopt a zoning ordinance.

Zoning is still a loaded issue among planners. Although many if not most contemporary planners embrace what is called "form-based" zoning, which encourages mixed-use and mixed-income development, the basic logic of Bartholomew's approach is still largely accepted. A majority of planners would argue that it is quite legitimate to separate industrial uses from residential and commercial ones. Moreover, most planners—even those who acknowledge the racist and classist impact of many past zoning practices—would support, for example, segregating mobile homes from single family housing on aesthetic or historic preservation grounds even though such an ordinance might have just as much racist or classist impact of traditional or "Euclidean"[47] zoning. What has become the accepted argument among planners is that no zoning, whether it is form-based or Euclidean, is racist or classist by definition. What is important is the intent of a zoning ordinance and whether the ordinance reflects the common consensus of what the citizens want. Even today, the concentration of multiple family housing and heavy industry in the city's South End and Alta Sita neighborhoods[48] (the traditional African-American communities) is a testament to the intent of past zoning ordinances by the then white majority to separate African-Americans from the rest of the city.

Sewers and Water Supply/The City's Appearance

The last two design chapters in the plan were the ones dealing with East St. Louis' utilities and infrastructure and strategies for improving the city's appearance.[49] Though relatively minor in the overall structure of the plan, both are reflective of Bartholomew's grand vision for how a city should be constituted. As with the earlier chapters, the notion that the city should be seen as an integrated whole with differentiated parts comes through loud and clear. But what also came through was the firm belief that while it might be permissible—and even desirable—that the races should be segregated, it was absolutely essential that the basic needs of all East St. Louisans had to be addressed if the city was going to function efficiently as an entity.

Like the chapter on zoning, the section on sewers and water supply is less than a page long plus an accompanying map. However, even though it is a very short chapter, Bartholomew struck hard to his main point, which was that for East St. Louis to operate effectively, all parts of the city— even those that were African-American—had to be healthy and fully functional. Just as with a human body, different parts could be "zoned" or "districted" as separate organs, but if they atrophied and died, they would ultimately cause the death of the whole body. In short what Bartholomew was telling East St. Louisans was that all parts of the city had to be adequately served, even those that were African American. The city simply could not sustain itself if some parts of the city had sewers and adequate water supply and others did not. Ultimately the health consequences of not serving all parts of the city equally would pull the city down, putting everyone at risk. Comparing maps of population and those showing adequate sewers and water supply, Bartholomew concluded that "water supply has at least kept pace with the expansion of population the construction of sewers, however, has fallen behind." But what he hoped was happening was that the riot had forced East St. Louisans to realize that the needs of all citizens had to be addressed. As he noted, garbage collection had been expanded greatly since 1917 as well as "contracts have recently been let and sewers are now under construction for a considerable portion of the populated area on either side of State Street east of 21st Street." But for Bartholomew, this recent flurry of activity still did not go far enough in addressing the sewerage needs of the whole city—including the "colored section." As he reminded his readers, "there is a large district, though, which lacks sewerage facilities, including Alta Sita, the colored section in the vicinity of Piggott Avenue, the northeast part of the city and the general vicinity of Washington Park."[50] But Bartholomew's larger argument went way beyond garbage collection and providing adequate sewers. It was that East St. Louis could no longer ignore the physical and social needs of all its citizens. The riot had many underlying causes. But to echo one of Andrew Theising's main points in *Made in USA*[51], Bartholomew seemed to be saying that the city's basic failure to uphold its "social contract" with its citizens had led to the unraveling of the core social fabric that kept the city together. For Bartholomew, time was running out. If the city did not act quickly and aggressively to address the basic needs of its citizens—both black and white—the dysfunctionality of those areas ignored would become a cancer that would ultimately bring about the downfall of the whole city.

The concluding actual planning chapter in the plan dealt with the City's Appearance. Many of Bartholomew's recommendations for East St. Louis have become standard fare in most comprehensive plans ever since. Yet while his main proposals for street trees, better sidewalks, limiting billboards, sinking utility lines, beautifying entrances to the city might seem rather commonplace for the modern reader, they were at the very heart of Bartholomew's vision for East St. Louis. For him, the city's

appearance was emblematic that East St. Louis—like any city—lived and died not as a collection of neighborhoods, but as an integrated whole. According to Bartholomew, if some parts of the city were attractive and others were decrepit, those parts that were decrepit gave the whole city an unpleasant feel. And for him, it was not just a matter of aesthetics. It was a question of dollars and cents.

It is now a generally accepted fact that the industrial city wishing to attract new industries as well as retain its present ones must offer to the manufacturer not merely good industrial sites, low freight rates and switching charges, and public utility services at economical prices, but the city must also offer to the employees of industries good living conditions,

good housing conditions, ample recreation facilities, and those other things that will tend to make life in that city pleasant for the *workingmen's* [italics mine] families.[52]

For Bartholomew, one of those amenities was a "pleasing aspect." And as Bartholomew noted, "it must be admitted that East St. Louis today offers anything but a pleasing appearance to its citizens and to those who visit the city."[53] Again, the point is that, for Bartholomew, while the city had parts, it was first and foremost a whole. The manufacturers could live in St. Louis or on the bluffs, but if the workers did not, or would not, live in East St. Louis, it would die.

Ultimately, what a city's appearance reflected was whether

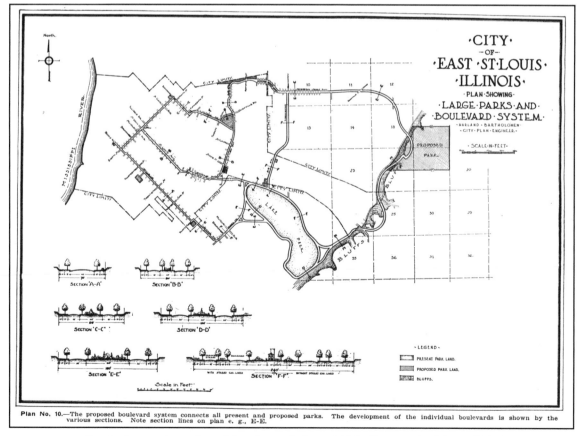

Plan No. 10.—The proposed boulevard system connects all present and proposed parks. The development of the individual boulevards is shown by the various sections. Note section lines on plan e. g., E-E.

Bartholomew's park and boulevard plan, 1920 Bowen Archives, SIUE

or not the citizens saw themselves as a community. If some parts of the city were strewn with litter, had blighted buildings, and had a basic unkempt appearance, it indicated both that the residents of that part of the city no longer identified with their own living space and that residents in the attractive parts of the city no longer saw the unsightly section being a reflection of themselves. This is why the most important of Bartholomew's beautification proposals was his last one for a civic center. Echoing the first comprehensive plans, Bartholomew called for a grouping of public buildings that would not only be an expression of the city's status and beauty, but of its existence as a unified community. Arguing that the present city hall would soon outline his usefulness, and that the city already needed a new library, as well as a new court house, Bartholomew urged East St. Louis to consider placing all three buildings on a common site close to the business district. Such an arrangement would not only generate a sense of architectural grandeur, it would also enhance efficiency by "concentrating public business at a common point" and "give expression to the community spirit."[54] In other words, the whole was greater than the parts and that the community center could be a source of pride for the whole city—both black and white.

Legal and Financial Aspects of the City Plan

The last chapter was not really part of the plan *per se* but a series of recommendations and appendices that outlined how it could be implemented. The thrust of Bartholomew's proposals was

that the city needed more legal power to coerce development in the manner in which the plan suggested and the power to raise more money to do the myriad needed projects.

In terms of legal or political changes that Bartholomew wanted to see made, one important one was a new city charter "to make possible the expedition of city planning work." According to him, the current charter did not have the legal and political capacity to undertake the scope of activities which he had suggested. For example, Bartholomew said, the city needed the capability to issue long-term bonds to finance major capital improvement programs like street widening and openings.[55] Another major recommendation that he made was to support the work of the Chicago City Club to push through enabling legislation at the State Constitutional Convention. Like progressive-era leaders of other major cities, the Chicago City Club was looking to expand municipal powers to include policies spanning from restricting occupancy to allowing cities to condemn excess land when using eminent domain and passing zoning ordinances.[56] But the main political action that Bartholomew wanted was the formation of a "permanent city plan commission." Such a commission would take the plan out of the hands of the city council and place it with a citizen board. For Bartholomew, a comprehensive plan was like an urban constitution and the planning commission was its supreme court. As matters came up—such as a proposal for a new building or a new development—

the planning commission would act as the protector of the plan as it reviewed new initiatives for compliance to the plan.[57]

Although Bartholomew was just barely polite to the city fathers throughout most of the plan, he saved his most scathing language for the last few paragraphs where he spoke of financial considerations surrounding the plan. In short, he accused the city of being cheap and implied quite strongly that it was this miserliness that had led to the rioting of 1917. While acknowledging challenges that the rapid growth of the city and the presence of the railroads created for the city, Bartholomew told East St. Louisans point-blank that "genuine public spirit has been almost unknown." And as a result, the city had grown in a willy-nilly fashion and the "lack of a systematic plan has been accompanied by a lack of regard for the very necessary matters of legislation and finance so vital to progress." In Bartholomew's mind, you got what you paid for, and the City had paid for precious little. "Public improvements cost money and perhaps," he commented, "the realization of the cost of the many things needed by the city has served heretofore to dampen enthusiasm for constructive accomplishments." However, he went on to say, "public improvements, though costly, bring their own reward and justification in the creation of new values and new business activity." Coming as close as he ever did in recognizing why the plan was being prepared in the first place, Bartholomew concluded his diatribe by suggesting that "it is undoubtedly this realization that has caused the recent community stock-taking and planning of the past two years."[58]

In Bartholomew's mind, the city simply had to raise more revenue to meet its responsibilities. Although it was hamstrung by archaic state and county laws that limited its ability to generate revenue, the city was not exercising the powers it did have to raise needed monies to remain viable. As Andrew Theising has noted elsewhere, East St. Louis manufacturers and railroads resisted being taxed at a legitimate rate to support services that their employees required in order to maximize their bottom line.[59] But Bartholomew made the argument even more forcibly. "Of the 131 cities in the United States having a population of over 50,000," Bartholomew exclaimed "East St. Louis has next to the lowest assets and value of public property and is very nearly the lowest in revenue receipts from taxes and in expenditures for governmental purposes."[60] Bartholomew concluded the plan by merely saying, "obviously the conclusion to be drawn from these figures is that East St. Louis can afford to raise revenues from which it may gradually make improvements at least comparable, if not superior, to those of other cities."

Aftermath of the Plan

So what came of the plan? Eventually, planning and zoning commissions started in East St. Louis. Collinsville Avenue now has a relatively straight connection with Collinsville Road—although the approach to the Eads and Municipal bridges is rather jagged (and of course, the Municipal Bridge no longer carries vehicular traffic). East St. Louis now has many of the regulatory powers that Bartholomew wanted such as the ability to take and execute options on property and to condemn land for the use of other corporations or agencies (both associated with Tax Incremental Financing districts, or TIFs). Most of the overhead lines have been removed downtown. The city has generally adequate sewer and water service (however, the state of the city's 107-year-old levees is being challenged by the federal government).

But for the most part, the majority of what Bartholomew had called for did not come about. His proposal for opening up a diagonal connection between State Street and Collinsville Avenue via Old Rock Road was never completed. Few community centers or playgrounds were ever built. East St. Louis was plagued by at-grade railroad crossings until the railroads eventually left the city. After the 1970's while the vast majority of housing units in the city now have indoor plumbing, East St. Louis' housing stock remained in distressed condition after 1920. Today most of East St. Louis' housing consists of poorly maintained public housing units or abandoned private houses. City finances are a disaster. Moreover, East St. Louis still does not have "a pleasing aspect." Of course, the most damning indictment of the plan is that it failed to remedy the two main problems that prompted its creation in the first place—racial tension and industrial viability. East St. Louis has become an American poster child for both institutional racism and the failure of American industrialization.

Would it have made a difference if the plan had been carried out almost a century ago? It is hard to imagine that it could have made things worse. East St. Louis has lost almost two thirds of its population, a casino is its largest employer, and a majority of its residents live in poverty. But in a sense, the plan did make things worse. Obviously, urban planners cannot be blamed for all of East St. Louis' problems. No matter what planners attempted to do, national and global social and economic trends could very well have resulted in the same consequences. Even though most of Bartholomew's plan was never implemented, the reams of planning studies since the 1920 plan have attempted to carry out Bartholomew's vision. Maybe Bartholomew did not get his way with State Street feeding directly into the downtown, but the interstate highways (of which he was a leading proponent) whisk automobiles across the East St. Louis landscape chopping up the city in their wake. And though Bartholomew did not actually propose a land use and zoning plan, East St. Louis planners have tried over and over again to separate the city into one-dimensional pieces to keep uses—and people—from contaminating each other.

The trouble has been that planners have tried to make East St. Louis into what it is not while never attempting to address its real problems. Bartholomew was a giant in the field of planning and his approach has worked remarkably well in many situations—especially for small towns and suburbs. But his approach could never work in East

St. Louis. The railroads did not cut up the city. The city intruded upon the railroads, squeezing into whatever empty spaces existed. Houses and factories were placed between the tracks and the rail yards by design, not by accident. They were there to take advantage of the placement of the railroads.

Not in spite of them. Bartholomew and the hundreds of planners who have followed him should have taken the city at face value. Instead of trying to untangle the city into neat conforming sections, they should have tried to make these so-called "non-conforming uses" work together, anticipating inevitable

changes in transportation and industrial design. And instead of trying to create racial harmony by cordoning off the races from each other, they should have tried to make the betterment of East St. Louis a common project that would have forced the races to come together as one.

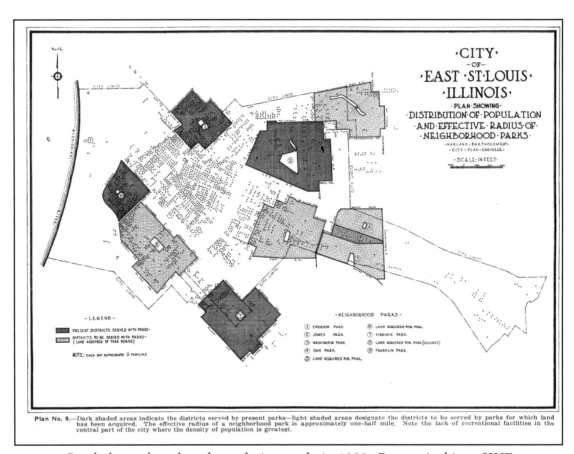

Bartholomew's park and population analysis, 1920   Bowen Archives, SIUE

End Notes:

1. Mary Edwards and Laura Lawson, "The Evolution of Planning in East St. Louis," *Journal of Planning History*, 2005 Volume 4, 357.

2. Harland Bartholomew, *A Comprehensive City Plan for East St. Louis, Illinois prepared for the War Civics Committee* (East St. Louis, Illinois: *The Daily Journal*, 1920).

3. Ibid., xiii.

4. Find citation for here

5. Ibid, xiii.

6. Ibid, xiii.

7. See Eldridge Lovelace, *Harland Bartholomew: His Contributions to American Urban Planning* (Urbana, Illinois: University of Illinois Office of Printing Services, Printing Division, 1992).

8. Ibid, A-23—A-31.

9. Ibid, A-20—A-22.

10. Bartholomew, v.

11. Ibid, v.

12. Ibid, 2.

13. Ibid, 2.

14. Ibid, 3.

15. After Bartholomew was no longer an active partner in the firm, HBA's "template" became even more rigid with the order of the chapters always appearing in the same order from city to city. Malcolm Drummond, personal interview, June 27, 2010.

16. Taken from an excerpt of the Memphis, Tennessee Plan of 1920 in Lovelace, Harland Bartholomew, A-10.

17. Bartholomew, *A Comprehensive City Plan for East St. Louis*, 5.

18. Ibid,5.

19. Ibid, 5-6.

20. Ibid, 6.

21. Ibid, 7.

22. Ibid, 29.

23. Ibid, 31.

24. Ibid.

25. Ibid.

26.Ibid, 33.

27. Ibid, 37.

28. Ibid.

29. Ibid., 39.

30. Ibid.

31. Ibid.

32. Ibid., 41.

33. Ibid., 41-47.

34. Ibid., xiii.

35. Ibid, 49.

36. Ibid.

37. Ibid, 17.

38. Ibid, 51.

39. Ibid.

40. Ibid., 17.

41. Ibid., 40.

42. Ibid., 28.

43. Ibid., 48.

44. St. Louis City Plan Commission, *Zone Plan Ordinance*, June 1919.

45. Bartholomew, *A Comprehensive Plan for East St. Louis*, 47.

46. See Colin Gordon, *Mapping Decline: St. Louis and the Fate of the American City* (Philadelphia: University of Pennsylvania Press, 2008).

47. Named in reference to the famous Supreme Court Case *Euclid v. Ambler Realty* (126), where the court recognized the right of municipalities to enact zoning ordinances.

48. See the zoning map (2009) in the "Maps of East St. Louis" prepared by the East St. Louis Action Research Project, http://www.eslarp.uiuc.edu/maps/CurrentZoning.pdf.

49. In the actual plan, the chapter on Housing is situated between the discussion on sewers/water supply and the one on the city's appearance.

50. Ibid., 48.

51. Andrew Theising, *Made in USA: East St. Louis* (St. Louis: Virginia Publishing Company, 2003)

52. Ibid. 55.

53. Ibid.

54. Ibid., 59.

55. Ibid., 61

56. Ibid., 61-62.

57. Ibid., 61

58. Ibid., 62.

59. See Theising, *Made in USA*.

60. Ibid., 63.

Murphy Building Detail Powell Photo

The End of the Line

Joseph L. Davis

Department of Social and Behavioral Sciences

Harris Stowe State University

The city was already dying. Oh, I didn't know it yet; I was only a boy of about seven. But then neither did East St. Louis. It was the mid 1950s and there were still jobs, still industry, still services, still a future, and even national recognition. Being named an "All America City" by *Look* magazine was a half dozen years off.[1] Mel Price was just starting his remarkable 41-year stretch in the U.S. House of Representatives and the incredible clout that Congressional seniority would bring to him and his district. But there was the sense that things had reached their peak and we were on the back slope. It's just that nobody, least of all a seven-year-old, knew how far or how fast things would slide.I was born in East St. Louis, in St. Mary's Hospital, and grew up there. My whole family had. My mother's family came from Germany. Her father, Henry Eickholt, came to the U.S. to see the World's Fair of 1904 and stayed to work in the stockyards. My father's family is Welsh and came to the area via West Virginia to work in the iron mines of Missouri, but Grandpa Davis moved to East St. Louis during The Great Depression because there were jobs. He started my family's three generation association with the city and the railroad. So, by 1955 my whole family, aunts and uncles, cousins and nephews, were all living and working and going to school and shopping and playing in East St. Louis. But, even for a seven-year-old, there was the discernable whiff of decay, and not just from the stockyards!

Freight Depot. East St. Louis, Ills.

Riverfront rail yards, c. 1915   Bowen Archives, SIUE

Perhaps it isn't fair to pick on East St. Louis. After all, the popular wisdom about its greater namesake to the west is that St. Louis peaked at the 1904 World's Fair and it's all been downhill since. And furthermore, a lot of East St. Louis economic decline, and other problems that would inevitably follow from that, were symptomatic of the U.S. in general as it shifted away from an industrial based society to . . . whatever we are becoming.

In a sense, East St. Louis is a microcosm, and a bellwether, of the decline of industrial America. Let's face it, people didn't move to East St. Louis – ever – for the "ambiance". It was neither the first American soil that immigrants touched nor the last frontier for pioneers to conquer. It was too Southern for ex-slaves (or ex-New Englanders) to feel really comfortable but too far north to avoid unions. It was too far east to be part of the West and too far west to be part of the Eastern Establishment. It was, and is, the crossroads of the nation, quintessential "middle (urban) America", and it was dying.

For whatever you can say about East St. Louis, it existed because there were jobs. They were hard jobs, dirty jobs, dangerous jobs, hands-on twenty-four-hour-a-day, seven days a week, three-hundred-sixty-five-days-a-year jobs. Driving through East St. Louis in summer in the 1950s, we had the windows down because no one had air conditioning (except for mysterious old Mr. Duffy who lived with his reclusive wife in a rundown mansion which was so off the main roads that no one bought it up and turned it into a funeral parlor like most old

mansions in town, and drove an emerald green Chrysler Imperial as big as the S. S. Admiral). I would wrinkle up my nose at the smell of pollution. I'll never forget my father's reaction. He said, "It smells like jobs to me." Most of those jobs were in heavy "smokestack" industries or existed because of those industries.

And many of those industries chose East St. Louis because it was a crossroads. Transportation was the key. First there were the rivers. We're only a few days riverboat ride north of the Ohio (Cairo was just too swampy to compete). We are literally at the confluence with the Missouri and Illinois Rivers, and only miles below the first falls of the Mississippi (the great Chain of Rocks).

I had often, as a child, heard the tale that when the famous paddlewheel steamboat "Robert E. Lee" switched its docking site from the east to the west bank of the Mississippi, Illinois Town (as East St. Louis was originally called) started to decline. I think that was a bit precipitous. Even though the St. Louis riverfront became the great passenger and freight center of the steamboat era, the extraction (coal) and produce (corn) loading facilities mostly stayed on the east side.[2]

There is no question that the rivers were the main reason St. Louis came to be, and grew to such national importance in the 19th Century. It truly was the Gateway to the West. Its original nickname "The Mound City" indicated that even the pre-Columbian Americans recognized the commercial importance of this area.[3] So did the French and later the United States (our

supposed "Spanish" heritage, contrary to the urging of former St. Louis Mayor Cervantes, was limited to a bookkeeping legal nicety of Napoleon to make a quick buck and perhaps the vague wandering of some incredibly lost conquistadors).[4]

All these "founders" saw the utility of the rivers and populated both sides of the river. The East Side also has its Indian Mounds (better preserved than St. Louis), its "French Village" and Cahokia, and its East St. Louis. Though the rivers never completely lost their transportation importance, they did end up as more of an obstacle than an advantage with the coming of the "new" transportation phenomenon that would really build East St. Louis – the railroads.

Indeed, it is argued that the main reason Chicago outgrew the St. Louis area was the delay in finally getting a railroad bridge across the Mississippi so that trains did not have to be broken up, loaded on the "Wiggins" Ferry (which still operated through World War II) and reassembled on the west bank of the Mississippi. Eventually three railroad bridges, including the fabulous Eads Bridge – one of the architectural marvels of the 19th Century and like the Brooklyn Bridge built so strong it is nine times as sturdy as it needed to be for even its peak traffic load of trains, cars, and people – would and still do cross the Mississippi at St. Louis. But that river and those railroads would ultimately build East St. Louis, determine its physical shape and form, and eventually lead to its economic decline.

One of the earliest memories of

this young boy was the slightly flat but persistent ding-ding-ding of the railroad crossings that laced East St. Louis in all directions. We were on the bus. My father worked nights and my mother never learned to drive. (And drive what? Dad had the car).

So we were on the bus heading home from a day of shopping at all the "downtown" St. Louis department stores – Famous, Stix, Kresge's dime store for a grilled cheese sandwich and 20 minutes twirling in circles on the counter stool, and finally Sears in East St. Louis.

The bus was stopped at a railroad crossing – and so was the train. The thing about the railroad crossings in East St. Louis was that trains didn't just pass, they stopped, backed up, stopped again. Occasionally, if the switch men were kind enough, they would uncouple the train, move the front part past the intersection and let people through until they got a signal to move on. And those were on the main streets through the city – State Street, Collinsville Avenue, Missouri Avenue.

The reason for so many crossings is that the city was built in and around and because of railroad yards. At one time as many as twenty-two different railroad lines operated in East St. Louis. This made us the largest railroad interchange point in the world. Unlike trucks and airplanes and even boats, that all operate on the same (public) thoroughfares, railroads built and maintain their own tracks. Yes, many railroads were given huge land grants by the government on which to build those tracks, and no I don't want to make the railroads sound like the poor unloved mode of transportation because the government doesn't maintain their rights-of-way at taxpayers' expense. I just state the fact that each road built and maintains its own lines.

The result of this fact is that many of the railroads ran almost parallel tracks (it's called competition) and roads that didn't serve the same destinations had to interchange traffic from one railroad to another. East St. Louis was one of the most important of those interchange points. Many/most major railroads that developed or conglomerated in the 19th century were either eastern roads (Baltimore & Ohio [B&O], Pennsylvania, New York Central) or western roads (Missouri Pacific [MoPac], St. Louis-San Francisco [SLSF], Missouri Kansas and Texas [MKT]). Most of them

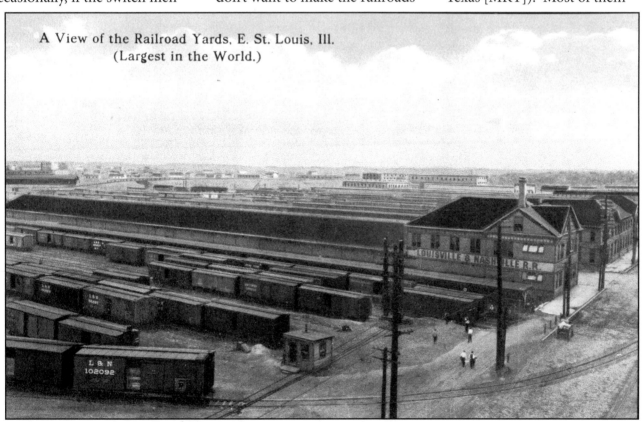

A View of the Railroad Yards, E. St. Louis, Ill.
(Largest in the World.)

The L&N facility, c. 1915   Bowen Archives, SIUE

began or ended their territory in East St. Louis.

Now I don't want to leave St. Louis out of the picture. After all, the railroads were attracted to that town because of its size and previous river importance. But it was also rather hilly and the ground was rocky. Since each of those railroads ended in a yard that was an extensive maze of tracks and covered a large area, each needed lots of (flat) land.

It is like sorting laundry. A train comes into the New York Central's Lower Yard or Pennsylvania's Roselake Yard with 100 cars from the East Coast, or added on to the train on the way (Buffalo, Cleveland, and Indianapolis). It must be sorted to all its destination cities (Kansas City, Denver, or Los Angeles). All of those destinations are served by other, and different, railroads. So the train must be broken up,

sorted (switched) on to different tracks, and then handed off to another railroad's yard where they are again sorted to different destinations.

This area was served by so many different railroad companies and required so many interchanges that three more railroad companies were created within the metropolitan area just to help handle interchanges. They were the Terminal Railroad Association (TRRA with their ubiquitous red switch engines), the Illinois Terminal Railroad (IT), and the Alton & Southern (A&S). And each of these needed yards too. Add to this the industries that owned their own railroads and rolling stock (railcars) like Anheuser Busch's "Manufacturers Railroad" and you have many very dirty, dangerous, and around-the-clock jobs . It also takes a lot of space to sort and store and

fix those 100-car trains going to dozens of different railroads and destinations. Well, the east side of the Mississippi at St. Louis is flat, thus a good place to build a railroad yard. It is also rather low and swampy so many yards were built on landfill over things like the Cahokia Slew (finally filled in with all the rock excavated from the foundations for the Gateway Arch) and needed flood walls to hold back the Mississippi.

I once worked as an international tour guide, and a question I often got from tourists was why the stupid Europeans built their castles and palaces so close to the railroad tracks. It's a chicken or egg thing. The railroads didn't build the yards in East St. Louis, East St. Louis was built in (or rather around and among) the yards. Why? Because that's where the jobs were. The workers needed houses, and stores, and the

New York Central locomotive at the Aluminum Ore Company site, c. 1925   Bowen Archives, SIUE

train crews needed lodging and cafes and those businesses needed water and electric power and fire protection and so you incorporate into a municipality to meet the needs.

Let's face it, with few exceptions cities are not planned and built like a house from a blueprint. Cities grow. It is truly organic.

I have been a professor of political science since 1972 and currently teach at Harris-Stowe stateUniversity. I have also taught at St. Louis University, St. Louis Community College, St. Charles Community College, St. Louis School of Pharmacy, University of Missouri-St. Louis, Southern Illinois University at Edwardsville, and the State Penitentiary in Pacific, Missouri. I often use in my classes a simulation that simply sets up the economic and geographic constraints a group of people face and within a day they will build a realistic city complete with an absolute jumble of land use with a seemingly disorganized (but economically logical) jumble of industry stores and homes all crammed together around a transportation hub, just like any old center city.[5]

City planning is for the most part an attempt to undo what is already built but no longer makes economic sense because the rules of the game (the land uses such as industry and transportation) have changed.

So, cities "grow" to meet the needs of people and the businesses that employ those people. But you don't kill the goose that laid the gold egg, so that municipality must also serve those railroads and the industries that those

railroads attract. After all, what better place to put a glass plant, or paint factory, or process aluminum ore (all heavy & bulky) than at a point where you can ship directly to almost any place in the U.S? So, the city becomes very business friendly (read few regulations) and concentrates on providing services and ignoring the vices that will keep the whole giant job-producing industrial machine well greased.

Even the shape of East St. Louis was dictated by railroads. It is bounded on the North by the Pennsylvania Railroads main line and more than 50-block-long Roselake Yards and on the South by equally massive Alton & Southern Yards. It never even had a "riverfront" until the railroads moved out. The waterfront consisted of a continual string of railroad yards from New York Central's Brooklyn Yards at the foot of the McKinley Bridge on the North to the Tolson Yards serving the Cahokia Power Plant on the South. While both Broadway and Missouri Avenues do technically run all the way to the river (or at least to Front Street and the flood wall) they were little more than company streets west of the approach to Eads Bridge. In fact "First" Street, which really is the first street of the city, is almost a half mile from the water. If you look at the street grid (what passed for urban planning in old East St. Louis) it makes little geographic sense. Most cities are laid out to compass points (North-South and East-West) or follow the geography (like St. Louis which attempted to keep streets parallel to the curving river). But East St. Louis streets all approach the river (and the compass) at an

angle, like a diamond pointed to pierce the river (if they would have gotten that far). Furthermore, the angle of the streets change three times so they spread out to the East like spokes. Of course, it does make sense if you draw in the railroad lines. The Southern part of the city runs southeast to parallel the Illinois Central and Southern Railways lines and yards. The central spoke of the city shifts to East-Southeast to follow the Louisville and Nashville lines (now used by Metrolink) and the Northern portion shifts to due east to stay parallel with the Pennsylvania Railroad.

The only municipal access to the Mississippi was a gate in the flood wall just south of the Eads Bridge. Front Street (with railroad tracks running down the middle of it) ran parallel to the flood wall which was so high you couldn't even see the water from a car. There was vehicle access to the water only via a steep ramp and over more tracks. So with effort you could drive onto the riverfront. It was a beautiful sight. You came out right across from the Arch construction site.

Since there was no other access to the river for miles up and down, it was always quiet except for the hum of tires on the exposed steel grating of the Eads Bridge, the lapping of the water and the banging of freight cars muffled by the massive concrete levee. It was also very safe because you were also protected by a solid mile of railroad yards crawling with railway police whose unique extra territorial jurisdiction made them as powerful as the FBI – and a whole lot tougher.

In Canada, federal and provincial

law regulates railroad police. In the United States, the appointment, commissioning and regulations of the rail police is primarily a state mandate; however, Federal Law allows Railroad Police Officers to enforce the laws of other states as found under the following provision:

Section 1704 of the Crime Control Act of 1990, effective March 14, 1994, provides that:

A railroad police officer who is certified or commissioned as a police officer under the laws of any state shall, in accordance with the regulations issued by the Secretary of Transportation, be authorized to enforce the laws of any jurisdiction in which the rail carrier owns property.[6]

So if your daddy was Assistant Terminal Trainmaster and grandpa was Freight-house Foreman so you know everybody and they know you (or at least your dad's car), it was a great place to picnic. Thus I spent many an evening in the 1960s watching the arch go up, munching on Nichol's barbeque (9th and Trendly Avenue, I went to high school with one of the sons). If it got late enough, and John Avault, another classmate and son of the Chief Clerk of the L&N, finished discussing the meaning of life, you could always jacklight rats with your .22's.

So what happened to this happy, busy, labor intensive, money making machine of a city? Well, I don't believe in one cause explanations of complex systems, Robert E. Lee included, but much of the decline of East St. Louis must be attributed to the decline and transformation of the railroads.

The first to go was passenger service. Until about 1960, there was really no other choice for inter-city travel than by train, and even within cities much public transportation was by street car. One hundred years before Metrolink, the East St. Louis-O'Fallon Interurban Railway and other "railbus" lines connected many small towns in Southern Illinois with East St. Louis and St. Louis beyond.[7] But the post-World War II growth of airlines and the building of the interstate highway system led most people to abandon the passenger trains for either the speed of flying or the convenience of driving their own cars. While East St. Louis was never a major passenger hub, much of the infrastructure supporting passenger trains (engine houses, repair shops, etc.) were located on the East Side.

The main passenger depot at East St. Louis, 1911   Bowen Archives, SIUE

Following closely on the decline of passenger service was the disappearance of LCL-less car loading. Again, until the 1960s, if you wished to ship a package – anything from a fruitcake to an entire prefabricated house ordered out of a Sears-Roebuck catalog – it went by train. The Railway Express Agency was the most famous LCL shipper but all railroads, and many other private freight forwarding companies maintained vast freight houses for sorting and shipping packages. Just like the sorting of railroad cars in the rail yards to their different destinations, LCL packages required that railroad cars carrying those loads be taken to a freight house, opened up and sorted package by package into other cars, sealed and switched to another railroad.

This was very time sensitive and labor intensive. My grandfather, Bill Davis, was general foreman for the L&N (Louisville &Nashville), then the NYC (New York Central) freight houses on Front Street, about where the casino's parking lot is now in the shadow of the Eads Bridge. He supervised almost 100 trucking crews (here we are talking 2-wheeled trucks, dollies) that man-handled everything from feather pillows to cast iron stoves from one freight car to another. The crews, black and white equally, were paid piecework. The more you moved, the more you were paid.

My father, Lloyd Davis', first railroad job after he got out of the army at the end of World War II was a weight checker. His dad hired him for what was officially known as a Timekeeper. But with piecework you didn't have

to time people because the more they moved the more they were paid. But you were paid by the pounds you moved and there were scales that each "crew" rolled their dollies over to weigh. Unlike the airlines, who worry about how much the plane can lift, or trucks who have axle limits, the railroads never cared how much your freight weighed. The locomotives themselves could weigh half a million pounds. But the men got paid by the tonnage they manhandled from car to car. My father's job was to record that weight and assign crews fairly so somebody didn't spend all day moving pillows and his kids didn't eat that week.

This entire industry no longer exists. You can't ship by rail today unless you lease a whole boxcar – bulk freight. All LCL shipping is now done by truck (UPS, FedEx) or air. The railroads did try to expand into those other modes of transportation. Piggybacking truck trailers on railroad flatcars was the most successful attempt and for awhile East St. Louis did boast at least a dozen Piggyback, Flexivan, and container loading yards.

My first railroad job, which my father got for me, was timekeeper for the New York Central Flexivan (truck trailer on railroad flatcars) yards that replaced the LCL Freight houses right on Front Street. But they too disappeared, and never were as labor intensive as less-car-loading anyhow.

As the railroad "business model" changed, East St. Louis got left behind. Many of those 22 railroads merged, which closed some yards. Steam engines, which required massive and

labor-intensive facilities to coal, water, clean and repair, were replaced by diesels which could run longer with less maintenance. The remaining railroads started sharing power so the same engines could haul a train all the way across the country without changing locomotives. Indeed, "unit trains" were introduced that didn't require switching cars from origin to destination.

Other industries serviced by the railroads also changed. My father graduated from East Side High in 1940 and joined the Illinois National Guard because it paid $5.00 when his field artillery battery would meet one evening each month in the basement of the Shriner's Temple to drill. This was still the Great Depression and who knew that they would all get Federalized a year later and be the first soldiers sent overseas to fight in World War II and not be released until 1945? He also went to work for J. C. Penney at their national warehouse. Every J. C. Penney store in the country was stocked from this massive facility, some of the shells of which still stand today on the south side of the city, west of Route 3. Of course, "box stores" now either warehouse in the individual retail store or literally "on the road" thanks to computerization of inventory. So those huge centralized national warehouses didn't move somewhere else, they just don't exist anymore.[8]

In general, that was the fate of East St. Louis. The "popular wisdom" that businesses moved away for any number of reasons, unions, politics, race, doesn't hold up. In general, businesses just changed and the old industries that supported the city didn't go somewhere else to do the same thing, they just ceased to exist in that form.

There were exceptions, as with the steel industry in our good neighbor to the north, Granite City. But those industries didn't just leave the area either, they left the country. So that is a national issue, not a local one.

Another industry that disappeared or morphed into another form that left East St. Louis out, was meat packing. At one time we were the second largest meat packing city in the U. S. (second only to Chicago) and what remains, including on a particularly warm summer night the smell, of those now abandoned slaughterhouses can still be seen on the north side. So what happened? Did people stop eating meat? No, the mode of production changed. No longer do mile-long trains of live cattle get shipped to giant processing plants. Nor do the products of those plants get shipped to market in refrigeration boxcars serviced by giant ice houses.[9]

Today, most slaughtering is done closer to the source. You don't move the cattle, you move the plant. It is then shipped by truck from farm to wholesaler. What is left of meat packing in the area are just those modest facilities needed to process whatever cattle are raised locally.

Unfortunately, all this decentralization, modernization, and computerization left East St. Louis behind. And, like many cities of the old "rust belt", of which we are the southern-most notch, we had to evolve or die. This was the dilemma the city faced, starting in the late 1950s. The problem was that no one told us that. It didn't all happen at once. It was so gradual that people thought it might not be important. After all, we made it through the Great Depression. It was just a glitch, not a fundamental shift in the economy. Businesses didn't announce to the city why they were closing, if they even really knew themselves.

Even academics fail to recognize many trends until, with the benefit of hindsight, they can gauge the cumulative impact of the subtle but inexorable shifting in those continental plates. So it was a lack of planning and foresight that led to the city's decline, but who do you blame? Do you blame the business community for abandoning the city in search of profit? Do you blame the politicians for focusing only

Riverfront rails, 2010 Powell Photo

on the present needs of their constituents? Do you blame the people for concentrating on their immediate lives and not re-tooling themselves for future careers?

In one sense East St. Louis now has a unique opportunity – to reinvent itself from scratch. There is almost nothing left of the "old" East St. Louis. The railroads are all but gone, and their former yards are vacant. The old industries are gone too, and provided we don't find too much residual pollution, there is more available acreage.

Much of the commercial property is abandoned or underutilized, as is the housing stock.

So we have lots of land and an ideal location to become . . . what? That is the dilemma facing East St. Louis. It could become a new industrial center (we have everything needed except an industry). It could gentrify and become a bedroom community to St. Louis (but like so many other examples, what do you do with the displaced?). There have been even more far-out suggestions

-- dome the whole thing, build a giant amusement park, or level it and make it all a park. A friend has even suggested that the land is more valuable as farmland. After all, it is the best horseradish growing area in the world.

The one thing it probably can't do is just sit back and react to whatever economic forces come along. That is what shaped the old East St. Louis, but that is also what killed it. The new East St. Louis will have to be of its own creation.

End Notes:

1. Bill Nunes, *Illustrated History of East St. Louis*, 1998.

2. Louis C. Hunter, *Steamboat on the Western Rivers: An Economic and Technological History*, 2nd ed., N.Y., Dover Publications, 1993.

3. William Allen & John G. Carlton, *St. Louis Post-Dispatch*, January 9, 2000.

4. Scott K. Williams, "Three Flags over St. Louis", 1999-2001, St. Louis History Museum.

5. Joseph L. Davis, "Community Land Use Game, An Evaluation" in *The Guide to Simulation/Games for Education and Training*, by Robert E. Horn and Anne Cleaves, editors, Sage Publications, 4th ed., 1980.

6. Special Agents Matt West and Paul Miller, Union Pacific Railroad Police, "The Railroad Police" website.

7. Paul H. Stringham, *Illinois Terminal, the Electric Years*, Interurban Press. Glendale, Cal., 1989.

8. Steve New and Roy Westbrook, eds., *Understanding Supply Chains: Concepts, Coverages, and Futures*, Oxford University Press, 2004.

9. Thomas Petraitis, *East St. Louis, Illinois: "Hog Capital of the Nation"*, Preservation Research Office, East St. Louis, Ill., 2010.

East St. Louis in Context: The Rise and Fall of America's Industrial Suburbs

Andrew Hurley, Ph.D.

Department of History, Chair
University of Missouri, St. Louis

For many Americans, East St. Louis is synonymous with urban blight, crime, and poverty. Informal surveys consistently rank it among the least desirable places to live in the United States and in the national media the city has come to symbolize the broken promises of the American Dream.[1] This unenviable reputation places East St. Louis in the company of other maligned locales like Camden, New Jersey; Gary, Indiana; and Newark, New Jersey. East St. Louis may have its problems, buti it is not alone. Indeed, those familiar with the city know that the surrounding towns of Brooklyn, Alorton, National City, and Washington Park suffer from many of the same afflictions. Strikingly, what all these places have in common is a legacy of industrial suburbanization, making the phenomenon worth closer investigation.

Murphy Building rear, 2010   Powell Photo

It would be correct but an oversimplification to attribute the recent decline of manufacturing suburbs to the wave of de-industrialization that devastated the country beginning in the 1970s. While industrial flight sapped the vitality of many manufacturing towns, not all shared the dismal fate of East St. Louis and its immediate neighbors. Moreover, urban decline followed divergent paths even in those places that continued to struggle in the aftermath of late 20th corporate restructuring initiatives. A person magically teleported from the intersection of Collinsville and Missouri Avenues in downtown East St. Louis to any street corner in Hamtramck, Michigan; Central Falls, Rhode Island; or Richmond, California, would quickly realize that he or she had materialized in a very different place.

This essay attempts to make sense of both the shared and divergent trajectories travelled by America's industrial suburbs, including those on St. Louis east side. The analysis operates on the premise that East St. Louis cannot be understood in isolation from its immediate neighbors and the ways in which the entire east side industrial district was connected to broader economic and social networks. As we shall see, industrial suburbs followed a fairly uniform course from their inception at the turn of the nineteenth century through era of de-industrialization. Much of the divergence has been recent.

The argument advanced here is that despite a common set of handicaps imposed by the legacy of manufacturing, the recent fortunes of industrial suburbs have varied according to the way that regions and metropolises have positioned themselves with respect to global flows of investment and population. Embedded within a relatively stagnant metropolitan setting, east side communities have had few resources and limited opportunities for redevelopment. As a result, East St. Louis and its neighbors have not taken part in the renaissance that some other industrial suburbs have experienced.

Industry Moves to the Suburbs

Places like East St. Louis experienced their formative development in an era of industrial peripheralization. Between 1870 and 1930, manufacturers sunk huge sums of capital in production facilities situated on the fringe of metropolitan areas. This emerging industrial geography involved both the migration of factories from inner-city to suburban location and the establishment of regional branch plants by large national firms.

The sequence of new factory openings at the Ford Motor Company in the early part of the 20th illustrates both processes. The spatial requirements of assembly-line production made the cramped quarters of Henry Ford's three-story building in the heart of Detroit obsolete by 1909.

On New Year's Day of the following year, his motor company transferred operations to a massive steel and glass structure two miles away in the suburban enclave of Highland Park.[2]

Within five years, however, the automaker's ambitions outstripped the capacity of the Highland Park plant and he began buying property seven miles west of downtown Detroit in sparsely populated Springwells Township. Sprawling across 2,500 acres, the River Rouge industrial complex epitomized the trend toward vertical integration. All the steps involved in the making of an automobile, from the collection of raw materials, to the making and shaping of steel, to the assembly of finished car parts took place on the same spot. This massive operation entailed the construction of nearly one hundred buildings and by the late 1930s, the employment of more than 100,000 workers.[3]

In pursuit of a national distribution strategy, Ford soon began building factories far beyond the Detroit area. Despite the economic efficiencies achieved at the Rouge Plant, Ford discovered that he could lower shipping costs considerably by scattering final assembly operations across the continent. The earliest of these branch plants were built shortly before World War I in or near downtown districts so they could also function as dealerships. Beginning in the late 1920s, however, the company veered toward suburban territories as it placed a higher priority on site acreage and transportation infrastructure. Some of the largest branch plants built in this period appeared in places like Chester, Pennsylvania; Edgewater, New Jersey; Richmond, California; and Long Beach, California, all of which were placed very close to big cities but in separate jurisdictions.[4]

Decades before Henry Ford grappled with the dilemmas of industrial plant location, the forces of metropolitan decentralization and national dispersal had already shaped the growth of St. Louis east side. A densely populated area, near the continent's geographic center, the St. Louis metropolis was ideally situated for firms with national ambitions. In the 1870s, a conglomerate of Eastern investors pooled their resources and established the St. Louis National Stock Yards Company on a 400-acre tract of land just north of East St. Louis. Some of the nation's largest packing houses, such as Armour, Swift, and Hunter soon followed and built hulking factories close by.[5] The Pittsburgh Reduction Company (later Alcoa) was the nation's leading producer of aluminum in 1902, when a bauxite refinery in Illinois became the latest addition to its continental holdings.[6] These national firms were joined by manufacturers with local origins. Early in the 1890s, William Niedringhaus, owner of the Granite Iron Rolling Mills and the St. Louis Stamping Company, moved his operations across the Mississippi River to a 3,500-acre tract of high ground that became Granite City, Illinois. Two decades later, another St. Louis firm, the Monsanto Chemical Company, picked a location just south of East St. Louis for its expanding product line.[7]

Wherever the phenomenon occurred, suburban locations offered manufacturers the advantages of cheap real estate, abundant land, proximity to a huge labor market, transportation infrastructure, and perhaps most importantly, political autonomy. During the late nineteenth century, city governments expanded their policing powers and became more responsive to the interests of working-class voters. Corporations found their actions in the community subject to closer scrutiny and tighter regulation. Many came to the conclusion that they were better off operating outside large cities where governmental oversight was more relaxed. The desire for political freedom was especially strong among firms that that generated noxious wastes and offensive odors. For this reason, manufacturing suburbs frequently attracted heavy industry and businesses that processed animal parts.[8]

The factors that drew manufacturers to the metropolitan fringe explain the defining

Swift and Company, National Stock Yards, c. 1915   Bowen Archives, SIUE

characteristics of these nascent industrial suburbs.

To maximize their insulation from external political influence, firms often drew tight boundaries around their jurisdictions. What emerged was a highly fragmented political landscape consisting of independent corporate fiefdoms interspersed with worker dormitory communities. Some of the new municipalities created in this process comprised no more than a square mile of territory. The tiny east side towns of Venice, Monsanto (later Sauget), Alcoa (later Alorton), and National City, had hundreds of counterparts across the nation. In many cases,

they also sprouted across either state lines or major bodies of water as they did in the St. Louis area. Devoted primarily to the making of industrial products, these places quickly earned reputations as primitive, dirty, rough, and corrupt. As the major taxpayers in these communities, corporations had a direct financial incentive to keep public expenditures to a minimum. Thus, many of these places were slow to acquire paved streets, sewer systems, and street lighting. Corporations, with a few notable exceptions, were equally reluctant to intervene in the moral affairs of these towns. Without the presence of an established middle class to provide

moral surveillance, working-class suburbs often bred vice and corruption. Especially after the implementation of Prohibition, many of these enclaves provided refuge for gamblers, prostitutes, and bootleggers. Although their remote locations kept these places out of sight and out of mind to most Americans, curiosity seekers who visited these places returned with remarkably similar reports emphasizing their depraved and slovenly character.[9]

The Heyday of the Industrial Suburb

At mid-century, the situation looked bright. A booming

Homes near Virginia Park, East St. Louis 2010   Powell Photo

industrial economy underwrote better living conditions for the residents of America's industrial suburbs.

Swollen profit margins loosened corporate purse strings and released money into municipal coffers and laborers' pockets. Prosperity, in conjunction with higher levels of civic activism among working-class families, increased both private and public investments in local communities. Manufacturing towns remained rough around the edges but real improvements in the quality of life made them sources of pride and springboards for upward mobility.

In her study of blue-collar suburbs in Los Angeles, Becky Nicolaides documented the upgrading of housing stock and civic amenities that took place after World War II. Earlier in the century, the ubiquity of owner-built homes gave these working-class suburbs a ramshackle and haphazard appearance. After the war, large-scale developers took over the field and applied uniform standards. In places like South Gate, California, working-class neighborhoods began to approximate their middle-class counterparts. At the same time, higher tax revenues allowed local governments to plow money into parks, athletic fields, street lighting, water mains, and sewer lines.[10] The steel town of Homestead, Pennsylvania witnessed similar changes; in 1955 its daily newspaper bragged about its "well paved" streets, "fine" police force, "full-time fire-fighting organization," and a shopping corridor that boasted

"more than three hundred stores, countless business offices, a daily newspaper office, and two large, progressive banks."[11]

It was also in this time period that East St. Louis basked in the national limelight by virtue of receiving an "All-America City" designation from the National Municipal League. Among the accomplishments cited to justify the honor were the city's strong civic spirit, its new schools, park improvements, and stable labor-management relations. The award was announced in the widely-circulated *Look* magazine, and proud citizens celebrated the achievement with a grand parade along State Street.[12]

The postwar years also saw industrial suburbs emerge as places where the American dream appeared to extend to African Americans. With the flow of foreign immigration slowed by restrictive legislation after 1925, manufacturers increasingly turned to African Americans to feed furnaces, butcher carcasses, and sweep shop floors. The phenomenon of black proletarianization spurred a mass migration from the rural south to the urban north in two great waves separated by the Great Depression.[13] For many who participated in this exodus, an industrial suburb often lay at journey's end. Not all blue-collar suburbs welcomed African-American migrants with open arms; Dearborn, Michigan and Cicero, Illinois, for example, were notorious for their efforts at racial exclusion.

Yet, most industrial areas saw significant increases in

racial diversity. Moreover, the black residential enclaves that flourished in and around Oakland, Newark, Gary, and East St. Louis were generally viewed as better places to live than inner-city districts undergoing cycles of overcrowding, dilapidation, clearance, and urban renewal.

The above-mentioned suburban areas in particular provided an unusually fertile setting for African American political and cultural expression in the postwar years. Oakland, Gary, and Newark were vital cores of the Black Power movement in the 1960s. East St. Louis was less politically prominent but contributed profoundly to the cultural ferment of the times by providing a platform for poets like Eugene Redmond, dancers like Katherine Dunham, and musicians like Miles Davis and Chuck Berry. In this respect, East St. Louis ranked with Oakland and Newark as top echelon nodes in the Black Arts Movement. Although more research is necessary, it is intriguing to postulate that the same loose regulatory environment that fostered vice and corruption also permitted more latitude with respect to cultural experimentation and innovation.

De-Industrialization and Devastation

Dramatic shifts in the manufacturing sector during the final decades of the twentieth century dealt a harsh blow to America's industrial suburbs. As scholars such as Thomas Sugrue and Howard Gillette have noted, structural changes within

American industry had begun to place strains on urban populations and communities as early as the 1950s and 1960s.[14] For the most part, however, the general prosperity of these years masked the social impact of increased levels of automation and plant relocation to lower-wage settings. For those paying close attention in the East St. Louis region, there were plenty of foreboding signs. The Aluminum Ore Company began cutting its work force in the mid-1950s and by the end of the decade, Armour and Company had shut down its slaughterhouse. The manufacturing sector staggered through the 1960s with plant closings or work force reductions at the American Zinc Company, Darling Fertilizer, the National Stockyards, and Swift and Company.[15]

Yet, it was not until the 1970s that de-industrialization hit with full force, crippling the local economies of towns dependent on industry. Continued industrial flight deprived communities of both jobs and tax revenues. While the national unemployment rate approached eight percent in the latter part of the decade, the corresponding figure was often twice as high in industrial suburbs. East St. Louis jobless rate of 21 percent compared unfavorably to the national figure of 7.1 percent in 1980. Meanwhile, strapped local governments were forced to cut back on basic city services. East St. Louis drew national notoriety for forsaking garbage collection in the late 1980s, but it was not alone in its predicament.[16] Ford Heights, a tiny suburban enclave outside Chicago, maintained garbage collection only by sentencing

misdemeanor offenders to trash detail.[17] The closing of Chrysler's Dodge Main plant in 1980 forced Hamtramck, Michigan to dismiss 300 municipal employees, leaving only 200 paid workers to run the city.[18]

The visible manifestation of this economic freefall was decay and abandonment. In the absence of renewed public or private investment, properties deteriorated, garbage accumulated, sidewalks cracked, potholes widened, and nighttime streets darkened. In one industrial suburb after another, the American Dream turned nightmarish and those who could afford to move away did so. Virtually all industrial suburbs witnessed population flight and growing impoverishment in the 1980s. Deprived of customers, businesses closed and once-thriving shopping strips were given over to vandals and graffiti artists. When Camden's mayor referred to his city as a "rat infested skeleton of yesterday" in 1973, he might have just as easily been describing Homestead, Gary, Highland Park, Michigan, or East St. Louis.[19]

Adaptation, Recovery, and Stagnation

In the wake of de-industrialization, America's manufacturing suburbs followed divergent paths. Some prospered by re-inventing themselves while others continued to bleed population and investment. Without question, local decisions and actions made a difference. But a national comparison suggests that some places had more options at their disposal than others. Industrial suburbs

had always functioned as specialized districts nested within larger metropolitan, regional, and national economic networks. At the dawn of a new millennium, geographic relationships remained absolutely critical and opportunities for exploiting new niches in a post-industrial economy were determined, to a large degree, by location.

From a national perspective, suburbs set within dynamic metropolitan settings had more room for creative maneuvering. As big coastal cities like New York, Boston, and San Francisco restructured their economies around high-tech industry, financial services, and high-end consumption, suburbs close to downtown business districts enjoyed spillover effects. Across the Hudson River from Manhattan, Hoboken, New Jersey had been immortalized as a gritty dockworker town in the 1954 film, *On the Waterfront*. Yet, as Wall Street bankers and financiers spiked the demand for luxury housing, Hoboken became a poster child for late twentieth century gentrification. First, it was artisans and bohemian-types who came to avoid skyrocketing Manhattan rents. Then it was Wall Street workers themselves who took up residence in the city's rehabilitated brownstones and tenements to take advantage of breathtaking skyline views.[20]

In many respects, Emeryville, California, developed as a west coast version of East St. Louis. As the San Francisco Bay terminus for the trans-continental railroad, Emeryville attracted an assortment of manufacturing firms including slaughterhouses, tanneries, and paint manufacturers. It also became San Francisco's illicit playground, with a flourishing trade in bootleg liquor, prostitution, and gambling. It was this sort of activity that prompted the future U.S. Chief Justice, Earl Warren, to label Emeryville, "the rottenest city on the Pacific Coast" when he served as Alameda County's district attorney during the Great Depression. Yet, a healthy regional economy, helped in no small part by the dot.com boom of the 1980s and 1990s, made it feasible for local planners to envision abandoned industrial property as a canvass for big box retailing and "new urbanist" mixed development. Although no more than 2,000 people had made Emeryville their home at any given time through the 1970s, new housing brought the residential population to 7,000 by 2004.[21]

Most industrial suburbs were less fortunate that Hoboken and Emeryville, either because they were embedded within weaker metropolitan economies or they were located too far from resurgent nodes within metropolitan areas. Faced with more limited resources and opportunities, many de-industrialized communities fell back on the vice trades that had long flourished in the shadow of factory smokestacks. If local politicians found incentive in the glory days of the 1950s and 1960s to clean up their towns in the pursuit of more wholesome and family-friendly reputations, they now faced pressure to look the other way or openly court commercial sin. Legal outlets for gambling and sexual titillation in the form of casinos and so-called "gentlemen's" clubs provided badly needed revenue and jobs. Not all such activity was legal, however. Probes of Los Angeles area card clubs, Cicero's massage parlors, and St. Louis east side striptease joints frequently revealed connections to organized crime.

Vice was not the only option for struggling municipalities and many turned to alternative dis-amenities for salvation. Shunned by middle-class communities, operators of trash incinerators, landfills, and private prisons found a welcome reception in places desperate for any sort of economic activity.[22]

Yet, even towns that turned to what one writer termed, economies of "urban extraction," showed wide variation with respect to population dynamics.[23] After several decades of population decline, some industrial suburbs experienced significant population increases, largely as a result of foreign immigration. With plenty of underutilized and relatively inexpensive housing, older manufacturing communities were able to accommodate the thousands of immigrants arriving from underdeveloped parts of the world. In the 1970s, Central

Housing amid abandoned factory, 2009   Powell Photo

Falls, Rhode Island, a depressed mill town outside of Providence, became a major destination for Colombians from Antioquia and Barranquilla provinces.[24] Mexico contributed more immigrants to the United States than any other country in the late 20th century and many settled in California's industrial suburbs. By 2000, Mexicans had become the dominant population group in the small municipalities of Bell, Bell Gardens, Cudahy, Maywood, and South Gate to the southeast of Los Angeles.[25] Industrial suburbs also attracted migrants from Asia and Africa.

Hamtramck, Michigan, once known for its large concentration of Polish immigrants became one of the nation's most ethnically diverse cities in the 1990s due to an influx of families from Yemen and Bangladesh.[26] Once again, however, this trend was geographically selective, occurring primarily, although not exclusively, on the east and west coasts.

St. Louis eastside typified those industrial suburbs that were not impacted by either strong economic recovery at the metropolitan scale or high

rates of foreign immigration. Although dynamic health care and bio-tech sectors contributed to a restructuring of the St. Louis metropolitan economy in the late 20th century, overall economic growth was relatively slack and did not create the sort of investment opportunities that revived communities like Hoboken and Emeryville. Indeed, St. Louis lost ground to most of its metropolitan peers in terms of average earnings during the 1990s and thereafter.[27] Nor did the region attract foreign populations in significant numbers, the relocation of nearly 50,000

A newer street in the Emerson Park neighborhood, 2010
Powell Photo

Bosnian refugees to St. Louis city notwithstanding. According to a 2006 study of 34 comparable metropolitan areas in the United States, only three contained lower percentages of foreign-born residents than St. Louis.[28] Fairmont City, which had a long history of Mexican settlement, was the only community in the vicinity of East St. Louis that witnessed much in the way of new immigration at the tail end of the twentieth century. Yet even with 35 percent of its population counted as foreign born in 2000, Fairmont City still contained about 13 percent fewer people than it did thirty years earlier. For most other municipalities in the area, population losses at the turn of the millennium were far more drastic.

Conclusion: The East Side in Context

At the end of the twentieth century, East St. Louis and its neighbors ranked among the poorest and most depopulated suburbs in the United States. They arrived at this lamentable destination after following a trajectory common to a subset of manufacturing suburbs weakly connected to dynamic metropolitan nodes within the post-industrial economy. Table I compares levels of population growth, poverty, and income across a geographically-dispersed sample of suburbs that were hit hard by late twentieth-century economic dislocations. The cluster representing East St. Louis and its environs shows modest internal variation, with Granite City and Wood River standing out as the most affluent. Yet, even these relatively prosperous municipalities performed well

below metropolitan norms and all lost population between 1970 and 2000. In these respects, the area had much in common with many communities on the outskirts of Chicago, Detroit, and Pittsburgh. By contrast, industrial suburbs within the orbits of San Francisco and New York supported populations with much higher levels of income. Very poor suburbs also ringed Providence and Los Angeles, but high rates of foreign immigration produced stable or growing populations in those places.

Despite endemic poverty, St. Louis east side conferred some relative advantages upon its residents. If the statistical data suggest any single factor capable of sparking an East St. Louis resurgence, it is most certainly affordable housing. Within the group of most severely distressed suburbs, the East St. Louis contingent boasted the cheapest housing. In 1999, the value of owner-occupied homes ranged from $31,000 in Brooklyn to nearly $60,000 in Wood River. (See Table II.) In the Chicago sample, the range shifts upward by more than $10,000 at the low end and $50,000 at the high end. Housing values were more comparable in Pittsburgh and Detroit, but slightly higher nonetheless. One way to measure the affordability of private housing is to compare home prices to local income levels. The ratio of median annual income to median home value calculates the number of years it would take for a household to purchase a private home, assuming it was able to commit all of its earnings to the purchase and assuming the home values correspond with sale prices.

In and around East St. Louis, the purchase of a local home required the equivalent of under two years' income for the average household in 2000. Only four communities in the entire sample could make the same claim. In coastal areas, where housing costs were higher, families typically applied four or five years' worth of income to a home purchase.

Not surprisingly, among the poorest industrial suburbs, St. Louis east side displayed relatively high rates of homeownership. Even in very impoverished communities like Brooklyn, Venice, and Alorton, between 44 and 53 percent of all occupied housing units were inhabited by their owners. Suburbs with similar socioeconomic characteristics in other metropolitan areas, for example Ford Heights outside of Chicago, Highland Park outside of Detroit, and Homestead outside of Pittsburgh, showed higher percentages of rental housing. In other words, fewer people held title to the places they lived. Likewise, homeownership rates in the slightly more prosperous municipalities of East St. Louis, Washington Park, Madison, and Fairmont City, compared favorably with analogous industrial suburbs around Los Angeles, New York, Providence, and Philadelphia. If the ownership of a private dwelling fosters civic responsibility and activism, as is often supposed, then citizens of St. Louis east side may be more motivated to address local problems than their counterparts elsewhere. Low population density has been another characteristic of the East St. Louis area that might be interpreted as an advantage over other industrial suburbs. With about 2,200 residents per square mile, East St. Louis was the densest east side community in 2000. Most other towns in the area contained far less people per acre. In other parts of the country, density levels tended to be much higher, typically ranging from about 3,000 people per square mile in some parts of the Midwest to well over 10,000 people per square mile in the Los Angeles and New York metropolitan areas. For all the urban ills that afflicted the East St. Louis area at the end of the twentieth century, overcrowding was not one of them. Even if housing conditions were substandard in many sections of St. Louis east side, residents there were spared the necessity of converting automobile garages into domestic domiciles as was in the case in the overflowing neighborhoods beyond Los Angeles southeastern border.[29] Abundant open space, of course, was a product of depopulation and abandonment, traits that were rarely seen as desirable. Low population density, then, should be seen as a characteristic that had ambiguous implications for the quality of life.

If this historical comparison of manufacturing suburbs shows anything, it is that over time suburban functions mattered as much as industrial character. The places investigated in this study have consistently been defined by their relationship to nearby central cities. Even as the nation's industrial economy faltered after World War II, most of these outlying districts continued to function as a refuge for undesirable activities. Those that managed to redefine their relationship to the larger metropolis did so only by taking advantage of profound social and economic transformations that occurred at the metropolitan level. What this means for struggling communities in and around East St. Louis is that radical changes in fortune are unlikely to occur until St. Louis repositions itself in international flows of population and investment. If such a scenario appears remote at the present time, it is worth remembering one of history's most important lessons, that people rarely have a sense of what awaits them around the next bend in the road.

TABLE I

Social Conditions in Selected Industrial Suburbs and Metropolitan Statistical Areas, 2000

Suburb	Metro Area	Percent Population Change Since 1970	Percent Population Below Poverty Line	Median Household Income
East St. Louis	St. Louis	-54.95%	35.10%	$21,324
Fairmont City	St. Louis	-12.88%	18.40%	$27,070
Granite City	St. Louis	-22.60%	11.30%	$35,615
Washington Park	St. Louis	-43.88%	44.80%	$21,132
Sauget	St. Louis	Not available	17.30%	$35,833
Alorton	St. Louis	-23.06%	47.30%	$17,860
Madison	St. Louis	-35.46%	12.40%	24828
Venice	St. Louis	-45.98%	39.60%	$19,853
Wood River	St. Louis	-14.33%	14.80%	$33,875
Brooklyn	St. Louis	Not available	48.50%	16630
St. Louis MSA		10.18%	9.90%	$44,437
Cicero	Chicago	27.67%	15.50%	$38,044
Ford Heights	Chicago	-30.88%	49.00%	$17,500
Chicago Heights	Chicago	-19.86%	17.50%	$36,958
Harvey	Chicago	-13.38%	21.70%	$31,958
Whiting	Chicago	-29.12%	12.30%	$34,972
Hammond	Chicago	-22.95%	14.30%	$35,528
East Chicago	Chicago	-31.01%	24.40%	$26,538
Gary	Chicago	-41.43%	25.80%	$27,195
Chicago MSA*		31.22%	10.50%	$51,046
Hamtramck	Detroit	-15.67%	27.00%	$26,616
Highland Park	Detroit	-52.75%	38.30%	$17,737
Detroit MSA*		29.92%	10.60%	$49,160
Homestead	Pittsburgh	-43.43%	26.60%	$16,603
Aliquippa	Pittsburgh	-47.33%	21.70%	$25,113
Munhall	Pittsburgh	-26.45%	11.90%	$32,832
Wilkinsburg	Pittsburgh	-28.32%	18.70%	$26,621
Pittsburgh MSA		-1.77%	10.80%	$37,467

TABLE I

Social Conditions in Selected Industrial Suburbs and Metropolitan Statistical Areas, 2000

Newark	New York	-28.47%	28.40%	26913
Bayonne	New York	-14.99%	10.10%	41566
Hoboken	New York	-14.99%	11.00%	62550
New York MSA*		83.20%	12.90%	$50,795
Camden	Philadelphia	-22.08%	35.50%	$23,421
Gloucester	Philadelphia	-21.91%	6.20%	36855
Philadelphia MSA*		28.45%	10.90%	$50,795
Central Falls	Providence	1.13%	29.00%	$22,628
Providence MSA		30.50%	11.80%	$41,748
Maywood	Los Angeles	65.23%	24.50%	$30,480
Commerce	Los Angeles	19.29%	17.90%	$34,040
Cudahy	Los Angeles	42.42%	28.30%	$29,040
Bell Gardens	Los Angeles	50.31%	27.30%	$30,597
Bell	Los Angeles	67.91%	24.10%	$29,946
Southgate	Los Angeles	69.35%	19.20%	$35,695
Los Angeles MSA*		132.84%	15.60%	$37,467
Emeryville	San Francisco	156.70%	13.20%	$45,359
San Pablo	San Francisco	40.79%	18.10%	$37,184
Pittsburg	San Francisco	174.90%	11.50%	$50,557
Crockett	San Francisco	Not available	7.40%	$48,574
Richmond	San Francisco	25.52%	16.20%	$44,210
Oakland	San Francisco	10.47%	19.40%	$40,055
San Francisco MSA*		126.38%	8.70%	$62,024

*Altered MSA boundaries between 1970 and 2000 may inflate population growth figures.

Source: U.S. Bureau of the Census.

TABLE II

Housing Affordability in Selected Industrial Suburbs, 2000

Suburb	Metro Area	Median Household Income	Median House Value	Ratio Income to House Value	Percent of Occupied Units Owned	Density (Avg. pop per square mile)
East St. Louis	St. Louis	$21,324	$41,800	1.96	53%	2,243
Fairmont City	St. Louis	$27,070	$45,000	1.66	73%	1,013
Granite City	St. Louis	$35,615	$57,200	1.61	71%	1,876
Washington Park	St. Louis	$21,132	$33,700	1.59	57%	2,180
Sauget	St. Louis	$35,833	$50,800	1.42	57%	60
Alorton	St. Louis	$17,860	$31,700	1.77	44%	1,545
Madison	St. Louis	$24,828	$38,000	1.53	59%	648
Venice	St. Louis	$19,853	$31,900	1.61	46%	1,349
Wood River	St. Louis	$33,875	$59,600	1.76	67%	1,865
Brooklyn	St. Louis	$16,630	$31,000	1.86	53%	802
Cicero	Chicago	$38,044	$111,100	2.92	55%	14,645
Ford Heights	Chicago	$17,500	$42,300	2.42	32%	1,955
Chicago Heights	Chicago	$36,958	$94,800	2.57	63%	3,424
Harvey	Chicago	$31,958	$70,500	2.21	56%	4,842
Whiting	Chicago	$34,972	$91,200	2.61	54%	2,914
Hammond	Chicago	$35,528	$78,400	2.21	63%	3,630
East Chicago	Chicago	$26,538	$69,900	2.63	45%	2,706
Gary	Chicago	$27,195	$53,400	1.96	56%	2,046
Hamtramck	Detroit	$26,616	$71,200	2.68	50%	10,901
Highland Park	Detroit	$17,737	$49,800	2.81	39%	5,623
Homestead	Pittsburgh	$16,603	$32,600	1.96	42%	6,282
Aliquippa	Pittsburgh	$25,113	$54,700	2.18	60%	2,868
Munhall	Pittsburgh	$32,832	$60,700	1.85	69%	5,311
Wilkinsburg	Pittsburgh	$26,621	$53,600	2.01	42%	8,335
Newark	New York	$26,913	$119,000	4.42	24%	11,495
Bayonne	New York	$41,566	$155,600	3.74	40%	10,992
Hoboken	New York	$62,550	$428,900	6.86	23%	30,239

TABLE II

Housing Affordability in Selected Industrial Suburbs, 2000

Camden	Philadelphia	$23,421	$40,700	1.74	46%	9,057
Gloucester	Philadelphia	$36,855	$79,500	2.16	74%	5,213
Central Falls	Providence	$22,628	$88,800	3.92	22%	15,652
Maywood	Los Angeles	$30,480	$156,100	5.12	29%	23,887
Commerce	Los Angeles	$34,040	$156,000	4.58	47%	1,914
Cudahy	Los Angeles	$29,040	$151,600	5.22	17%	21,628
Bell Gardens	Los Angeles	$30,597	$175,000	5.72	24%	17,721
Bell	Los Angeles	$29,946	$167,100	5.58	31%	14,803
Southgate	Los Angeles	$35,695	$161,400	4.52	47%	13,085
Emeryville	San Francisco	$45,359	$161,600	3.56	37%	5,646
San Pablo	San Francisco	$37,184	$146,100	3.93	49%	11,727
Pittsburg	San Francisco	$50,557	$165,100	3.27	63%	3,639
Crockett	San Francisco	$48,574	$204,100	4.20	59%	635
Richmond	San Francisco	$44,210	$171,900	3.89	53%	3,310
Oakland	San Francisco	$40,055	$235,500	5.88	41%	7,127

Source: U.S. Bureau of the Census.

End Notes:

1. See for example, "The Six Worst Cities In the United States," The Worst of Everything website, July 6, 2009, http://worstofeverything.blogspot.com/2009/07/6-worst-cities-in-united-states.html, accessed June 17, 2010; "These are the 25 Worst Cities in the United States," *Yahoo Answers* website, http://answers.yahoo.com/question/index?qid=20060822144946AA1wcVK, accessed June 17, 2010. For example of national media portrayals, see, Lee Griggs, "East St. Louis, Illinois," *Time* 133 (June 12, 1989), http://www.time.com/time/magazine/article/0,9171,957921,00.html, accessed June 17, 2010; Evelyn Nieves, "Poverty Tour Revisited," *New York Times*, September 26, 2000, A18; Isabel Wikerson, "Ravaged City on Mississippi Floundering at Rock Bottom," *New York Times*, April 4, 1991, A1.

2. Allan Nevins, *Ford: The Times, The Man, the Company* (New York: Charles Scribner's Sons), 1954, 372,452.

3. Allan Nevins and Frank Ernest Hill, *Ford: Expansion and Challenge, 1915-1933* (New York: Charles Scribner's Sons, 1957), 201-204.

4. James M. Rubenstein, *The Changing U.S. Auto Industry: A Geographical Analysis* (London: Routledge Press, 1992), 47-71.

5. Ellen Nore, *St. Louis National Stockyards Company: East Side Story* (National City: St. Louis National Stockyards Company, n.d.), 2, 11-15

6. George David Smith, *From Monopoly to Competition: The Transformation of Alcoa* (Cambridge: Cambridge University Press, 1988), 98.

7. Andrew J. Theising, *Made in USA: East St. Louis, the Rise and Fall of an Industrial River Town* (St. Louis: Virginia Publishing, 2003), 105-110. Dan Forrestal, *The Story of Monsanto: Faith, Hope and $5,000, The Trials and Triumphs of the First 75 Years* (New York: Simon and Schuster, 1977), 29-30. Doris Rose Henle Beuttenmuller, "The Granite City Steel Company: History of an American Enterprise," *Bulletin of the Missouri Historical Society* 10 (January 1954), 143-45.

8. Richard Walker and Robert Lewis, "Beyond the Crabgrass Frontier: Industry and the Spread of North American Cities, 1850-1950," *Manufacturing Suburbs: Building Work and Home on the Metropolitan Fringe*, ed. Robert Lewis (Philadelphia: Temple University Press, 2004), 16-31.

9. See for instance, Graham Romeyn Taylor, *Satellite Cities: A Study of Industry Suburbs* (New York: D. Appleton and Company, 1915). Margaret F. Byington, *Homestead: The Households of a Mill Town* (New York: Charities Publication Committee, 1910). John A. Fitch, *The Steel Workers* (New York: Charities Publication Committee, 1911).

10. Becky M. Nicolaides, *My Blue Heaven: Life and Politics in the Working-Class Suburbs of Los Angeles, 1920-1965* (Chicago: University of Chicago Press, 2002), 207-212.

11. Cited in William Serrin, *Homestead:The Glory and Tragedy of an American Steel Town* (New York: Random House, 1992), 292-93.

12. "All America-City," *Look* 24 (March 1, 1960), 82. Theising, *East St. Louis*, 193-94.

13. August Meier and Elliot Rudwick, *Black Detroit and the Rise of the UAW* (New York: Oxford University Press, 1979). Joe William Trotter Jr., *Black Milwaukee: The Making of an Industrial Proletariat, 1915-45*(Urbana: University of Illinois Press, 1985). Dennis Dickerson, *Out of the Crucible: Black Steelworkers in Western Pennsylvania, 1875-1980* (Albany: State University of New York Press, 1986);

14. Thomas J. Sugrue, *The Origins of Urban Crisis: Race and Inequality in Postwar Detroit* (Princeton: Princeton University Press, 1996). Robert O. Self, *American Babylon: Race and the Struggle for Postwar Oakland* (Princeton: Princeton University Press, 2003), 170-173. Howard Gillette, Jr., *Camden After the Fall: Decline and Renewal in a Post-Industrial City* (Philadelphia: University of Pennsylvania Press, 2005), 40-61. Also see numerous essays in, Jefferson Cowie and Joseph Heathcott, eds., *Beyond the Ruins: The Meanings of Deindustrialization* (Ithaca: ILR Press, 2003).

15. Theising, *East St. Louis*, 193.

16. Jonathan Kozol, *Savage Inequalities: Children in America's Schools* (New York: Crown Publishers, 1991), 7-8.

17. Dirk Johnson, "The View from the Poorest Suburb," *New York Times*, April 30, 1987.

18. Barrett Seaman, "In Michigan:

Goodbye, Dodge Main," *Time* (February 11, 1980), 8-14.

19. Cited in, Gillette, Jr., *Camden After the Fall*, 89.

20. Ruth Rejnis, "Buyers Renovating Homes Revive Inner City Areas," *New York Times*, September 10, 1972, 94.

21. William Hudnut III, *Halfway to Everywhere: A Portrait of America's First-Tier Suburbs* (Washington, D.C.: The Urban Land Institute, 2003), 340-343. Morris Newman, "A Onetime Industrial Field Now Sprouting Storefronts," *New York Times*, January 7, 2004, C4. Alfred J. Bru, "Phoenix from the Ashes," *The Registry, The Bay Area Real Estate Journal*, n.d., http://www.theregistrysf.com/emeryville.html, accessed June 9, 2010. Dana Perrigan, "Emeryville's Transformation," *San Francisco Chronicle*, June 21, 2009, N1.

22. William Fulton, *The Reluctant Metropolis: The Politics of Urban Growth in Los Angeles* (Baltimore: Johns Hopkins University Press, 2001), 87-90. Bruce Rushton, "Welcome to Brooklyn," *Riverfront Times*, July 5, 2000. Dirk Johnson, "Cicero Journal; In a Town of Scandal, Yet One More," *New York Times*, May 12, 1998, A12.

23. William Fulton, *The Reluctant Metropolis: The Politics of Urban Growth in Los Angeles* (Baltimore: Johns Hopkins University Press, 2001), 77.

24. Martha Martinez, "The Latinos of Rhode Island," *Rhode Island Latinos: A Scan of Issues Affecting the Latino Population of Rhode Island*, ed., Miren Uriarte (Boston: University of Massachusetts, Boston, Mauricio Gastón Institute.

2002), 33-50.

25. U.S. Bureau of the Census, Summary Files 1 (SF 1) and Summary Files 3 (SF 3), *American Fact Finder* website, http://factfinder.census.gov, accessed January 9, 2009.

26. Sarah Kershaw, "Queens to Detroit: A Bangledeshi Passage," *New York Times*, March 8, 2001, 1. Jodi Wilgoren, "A Nation Challenged: Arab Americans," *New York Times* November 4, 2001, D1.

27. East-West Gateway Coordinating Council, *Where We Stand: The Strategic Assessment of the St. Louis Region*, 4th edition (St. Louis: East-West Gateway Coordinating Council of Governments, 1999), 23. East-West Gateway Council of Governments, *Where We Stand: The Strategic Assessment of the St. Louis Region*, 5th edition (St. Louis: East-West Gateway Council of Governments, 2006), 39.

28. East-West Gateway Council of Governments, *Where We Stand: The Strategic Assessment of the St. Louis Region*, 5th edition (St. Louis: East-West Gateway Council of Governments, 2006), 19.

29. Nicolaides, *My Blue Heaven*, 330-32.

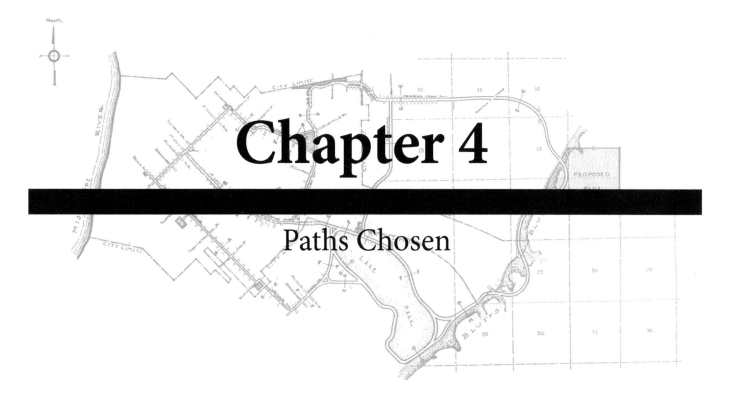

Chapter 4

Paths Chosen

Three Lives That Defined a City: East St. Louis' First Sixty Years

Andrew J. Theising, Ph.D.

Institute for Urban Research,
Southern Illinois University Edwardsville

The early history of East St. Louis is best defined by the biographies of three men; the influence of each lasted about 20 years but the legacy of each lasting forever in the city's memory. These men were influential because they each had something in common: the ability to capitalize on a particular situation. They were all entrepreneurs in a sense—though the outcomes and impacts were very different for all of them. One was focused on the whole, another focused on self, and the third was focused on both. One brought controversy. One brought peace. One brought tragedy.

John B. Bowman

The city's founder, John B. Bowman, c. 1870   Bowen Archives, SIUE

"A Meteor of the Skies"—John B. Bowman 1860-1880

"Pages could be devoted to the accomplishments of the man-meteor who flashed through the sky...imbued with a spirit of enterprise that has immortalized his name in the annals of his city...." Adolph Seuss on John Bowman, 1943 [1]

John B. Bowman was born Johannes B. Baumann near Mannheim, in the Duchy of Baden, on April 9, 1833. He was a student at the University of Heidelberg and participated in the Hecker Uprising to overthrow the monarchy and establish a republic during the revolutionary movements of the German States in 1848. He was an intelligent man, educated in civil engineering and law, and an outstanding orator. By1854, but perhaps as early as 1852, Bowman had anglicized his name and moved to Cahokia, Illinois.[2] He made his way to St. Louis, and through some stroke of great fortune became the personal secretary to one of Missouri's most prolific politicians, Thomas Hart Benton. Benton, who was Missouri's first Senator (serving until 1851) and served one term in the House of Representatives (1852-1854), was likely retired from public service when Bowman was in his employ (though he ran for Missouri governor in 1856).

Benton, however, was still able to pull strings for his rising young protégé. Upon Benton's recommendation, President James Buchanan appointed Bowman the postmaster of Manchester, Missouri in 1857—a small town about 20 miles west of St. Louis along the Manchester Road.[3]

Bowman had won favor with a powerful man, and like a meteor, he was about to rise for all to see.

The first official presence of John B. Bowman in what is now East St. Louis was his election as Police Magistrate on April 1, 1861,[4] which is the very day East St. Louis was born by name. However, he probably came to East St. Louis on November 10, 1859, when former Civil War General Lewis B. Parsons Jr., then president of the Ohio and Mississippi Railroad and acting on behalf of the defunct Page and Bacon Bank, led an auction of land in what is now East St. Louis (and where the Ohio and Mississippi Railroad already had holdings). Bowman describes the transaction in unusual detail in the appendix he wrote for Reavis' *Future Great City of the World*: "The average price at which property was disposed of at that sale did not exceed one dollar and twenty-five cents per foot front. What has proved since to be the most valuable property then brought the least price."[5] This auction with such cheap land included the area that was once called "Illinois City"—400 acres of land that, in 1873, John B. Bowman sold to New York capitalists to establish the National Stock Yards, right about the time he would have been writing for the Reavis history.[6]

By 1865, Bowman had written a new city charter, pushed it through the Illinois Legislature, and won his first term as mayor of the newly re-chartered "East St. Louis." Within another ten years, in addition to being mayor, Bowman was also an attorney in private practice, a real estate and insurance agent for the

Connecticut Land Company, owner of title and abstract offices in Belleville, publisher of the *East St. Louis Gazette*, financier of the East St. Louis Gas Light and Coke Company, and attorney for such disparate interests as the Illinois and St. Louis Bridge Company, the Wiggins Ferry Company, the National Stock Yards, the Vandalia Railway, the East St. Louis and Carondelet Railroad, and the Western Union Telegraph Company.[7] This was exactly the type of person the State of Illinois needed.

To understand Bowman's importance in the 1860s, one must understand the objectives of the State of Illinois in the 1840s. When Illinois was admitted to the Union in 1818, the United States Congress was already constructing the first interstate highway—the National Road. It was slowly creeping toward Illinois with the goal of creating a land connection between the great rivers of the country, and by 1820 Congress authorized the road to reach all the way to the Illinois shore of the Mississippi.[8] This led to a great interest in both the overall development of infrastructure in the state as well as direct public investment in that infrastructure. Today, it is commonplace for government to build infrastructure, but in the early 19th century, such public investment was rare and controversial. Private firms built roads and bridges—not cities, not states. Governor Joseph Duncan (1834-1838) pushed the state legislature to begin the Internal Improvement Program. This led to massive amounts of bonded debt that was intended to build bridges, ports, roads, canals, and other commercial improvements.[9] The program was a disaster, racking up $14 million in bonded debt for a state of less than 500,000 inhabitants. By 1842, program construction was suspended. Illinois had nearly bankrupted itself and politicians were feeling tremendous pressure to develop a fix.

The solution was simple—let the marketplace develop the state's infrastructure. The state put through a new constitution in 1848 that drastically relaxed power. The legislature could not authorize spending in excess of $50,000. Debt repayment schedules were fixed by law, as were public salaries. Hundreds of patronage positions at the county level were made elected positions.[10] This, along with subsequent constitutional changes during this period, functionally pushed traditional state power down to the local level. Entrepreneurs showed up in Illinois in droves, and municipal incorporations spiked in the 1870s.[11] Illinois became a no-holds-barred state, and East St. Louis was established at a time when there were few rules and "the merger of public and private prosperity"[12] was accepted and encouraged.

John Bowman envisioned an industrial city. He knew the location of East St. Louis across from the fourth largest city in the United States in the 1870 census would ensure its greatness for decades to come. He was always looking for East St. Louis' advantage, be it in infrastructure, industry, or utility. He sought economic opportunity (professional, political, and personal) and was a driving force behind most major efforts such as bridge construction, dike construction, and railroad construction. He pushed for new industries (being personally responsible for the arrival of the National Stock Yards), new institutions (he gave the land for creating St. Patrick's and St. Henry's churches and was president of the first library in the

Bowman's signature, 1878
Theising image,
Bowen Archives, SIUE

city), and new government. He was constantly tweaking the city's charter so that it could take full advantage of new state laws and powers.

Bowman started something big, but he eventually lost control of it. Railroads flocked to the city, and the Wiggins Ferry was the only way across the river to St. Louis. When the first bridge connecting St. Louis to Illinois was completed, it connected to East St. Louis. By river or rail, freight moved through East St. Louis. Money flowed freely and soon shady opportunists arrived in the form of gambling dens, brothels, municipal corruption, and general lawlessness. Fierce competition emerged over railroad rights-of-way and access to new infrastructure.

His attempt to create an expanded charter under new Illinois general law in 1877 backfired. The mayor at the time was Samuel S. Hake, Bowman's friend who "favors all movements" toward "material prosperity" and "actively engages personally and officially in their promotion and accomplishment."[13] The new general law charter was approved by special election, and Bowman ran for mayor under the new charter's provisions. Unfortunately, a large section of politicians (all opposed to Bowman—called by the press "Anti-Bowmanites") did not recognize the special election and the general law charter. The Anti-Bowmanites refused to give up power, recognized the old charter, and functionally ran an old "charter government" alongside the Bowmanites' "general law government."

East St. Louis was a political disaster from 1877 to 1879. The Anti-Bowmanite charter government was led by Ernest Wider with the support of Maurice Joyce and John J. McLean. In a direct effort to spite Bowman, one of the first actions of the charter government under Wider was to abolish the city library that Bowman had created.[14] The Bowmanite general law government was led by John Bowman with the support of Thomas Winstanley and Malbern M. Stephens. Bowman was furious over the charter government's actions and lawsuits flew back and forth.

Amid this trial, personal tragedy struck Bowman's family. On December 23, 1877, Bowman's wife, Annie Goings Bowman, accidentally killed herself. She feared for her safety and kept a gun tucked in the bodice of her dress. She was removing it when it discharged, killing her instantly.

She had just celebrated her 26th birthday. Bowman was widowed (likely for the second time) at age 44.

On July 19, 1878, the Illinois Supreme Court ruled against Bowman and determined the special election was invalid (as was the charter that had been approved). Lawsuits between the Bowmanites and the Anti-Bowmanites kept the final implementation of the decision at bay until the end of terms the following spring. By the spring of 1879, the dual government crisis was nearing an end. On election day in April, the two governments held separate elections at separate polling places. The Bowmanites recognized the election of Thomas Winstanley as mayor, and Bowman surrendered all official documents and responsibilities to him. The Anti-Bowmanites recognized the election of Maurice Joyce, who immediately sought a court order for Bowman to surrender all documents and responsibilities to him.[15]

Winstanley's Bowmanite government was ordered by the court to disband, which it did. Joyce and the Anti-Bowmanites held control of East St. Louis for the next six years. Bowman was without political power for the first time since the city was created. He had lost control of his creation.

Years of lawlessness emerged. The city council was characterized by corruption, particularly the influence of the Wiggins Ferry Company and its president Sam Clubb. Gamblers flocked to the free-wheeling city. Public officials robbed the city treasury. Railroad detective Thomas

Furlong described the city at this time as being a "wide-open town, with the accent on the words 'wide' and 'open.'"[16] Bowman retreated to his law practice and his newspaper, *The East St. Louis Gazette*—which employed a young manager named James W. Kirk, who was quick to publicize crooked politicians and publicly lament the condition of the once-promising city.

The lawlessness reached its height on November 20, 1885. John Bowman, described as a very methodical man, was making his way home from his office near the intersection of Missouri and Collinsville avenues along his usual route at his usual time— 6:30 p.m. When he reached his home on 10th Street, a gunman approached him from behind. A single shot was fired at close range and Bowman fell dead outside the gate to his front lawn.[17] He was 53 years old. His third wife, age 25, was now a widow.

The police made little or no effort to investigate the matter. The family, led by eldest son Frank B. Bowman, immediately hired the finest investigator in St. Louis, Thomas Furlong, who was railroad detective for the Missouri Pacific and the other Gould interests. The facts of the case were few, and Bowman's many enemies were preparing their alibis.[18] Furlong and his men investigated the matter carefully and discovered two witnesses, Christian Schmidt and William Banks. The two men were actually returning from their own crime of sorts—they were securing tobacco recently stolen from a freight car and hidden inside a haystack.[19] They witnessed the gunshot, saw Bowman fall, and recognized the

perpetrator as being George W. Voice, an East St. Louis police officer.

It should come as no surprise that a member of the city police would commit a ghastly crime, but the motivation was never fully documented. The strongest evidence from the scant historical record points to this as a murder-for-hire, with Samuel C. Clubb as the leader.[20] Clubb enjoyed near-total control of city government. The Wiggins Ferry Company was a powerful force in the city and Clubb was not reticent to wield his influence. The *East St. Louis Gazette* regularly criticized Clubb and his abusive power.

Clubb was entering the ferry company into leasing agreements with different railroad interests, putting the company at large financial risk and taking it outside its core business. This was bothersome to a group of shareholders led by H. C. "Clem" Creveling. Creveling issued a letter to shareholders on June 16, 1885, that outlined his concerns. James W. Kirk published the letter in the *Gazette* two weeks before Bowman's murder.[21] The suit was filed under a new provision of the Illinois constitution that addressed railroad competition. The law was untested, but Clubb felt confident that he could prevail. However, Creveling had only recently hired a new attorney to represent him— John B. Bowman. Bowman had been the Wiggins Ferry attorney for many years, until Samuel Clubb came to power. Though Bowman was forced out as corporate counsel, he still retained a vast knowledge of the company's operation. Bowman's death would ensure a Wiggins Ferry victory in the case.

Creveling's stock certificate, 1867   Bowen Archives, SIUE

Clubb denied any involvement. Voice was indicted for murder, and a second police officer, Patrick O'Neil, was indicted as an accessory. At a preliminary hearing, the witnesses testified and Voice was returned to jail without bond. Shortly after this preliminary hearing, witnesses Schmidt and Bank were threatened by associates of Voice and O'Neil. Fearing for their safety, Schmidt and Bank fled the county and the charges were dismissed against Voice and O'Neil. [22] The case was never solved. The $5,000 reward money was never claimed, so it was used to finance the casting of two bronze busts of Bowman—one that rested atop a pedestal many years in the East St. Louis

Public Library (from which it was stolen in the 1990s) and the other that rests atop Bowman's grave in Bellefontaine Cemetery in St. Louis. Bowman was buried next to his previous wife Anne Goings Bowman in Bellefontaine Cemetery. His will directed that his head be turned so that it faced his beloved East St. Louis. Samuel Clubb suffered deep emotional problems and was declared insane by the Probate Court of St. Louis the following spring.[23] An attempt was made on the life of James W. Kirk on June 19, 1886, from which he narrowly escaped.[24] He continued to publish the *Gazette* until starting his own paper—the *East St. Louis Daily Journal* in 1890, the city's first daily paper. John Bowman was

"a meteor in the skies," and like a meteor his light was bright but brief. His obituary ends with the line: "In his death, East St. Louis is deprived of her greatest benefactor, whose place will not soon be filled."[25] It was not too long, though, before a knight in shining armor came along.

"City Builder"—Malbern Monroe Stephens 1880-1900

"If my memory serves me right, Mayor [Stephens]…did much to make East St. Louis the city it is today. But this work was not accomplished without much hard labor on his part and on the part of those who assisted him, for the gamblers and crooks did not give up without a struggle. Mayor [Stephens], however, made it as

law-abiding a place during his administration as any other city in the country of its size." Thomas Furlong on Malbern Stephens, 1912 [26]

The only periods of peace and prosperity that East St. Louis ever knew were under the reigns of M. M. Stephens. An 1892 biographical volume described him as "one of the most agreeable of men" with "a heart of gold" and "ever ready to extend a helping hand to the needy and suffering."[27] He was truly an amazing man. He was honest and forthright, had a good sense for management and leadership, and led by example. An 1895 review noted that "in every movement for the welfare of the community and the improvement of the city... Stephens is always to the front."[28] It was the railroad industry that first brought M. M. Stephens to the city where he would spend the rest of his life. Like his father back in Pennsylvania, he was a railroad man—not an executive in the front office, but rather an engineer sweating behind the great boiler of an Ohio and Mississippi steam engine.

He arrived in East St. Louis in 1868 and married a French immigrant, Mary Elizabeth Tomkins Beam, four years later.[29] Beam had been married previously and brought two children to the marriage (Lillie, who later married Edward Cuddington, and Emma, who married into the politically prominent Jackeisch family), and in 1882, their daughter Leonora was born. In 1874, Stephens stepped away from railroading and opened a hotel (as his father did in Pennsylvania), called the Fourth Ward House. It stood at the corner of Collinsville and Summit avenues.

He first won elected office in the turbulent year of 1877. He was a fourth ward alderman on the city council, and an ardent follower of John B. Bowman. During the tumult that erupted, Stephens followed his friend Bowman and served on the Bowmanites' general law council. When the general law council was dissolved by court order, Stephens and the Bowmanites were sidelined. Stephens worked with the Bowmanites to create the "Citizens Party," which had its debut in the aldermanic elections of 1884. (There were two aldermen elected from each of four wards serving two-year terms, with one elected in odd years and one elected in even years; mayoral elections were held in odd years.) The new party won all four aldermanic seats up for election. The Anti-Bowmanites still controlled half of the council and their candidate, Dr. O. R. Winton, was still serving as mayor, but support for the Anti-Bowmanites was faltering due to outlandish stories of corruption that were emerging from the Winton Administration. Stephens was a voice of opposition. Though there was considerable evidence of influence-peddling and official graft, there is absolutely no evidence of Stephens being part of any of it.

The Bowmanites looked forward to further victory in the April 1885 elections—specifically recapturing the mayoralty from the corrupt Anti-Bowmanites. They were shocked at the results: the Citizens Ticket lost every office.[30] Bowman's arch-nemesis Maurice Joyce was mayor, and Anti-Bowmanites claimed half of

*M. M. Stephens, c. 1900
Bowen Archives, SIUE*

the city council. The Bowmanites blamed Sam Clubb, lamenting that "The Captain did it with his magic wand, and the like, you know."[31] The technique was a familiar one: the Anti-Bowmanites flooded the polls with transients within the city limits. "These tramps have wandered aimlessly [and] have now organized," and will be "on a par with Gypsies and other Nomadic tribes."[32] They overwhelmed the polls on election day, with instructions to elect the Anti-Bowmanites to office. The *Gazette* mocked the new mayor: "Long live Maurice I, King of Tramps."[33]

After John Bowman's murder in late November 1885, Stephens inherited Bowman's mantel of reform and the leadership of the Bowmanite movement. He was the target of a smear campaign shortly after Bowman's murder. Accusations were widely circulated in the *East St. Louis Signal* (the Anti-Bowmanite newspaper that existed briefly in the 1880s) that Stephens had

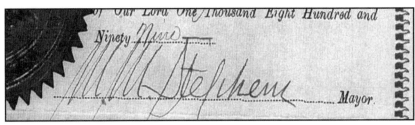

Stephens' signature, 1899   Bowen Archives, SIUE

accepted a payment from a man named Caves for illegal gambling privileges in East St. Louis. The *East St. Louis Gazette* vigorously defended Stephens. Even the man who was supposedly negotiating the deal came forward to deny any wrongdoing by Stephens. The *Signal* eventually printed an editorial statement that "we know nothing of the truth or falsity" of the charges against Stephens.[34] Though many threw mud, to the impeccable Stephens it would not stick.

Stephens knew that genuine reform would not happen until the corrupt electoral system that enabled greedy politicians was overhauled. Stephens and other Bowmanites designed legislation that would require, among other rules, voter registration. Election reform, as it was called, became a divisive issue and the subject of extensive editorials. Somehow, Stephens' Citizens Party was able to advance this critical piece of legislation successfully in November 1886.[35] It was immediately challenged in court by the Anti-Bowmanites, but was upheld as legal by the Illinois Supreme Court in January 1887.

Support for reform in East St. Louis expanded with the assistance of St. Clair County and the indictment of three former public officials on conspiracy to commit fraud, all Anti-Bowmanites: former City Clerk

Timothy Canty, County Recorder Dennis Canty, and former Mayor O. R. Winton.[36] It was probably the most egregious case of public corruption ever to surface in East St. Louis. Public officials conspired to loot the city treasury of thousands of dollars in a complicated scheme that would involve heavy orchestration, the authorized movement of public funds, and a devious safe-cracker from St. Louis. In the end, the money was gone and the records destroyed.

James W. Kirk, manager of the *East St. Louis Gazette*, openly lambasted the city in his newspaper, declaring in 1886 that the city was under a "Reign of Terror," lamenting brazen daytime crime and nicknaming the town "Burglarville" due to its unabashed criminality.[37] The Anti-Bowmanites were feeling the pressure. Newspaper headlines exposed the trickery of public officials. Prosecutors were investigating corrupt practices and indicting officials. The new election reform law meant that long-standing election tactics could not be employed. Finally, John Bowman had been made a martyr for the cause of reform. The tide had turned.

In the election of April 1887, the Citizens Ticket won every office for which it ran a candidate.[38] Stephens was now mayor, and East St. Louis in the late 1880s

was on the cusp of unprecedented prosperity. He held the confidence of the electorate. "He was not a man trained for leadership or statesmanship when he undertook the responsible duties of the mayoralty. He was a plain man of the people, with no pretension not justified by the confidence and compliments of his fellow citizens."[39]

As mayor, change began almost immediately. Under Joyce, the city had become "a lamentable, complicated and embarrassed condition of affairs."[40] The city's credit was in ruins. Revenue was collected months in advance and squandered by public officials.[41] Stephens began by settling the city's debts, which had been at least $750,000 (possibly higher), for the reduced sum of $628,143.10.[42] He abolished the city "scrip," treasury warrants that were sources of corruption and basically worthless.[43] Streets were paved with granite block and lighted with electricity for the first time.[44]

His city was growing too. The first daily newspaper, *The Daily Journal*, appeared in 1890. Catholic and Protestant churches were opening up, St. Mary's Hospital was established in 1890, and the Henrietta Hospital (later Christian Welfare) in 1897.[45] The First National Bank (still operating in East St. Louis) was created, the East St. Louis Electric Railway was developed, and the new Merchants Bridge (for railroads) opened across the Mississippi.[46] Stephens was actively engaged with Congressman W. S. Forman and led a corporate interest to establish a third bridge across the Mississippi (which did not materialize).[47] Stephens traveled extensively and worked to bring new investment to East St. Louis. The city always had significant national investment (the National Stock Yards, for example, was tied to east coast investors that included Cornelius Vanderbilt), but Stephens made the city attractive to foreign investors, particularly from Great Britain.[48]

He moved government institutions forward on all fronts. He appointed "good men to the official positions," enjoyed a majority support of the city council, put the city on a cash basis. He created a "courageous and competent" police force and established the first "effective" fire department for the city.[49] Five new school buildings were opened by 1895, including a new high school. He re-established the public library (which had been abolished by Anti-Bowmanites several years earlier).[50]

The grandest of projects, though, was the implementation of John Bowman's "high grade" proposal to pave and raise the levels of key thoroughfares. The city could not prosper, argued Bowman and those who shared his industrial vision, until the town was raised "out of the mud."[51] The high-grade movement was controversial, with many complaining that the land being protected was simply not worth the investment,[52] but Stephens knew better. The work commenced with Broadway, the

primary thoroughfare between the downtown commercial center and the river. The street was raised from five to 15 feet, and then paved with granite block. Missouri Avenue was raised by 1890, and other downtown streets continued to be raised for a period of years.[53] The engineer for the project was Henry Flad, who had been James Eads' right-hand man during bridge construction in the 1870s. To this day, the lots of downtown East St. Louis still sits below street grade in many places.

Stephens brought an unprecedented period of prosperity to East St. Louis. He served for a sixteen-year period—with a small gap of defeat in the election of 1895. Stephens lost the election that year to Henry F. Bader, a druggist by trade, but readily won re-election to the mayoralty in 1897. During his term out of office, he was appointed Postmaster of East St. Louis by President Grover Cleveland. He also had personal tragedy emerge. His wife of 22 years died on September 2, 1894— about six months before the 1895 election—leaving him widowed at age 47 with a 12-year-old daughter and two older stepdaughters. He married Sarah J. Bolte (age 19, who had the nickname "Stevie" after marriage) on January 8, 1896—just 16 months after Mary Elizabeth's death and in plenty of time to prepare for the 1897 election.[54]

He was handily re-elected in 1897, 1899, and 1901. Reviews of his performance were consistently glowing: "From the very inception of the reform movement to the present date, Mayor Stephens has displayed the rarest executive ability, and has

at the same time demonstrated his capacity for public affairs to an extent which marks him as a coming man in the larger sphere of State government…. He has not been offensive, dictatorial, or presumptuous in dealing with his subordinates, his critics, or his friends."[55] By the turn of the century, though, Stephens found himself where Bowman was in the 1870s: the city he loved and built was no longer something he could control. New forces were at hand—and they were not friendly.

A beautiful new city hall building was dedicated on January 19, 1900, and Mayor Stephens was its first occupant. He was not in the building for long, though. A group of men emerged about this time, one or two of them having already been established but others relatively new to the city, and they laid plans to take over city government. Mayor Stephens wasn't really needed anymore in East St. Louis. He had done the heavy lifting: he stabilized government services, restored the city's finances, built the major infrastructure, and pushed the local economy forward. The city had so much economic momentum that it did not need M. M. Stephens to ensure its success. It would be easy to convince voters that it was time for a change. Stephens lost the 1903 election to Judge Silas Cook, who had arrived in East St. Louis in 1898 and who immediately won election to the city court. Cook would be the face (but not the power) of a new political machine.

Stephens took the opportunity to become a full-time capitalist. On July 1, 1902, he leased his hotel (now called Stephens House, which later became the Summit

Hotel) and moved to an opulent residence on the finest street in the city (in the Philip Wolf subdivision) at 1010 Pennsylvania Avenue.[56] For years he had been investing his hotel proceeds in area real estate. He now turned his attention to his large real estate empire, railroad construction (like his father), and the State Savings and Loan where he was president. The Stephens Office Building stood at 316-318 Missouri Avenue. Ironically, his defeat was enabled by the switching of loyalty of Frank B. Bowman—eldest son of John Bowman, Stephens' close friend and benefactor.

The "Controlling Factor"— George Locke Tarlton 1900-1920

"Mr. Tarlton was the acknowledged 'one-man political regime' in St. Clair County. ... Close observation...left little doubt but that Mr. Tarlton was the controlling factor in county and city organizations of both major parties." Locke Tarlton's obituary in the Journal, 1943[57]

Within a month of Stephens'

G. Locke Tarlton, c. 1907
Bowen Archives, SIUE

departure from city government, the Mississippi River rose from its banks in one of the worst floods on record—quickly overcoming dikes and nearly reaching the mayor's office itself. It seems symbolic of the transition East St. Louis was about to face from an era of peace and prosperity to one of greed and corruption. The floodwaters ravaged parts of town, especially a low-lying area of homes near "Whiskey Chute"— the line of taverns along St. Clair Avenue leading to the Stock Yards. Families fled the flooding and land speculators moved in to buy up the cheap housing stock. One of those speculators was George Locke Tarlton.

Locke Tarlton (he went by his middle name) had only recent gone into business. He was only 20 years old when he entered into a real estate partnership with 43-year-old Thomas Jefferson Canavan. One biography described young Locke as being "always attentive to his studies," and that "few members of his class were better qualified to battle with the elements of an education than he."[58] It continued, stating that he "is one of the most popular men in the city with all classes of citizens" and that "his social disposition is largely responsible for the great success of the firm with which he is associated." In 1903, the firm Canavan and Tarlton was established. Its offices were at 114 North Main Street and called itself "the enterprising real estate firm."[59] While the partnership was indeed engaged in real estate, it also financed real estate and provided fire and property insurance. It was very successful. By 1912, Tarlton had moved to a fine residence at 600 Washington

Place—a wealthy street that was a tangent of powerful Pennsylvania Avenue.

Tarlton was born in East St. Louis in 1882 to Ralph B. Tarlton and Mary E. Locke. The family resided at 636 or 638 North Ninth Street. Ralph Tarlton was an adventurous man, having left his family's prominent farm in Missouri for the wilds of Kansas. He went further west to hunt buffalo, removed to the wild-west town of Dodge City at its beginning, and eventually became involved in various Stock Yards interests.[60] He connected with various commission firms at the National Stock Yards and eventually opened his own firm in partnership with Nick Moody. Moody and Tarlton were among the most prominent names in the commission business at the National Stock Yards.

Tarlton's business partner was Thomas Canavan. Canavan was born in Milwaukee in 1859. His father enlisted in the 5th Wisconsin Cavalry in the Civil War and was killed in action. By 1866, the family moved back to East St. Louis (it was Illinoistown when they left) and Canavan was part of the first graduating class of East St. Louis High School. He opened a grocery store in 1891 and operated it throughout the Stephens years, until his switch to real estate in 1902-1903. During the Stephens era, he developed a taste for politics—serving two terms as alderman and on the first board of education of District 189 as well as marrying into the Shea family (Anti-Bowmanites, though there is no evidence that Canavan was one).[61] One of the very first transactions of Canavan and Tarlton was the speculation surrounding flooded out homes.

Tarlton purchased the properties at fire-sale prices. He had no intention of re-populating the homes with families; rather, he allowed criminal elements to enter and, before long, he was the landlord, property manager, and/or rent collector of a string of brothels. This flooded-out neighborhood became known as "The Valley," and it was one of the most infamous red-light districts in the United States.[62]

Surrounding the brothels in The Valley were various taverns and gambling dens (and often those functions were co-mingled). The Valley and its operators were unmolested by the police. Politicians were well aware of the vice going on in the city and willingly turned a blind eye to it all. The political machine of Mayor Silas Cook (which was headed by his chief of police, George Purdy) refused to be involved. One problematic saloon was called "The Monkey Cage" and was operated by known criminals George "Potts" Nevins and George Neville.[63] Cook ordered the place closed due to "many complaints regarding its character." However, after representatives of major liquor firms lobbied the mayor, the saloon was re-opened because Cook was assured that criminal activity would stop—which it did not.[64] Tarlton was openly involved in such enterprises owning the buildings, collecting the rents, or managing the properties. Tarlton went so far as to hire a particular man from St. Louis—with a record of establishing profitable brothels in St. Louis—to launch one for a particular East St. Louis land owner.[65]

One of the most brutal stories

of the lawlessness of The Valley involved the son of an Armenian baker, Alphonse Magarian. The bakery was adjacent to one of The Valley's busy brothels. The elder Magarian tired of the criminal activity next door and repeatedly complained to public officials about his neighbor's illegal practices. Pressured to act, police raided the brothel and shut it down. Shortly after the raid, Alphonse disappeared. He had just turned three years old. Magarian offered a $2,000 reward for his son's safe return, but the kidnappers would have none of it. The child was being used as a lesson to all who dared complain about business in The Valley. The boy's decapitated body was found in a gunny sack. His head was found in the city dump over a week later.[66] Berta Franz, a prostitute at the brothel in question, was framed for the murder. She herself was murdered and the body placed on the railroad tracks to make it appear as a suicide. The brothel was owned by Thomas Canavan and Locke Tarlton.[67]

A great opportunity occurred in 1907, when the Illinois legislature passed enabling legislation to set up special taxing districts with the authority to develop levees to protect flood-prone areas. East St. Louis, with its long history of flooding, was a prime target of such legislation and the necessity of establishing a flood control district was an easy case to make. Locke Tarlton, a man who understood property values and flood plains, immediately became involved. Tarlton won his first election to public office in 1908, when he became a founding member of the East Side Levee

and Sanitation District.

Tarlton used the position to enrich himself. The Levee District made extensive plans to develop infrastructure and drain wetlands, and using insider information, intervened in land deals. In

Tarlton's signature, 1909
Bowen Archives, SIUE

one case, Tarlton purchased a large amount of swamp land at minimal price just before the Levee Board announced that it was going to drain the land to make it developable.[68] In another case, when the Levee Board expressed interest in buying land for a right-of-way, a Tarlton agent approached the owner (a widow) and bought the land from her for $5,000. Three weeks later, he sold the land to the Levee District for $20,000.[69] As president of the Levee Board, Tarlton kept Levee District funds in bank accounts that bore no interest. In return, these banks established slush funds that Tarlton could use for his illicit political activities.[70] The Levee District, under Tarlton's leadership, became an instrument for corruption.

The political machine of Cook and Purdy was weakening, but managed to cling to power. Cook won the 1905 election by less than 250 votes.[71] Thomas Canavan challenged Cook unsuccessfully in 1907. The *Daily Journal* noted that Congressman William Rodenberg, long a supporter of Silas Cook, stated publicly that he preferred Canavan. The endorsement, however informal, was not enough. In 1909, Cook survived a three-way race. M. M. Stephens attempted a comeback, while Charles Lambert—Anheuser-Busch sales representative for East St. Louis and Cook's city clerk—bolted from the machine to run against his boss. There was enough disenchantment with Cook to enable his defeat, but he won a plurality in the three-way race. Tarlton, safely ensconced in his Levee Board position, decided to get involved.

He chose Lambert, a Republican, as his pawn. (Canavan was a Democrat. Tarlton was equally influential in both parties.) Through sheer political maneuvering, Tarlton and Lambert ousted the Cook-Purdy machine and Tarlton was now enjoying dominance of city hall as well as the Levee Board. Tarlton was known to stand in the street and openly pay five dollars for a vote.[72] He later bragged aloud that he controlled the mayor.

The administration of Charles Lambert was probably the most corrupt in the city's history. Lambert's chief of police was George Washington "Wash" Thompson, who himself was the owner of a saloon and gambling den in The Valley. Just as in the early 1880s, the city was nearly bankrupt, $250,000 in city funds disappeared, and bribery was commonplace—even brokered by the mayor himself. In an astonishing case of public malfeasance, Lambert and the council established the East St. Louis Finance Committee (no member was an accountant). The committee examined the books of the Lambert Administration, declared all money to be accounted for, and then ordered

the financial records to be destroyed.[73] Thanks to media intervention, the records were not destroyed but rather secured in the comptroller's vault for later inspection. They mysteriously disappeared when authorities went to claim them.

The law almost caught up with the Tarlton machine in 1912. Charles Webb, State's Attorney for St. Clair County, raided the saloon of police chief "Wash" Thompson. Being a county official, Webb was independent of the political arrangements that kept city officials away from the graft and corruption. It led to a massive multi-year investigation of corruption in East St. Louis, landing indictments for six city officials including Police Chief Thompson and Mayor Lambert.[74] Helping push the investigation along was the East St. Louis Protective Association, a good government group sponsored by M. M. Stephens.[75] Tarlton personally was never threatened. Astonishingly, despite years of investigation and seemingly astounding evidence, the jury acquitted the men.[76] Tarlton controlled the jury, and Prosecutor Webb announced that he would drop further prosecution.

Tarlton had to find a new mayor to replace Lambert. He chose former State Senator John Chamberlin, whose family had been leaders of McKendree College in nearby Lebanon, Illinois. Chamberlin was a good man at heart and, to Tarlton's chagrin, cooperated with the Webb investigation. In 1915, Tarlton saw to it that both Chamberlin and Webb were defeated by more agreeable candidates.[77]

Tarlton's choice for mayor in 1915 was Fred Mollman, whose family ran a harness and leather shop on Missouri Avenue. He was challenged by incumbent mayor John Chamberlin, who ran on the slogan "Make East St. Louis a little more like home and a little less like hell," but went down to defeat handily.[78] Mollman was an inept leader, described by the newspaper as a "good man" with "questionable associations."[79] His fear of leadership and his inability to control city government would prove disastrous in 1917, when mobs rioted on the streets slaughtering innocent black residents. Yet, thanks to Tarlton, he won the 1917 election by the largest majority ever recorded.[80]

After the pogrom of 1917, the congressional committee that investigated it condemned Tarlton and the corruption of East St. Louis. The committee said that the city "wallows in a mire of lawlessness and unshamed corruption."[81] Much of the blame was laid at Tarlton's feet. His obituary, which largely ignored his controversial past, simply stated that his name was "one of those mentioned" in the report.[82] The riot marked the end of Tarlton's power in city hall, but not the end of his political involvement. He remained a force on the Levee Board, being re-elected as late as 1920. He helped his brother-in-law, Edwin Schaefer, win a seat in Congress (that would later be held by Mel Price for 44 years). Tarlton's construction company thrived. It won several lucrative contracts—including replacing all of the light standards in the City of St. Louis and the construction of military camps at Neosho, Missouri, and Little Rock,

M. M. Stephens, c. 1925
Bowen Archives, SIUE

Arkansas. The firm Canavan and Tarlton also existed up to Canavan's death at age 81 in 1940. Tarlton died of heart and kidney ailments in 1943. He was only 61.

Epilogue: The Last Hurrah — The 1920s

After the horrid riot of 1917, East St. Louis leaders pushed for reform. The voters quickly approved changing the charter so that it would become a commission form of government—with the intent of making city government more accountable for its actions. The city would be run by five commissioners, one of them being the Mayor (who would hold the title of police commissioner) and the other four dividing up the other duties of city government: streets, finance, buildings/fire protection, and public relations. The change would take place in 1919, when Fred Mollman's term as mayor would end.

To whom could the city turn to heal the great divisions caused by years of corruption and violence? The city fathers approached the only man who could bring peace and prosperity to a broken city— Malbern M. Stephens, now age 72. Stephens only grudgingly accepted the position. He had worked too

hard and was invested too deeply to say no.

The situation he faced in 1919 was far different than when he had last held the office. Professionally, the city was in ruins. The corruption and mismanagement had squandered the city's resources. In the 1918 census of governments, East St. Louis was the second poorest city government in the United States.[83] Personally, he had lost considerable stature. Mayor Stephens, who once was considered the wealthiest man in East St. Louis and amassed a real-estate fortune worth $500,000 (double the estimate of Bowman's wealth), declared himself penniless in a May 17, 1916 court filing—attributing his loss to the failure of a New York investment called the Victoria Building.[84] Stephens, like his city, was at the end of the rope.

Despite the immensely frustrating job of being mayor, Stephens was able to bring relative peace, calm, and, to a degree, prosperity to the city, much as he had done in the 1890s. Stephens hated the commission form of government. He said in 1920, "How do you expect me to act as a Mayor should when I have four Commissioners to vote against me at the Council meetings?"[85] The ability to hire and fire employees rested with each individual commissioner. It was as if the city had five mayors, not one; discipline at city hall was weak and loyalties divided. Stephens said in 1922, "things have come to such a pass under the commission form of government that if I walked into the office of our Chief of Police he'd likely as not tell me to go to hell."[86]

Stephens was defeated in his bid for re-election in 1927. He failed to get his party's nomination because of the challenge posed by M. L. Harris—who received enough votes to win the primary but failed to get enough votes to defeat Republican Frank Doyle in the general election. Harris' victory over Stephens was orchestrated by his brother-in-law, Locke Tarlton. Had he won, Stephens would not have survived his term. He died August 20, 1928. As it turned out, Frank Doyle did not survive long either—he died in office in 1933. Despite the ups and downs represented by these three lives, East St. Louis moved on. The city has been dragged through unspeakable horror, blatant corruption, and frustrating reforms; yet it remains. It would be wrong to call it resilience; "survival" would be a better term.

So much of the physical space these men occupied has disappeared over the century. The stately Howe Institute that John Bowman called home (and where he met his fate) near 10th and Ohio was flattened in the 1896 tornado and has long since been redeveloped. The opulent mansion Mayor Stephens built at 1010 Pennsylvania was the Oganski Funeral Home for some time, and is now just an open field. Locke Tarlton's home in the 600 block of Washington Place is now just a grassy corner. Still, their legacy is with us.

The place that John Bowman chartered at the outset of the Civil War now celebrates its sesquicentennial. The commercial streets that Malbern Stephens raised from the floodplain are still ten feet higher than the lots downtown (notice that the East St. Louis federal building is still entered from the second floor). The lax rules under which Locke Tarlton's empire thrived still remain only partially enforced. In a very real sense, the people of East St. Louis today are living with the consequences—good and bad—of decisions made long, long ago. Yet, like the river alongside it, East St. Louis just keeps rolling along.

End Notes:

1. Adolph B. Seuss. 1943. *The Romantic Story of Cahokia, Illinois*. Belleville, IL: Buechler Publishing. 105.

2. Seuss (1943) states 1852; the *Globe* obituary (1885) states 1854. Both imply that Bowman went to England first, and the *Globe* adds that there were other stops in Europe—but both concur that Bowman's destination in the US was the St. Louis area.

3. The historical record on both the time and place of Bowman's service as postmaster is unclear. This note will lay out the best information and argument to clarify Bowman's service. Bowman's obituary in the *St. Louis Globe Democrat* and the reprint of it in the *East St. Louis Gazette* refer to Bowman as being the postmaster of Knob Noster, Missouri—a small town in Johnson County near Sedalia. This is most likely an error, and this error was repeated in my book, *Made in USA: East St. Louis* (2003). The record has been set straight for me by Raymond "Sandy" Peters, great-grandson of John Bowman, through a story of amazing coincidence. The building that housed the Manchester Post Office where Bowman worked still stands at 14328 Manchester Road, Manchester, MO 63011. Unknowingly, this historic building was acquired by a Bowman descendant in the 1980s and during renovation, papers were found in the wall that had been signed by John Bowman as Postmaster. This should set the record straight regarding the location of Bowman's service. Adolph Seuss (1943) states that Bowman was indeed the postmaster of Manchester, and that Bowman assumed that office in 1854. The *Globe* obituary does not give a date for Bowman's appointment, but states that Bowman received his appointment from President James Buchanan—who did not assume the presidency until 1857. It would make sense that Bowman received his appointment in 1857. Such appointments were usually two years in length, and Bowman does not show up in East St. Louis until about 1860. The timing fits. Further, Senator Benton likely knew both Presidents who would have appointed Bowman—Pierce (if 1854) and Buchanan (if 1857) from their service together in the U.S. Senate in the 1840s. Though all were Democrats, Pierce was out of favor with his party and Benton supported Buchanan's presidency (even though his own son-in-law, John C. Fremont, was the Republican candidate against Buchanan!). Hence, it was probably Buchanan who made the appointment—making Bowman's term from 1857 to 1859. Benton died in 1858, which indicates that Bowman likely would not be reappointed in 1859 and, therefore, should move on to new opportunities—such as East St. Louis.

4. Robert A. Tyson. (1875) *History of East St. Louis*. East St. Louis, IL: John Haps and Company. 31. As noted on page 90 of *Made in USA: East St. Louis*, Bowman might have been introduced to East St. Louis real estate through Senator Benton. Gregoire Sarpy was a large landholder in colonial St. Louis, with considerable acreage in what is now Webster Groves, Missouri and East St. Louis, Illinois. Sarpy died in 1824, but Benton bought a considerable portion of Sarpy's Webster Groves holdings—later selling some of this land to Pierre Chouteau Jr., son of St. Louis' founder. It is conceivable that Bowman was introduced to the Sarpy holdings through Benton or Benton's estate.

5. L. U. Reavis. 1876. *The Future Great City of the World*. St. Louis: C. R. Barnes. Appendix, 65. John Bowman was the author of the "East St. Louis" portion of this volume's appendix. Though Reavis does not attribute it to him, the historical record does. See, for instance, *East St. Louis Today* (the Chamber of Commerce publication), January 1938, page 6.

6. Tyson (1875), 121-122.

7. "A Cowardly Assassin," *St. Louis Globe-Democrat*. November 21, 1885. 3.

8. For more on the National Road in Illinois, see Andrew Theising, "America's First Interstate: The National Road and its Reach Toward St. Clair County, Illinois," *The Confluence*. Jeffrey Smith, ed. Spring/Summer 2010. 4-15.

9. For a more thorough explanation of the Internal Improvement Program, see Andrew Theising. 2003. *Made in USA: East St. Louis*. St. Louis: Virginia Publishing. 67-68.

10. L. E. Robinson and Irving Moore. 1909. *History of Illinois*. Chicago: American Book Company. 112-113, 118. Also, Henry Hitchcock. 1887. *American State Constitutions*. New York: Putnam and Sons. 35-36, 44.

11. James Brasfield. 1997. "Local Government," *St. Louis Currents:*

A Guide to the Region and Its Resources. James O'Donnell, ed. St. Louis: Missouri Historical Society Press. 46.

12. Term from Daniel Boorstin, in Dennis Judd and Paul Kantor, eds. 1992. *Enduring Tensions in Urban Politics.* New York: MacMillan Publishing. 78-79.

13. Tyson, *History of East St. Louis,* 103.

14. "Across the River," *St. Louis Evening Post.* August 6, 1878. 1.

15. For a detailed description of these events, see Theising, 2003, *Made in USA,* pp. 72-83.

16. Thomas Furlong. 1912. *Fifty Years a Detective.* St. Louis: C. E. Barnett. 165.

17. Furlong, 1912, 174-175; "A Cowardly Assassin," November 21, 1885, 3.

18. Furlong, 1912, 174-175.

19. Furlong, 1912, 175.

20. A lengthier account of Clubb's role appears in Theising, 2003, *Made in USA: East St. Louis.* 80-88.

21. Multiple articles in the *East St. Louis Gazette,* November 7 and November 14, 1885; 2.

22. Furlong, 1912, 176.

23. "Is it Retribution? Captain Samuel C. Clubb, Upon an Inquiry Had in the St. Louis Probate Court, is Declared Insane," *East St. Louis Gazette.* April 24, 1886. 2.

24. "Attempted Assassination," *East St. Louis Gazette,* June 19, 1886. 2.

25. "A Cowardly Assassin," 3.

26. Furlong, 1912, 180.

27. Chapman Brothers. 1892. *Portrait and Biographical Record, St. Clair County, IL.* Chicago: Chapman Brothers. 137.

28. *Historical and Descriptive Review of Illinois, Volume I.* 1895. St. Louis: John Lethem. 200.

29. Chapman Brothers, 1892, 137-138.

30. See "The Tramp Element," *East St. Louis Gazette,* April 11, 1885. 2.

31. "The Captain," *East St. Louis Gazette,* April 11, 1885. 2.

32. "The Tramp Element," *East St. Louis Gazette,* April 11, 1885. 2.

33. "The Tramp Element," *East St. Louis Gazette,* April 11, 1885. 2.

34. See "A Damning Confession," *East St. Louis Gazette,* January 23, 1886. 2.

35. It is unclear to the author how such legislation could have passed the council where Bowmanites did not have a majority, or survive the veto pen of Mayor Joyce. The vote took place weeks before Bowman's murder—so the community had not yet swung behind the Bowmanites as strongly as it would after the assassination. Perhaps there was an extended absence that swung the council vote in favor of the Bowmanites. This could have been possible since two Anti-Bowmanite council members, Shea from Ward Two and Cunningham from Ward Three, were indicted during this time period and Shea does not return to the council in 1887 (though Cunningham does); the record also shows considerable absences for Alderman Bird

(Ward Four), elected in 1886 and who served only one term.

Another plausible explanation is that Anti-Bowmanites attempted to save face by supporting the legislation and then defeat it with a court challenge—which did move forward shortly after passage.

36. See series of articles in *East St. Louis Gazette,* May and June, 1884; and Furlong, 1912, 165-173.

37. See *East St. Louis Gazette,* June 19, 1886. 2.

38. "Deliverance at Last," *East St. Louis Gazette,* April 9, 1887. 2.

39. Chapman Brothers, 1892, 137.

40. Chapman Brothers, 1892, 137.

41. Chapman Brothers, 1892, 137.

42. Fekete, Thomas. 1907. "City of East St. Louis," *Historical Encyclopedia of Illinois and History of St. Clair County.* A. S. Wilderman and A. A. Wilderman, eds. Chicago: Munsell Publishing Company. Stephens' obituary in the *St. Louis Globe Democrat,* August 21, 1928, puts the indebtedness at $950,000, but corroborates the settlement amount. The Stephens biography by Chapman Brothers puts the indebtedness at $850,000. Fekete is probably the most reliable source on this, since he appears to be drawing information from primary records here and elsewhere in his essay.

43. "Death Comes at 10 a.m. at Hospital," *East St. Louis Daily Journal,* August 20, 1928. 2.

44. Fekete, 1907, 755.

45. Fekete, 1907, 755.

46. Fekete, 1907, 755.

47. *Historical and Descriptive Review of Illinois*, 1895, 200.

48. *Historical and Descriptive Review of Illinois*, 1895, 189.

49. Chapman Brothers, 1892, 137.

50. *Historical and Descriptive Review*, 1895, 189.

51. "M. M. Stephens, City Builder," *St. Louis Post-Dispatch*, August 21, 1928. Editorial.

52. "M. M. Stephens, 81,…," *St. Louis Globe Democrat*, August 21, 1928, 24.

53. "M. M. Stephens, 81,…" *St. Louis Globe Democrat,* August 21, 1928, 24.

54. This information is from the Stephens family history provided by his granddaughter, Betty Allen of Louisiana, MO; and from "Death Comes at 10 a.m. at Hospital," *East St. Louis Daily Journal*, August 20, 1928. 1, 2.

55. Chapman Brothers, 1892, 137.

56. "Death Comes…," *East St. Louis Daily Journal*, August 20, 1928. 1.

57. "G. L. Tarlton is Dead at Age 61," *East St. Louis Journal.* May 7, 1943. 2.

58. "George L. Tarlton," *Queen City Directory of East St. Louis and the East Side.* 1912. N/A. 1459.

59. "Canavan and Tarlton" (advertisement), *East St. Louis Daily Journal.* January 20, 1909. 6.

60. Chapman Brothers, 1892, 516-517.

61. "T. J. Canavan, Realtor, Dies," *East St. Louis Daily Journal.* March 3, 1940. 1.

62. For a more-detailed description of The Valley, see Theising, *Made in USA: East St. Louis*, 141-144.

63. Malcolm McLaughlin. 2005. *Power, Community, and Racial Killing in East St. Louis.* New York: Palgrave McMillan. 58.

64. McLaughlin, 2005, 58.

65. McLaughlin, 2005, 58.

66. McLaughlin, 2005, 60. I am indebted to Malcolm McLaughlin for bringing this story out of the pages of obscurity and identifying the primary sources associated with it. For more information, see his outstanding book referenced herein.

67. McLaughlin, 2005, 60.

68. U. S. House of Representatives, *Congressional Record.* Volume 56. 1918. Washington: Government Printing Office. 8830.

69. US House of Representatives, 1918, 8830.

70. US House of Representatives, 1918, 8830.

71. "A Divided Victory," *East St. Louis Daily Journal.* April 5, 1905. 2.

72. US House of Representatives, 1918, 8830.

73. Elliott Rudwick. 1964. *Race Riot at East St. Louis.* Chicago: University of Illinois Press. 176-177, 178, 180. See also Theising, *Made in USA: East St. Louis*, 137.

74. "Former East St. Louis Officials Go to Trial," *St. Louis Post Dispatch.* Feburary 4, 1915. 1.

75. "East Side Former Mayor Reveals a Big Vice System," *St. Louis Post Dispatch*, November 29, 1912. 1.

76. "Six Acquitted of Graft Charge in East St. Louis," *St. Louis Post Dispatch*, February 16, 1915. 1.

77. McLaughlin, 2005, 63; and Theising, 2003, 137-140.

78. Theising, 2003, 137.

79. Rudwick, 1964, 185.

80. "Mollman Polls Largest Majority on Record," *East St. Louis Mail.* April 6, 1917. 1.

81. US House of Representatives, 1918, 8830.

82. "G. L. Tarlton is Dead at 61," *East St. Louis Journal.* May 7, 1943. 1.

83. Theising, 2003, 187.

84. "M. M. Stephens, 81, Former Mayor of East St. Louis, Dies," *St. Louis Globe Democrat.* August 21, 1928. 24, and "M. M. Stephens, 9 Times Mayor of E. St. Louis, Dies," *St. Louis Post-Dispatch*, August 20, 1928.

85. "M. M. Stephens, 81, Former Mayor of East St. Louis, Dies," *St. Louis Globe Democrat.* August 21, 1928. 24.

86. "M. M. Stephens, 81, Former Mayor of East St. Louis, Dies," *St. Louis Globe Democrat.* August 21, 1928. 24.

Murphy Building Detail   Powell Photo

"East Boogie": As American as Cherry Pie

James T. Ingram

Columnist
St. Louis American

In 1960, a young, charismatic president by the name of John Fitzgerald Kennedy inspired America and, with his elegant wife and young family, ushered in the age of "Camelot" (at the White House) and, along with it, a sense of hope and optimism. His was the classic "American story"; born the heir to a political dynasty, a Harvard graduate, a war hero, his father a former ambassador and multimillionaire. Yet, and equally as American, was the unspoken Kennedy legacy: wealth gained as the result of patriarch Joseph Kennedy's days as a bootlegger and a not-so-public reputation as a philanderer, a trait that the Kennedy men all seemed to inherit from their father.

Malcolm Martin statue, 2010   Powell Photo

But, tragically and just as publicly as President Kennedy was worshipped and admired, his life was just as publicly snuffed out on the streets of Dallas, Texas, by an assassin's bullets.

In a parallel universe, East St. Louis, Illinois was as synonymous in its reputation as an all-American city as the Kennedy's were in their reputation as aristocrats.

In fact, in 1960 *Look* magazine and the National Municipal League named East St. Louis as an "All-America City".[1]

And as anyone who lived in, frequented, passed through, or migrated to East St. Louis during that period will tell you, that reputation was well-earned.

In 1960, East St. Louis (or "East Boogie" as she has become affectionately known) was a community of hard-working and family-oriented blue-collar workers.

East Boogie was home to an abundance of profitable businesses, solid schools, strong, close-knit neighborhoods, and churches.

An industrial giant, East St. Louis was home to the Swift, Armour Company and other meat packing plants, National Stockyards (so famous that John Kennedy made an obligatory stop there during his presidential campaign) and Aluminum Ore Corporation which, at that time, was the world's largest aluminum processing center.

It was the reason that my grandfather, my father, and other poor black southerners migrated to East Boogie, knowing that within a few days of their arrival, they would be assured steady and gainful employment; a far cry from their slave-like existence in the deep south.

It was the epitome of what white America defined as successful: steady jobs, homeowners with white picket fences, men working while the women, by and large, were housewives and homemakers. Everyone knew their role and stayed in their respective lanes.

Racially, the lane for African-Americans (prior to the mid 1960s) was the south end of East Louis, while whites lived wherever their wallets could afford.

Much of that was the residue of America's segregationist legacy and exacerbated by the legacy of America's most savage "race riot"(or massacre) of July 2, 1917, in which blacks were slaughtered

Collinsville Avenue, 2010   Powell Photo

by whites for daring to displace disgruntled white laborers.[2]

The aftermath was horrific, with black men, women, and children ruthlessly murdered simply for having the audacity to be black and the temerity to be in the path of white outrage.

That travesty was further exacerbated by the racism of President Woodrow Wilson, whose benign neglect was captured by myriad national newspapers of the day.

This is the post-riot legacy that, to this day, exists in East St. Louis and served as the catalyst for the eventual mass exodus of whites (from East Boogie) to the surrounding communities of Belleville, Fairview Heights, O'Fallon, and Shiloh during the 1960s and 1970s.

And that exodus was the beginning of the erosion of East St. Louis' "All-America" status and emergence as a depleted, deteriorated, shell of its former self, replete with corrupt politics, next to a non-existent tax base and a reputation as the violent, forlorn epicenter of hopelessness for its, nearly, all-black residents.

Nothing better personifies that deterioration than "downtown" East St. Louis, Collinsville Avenue, a collection of check cashing facilities, wig shops and hair supply joints, typical of urban decay; with the highlight being the once prominent Spivey Building, a 13-story boarded up, crumbling, eyesore (and the city's tallest building).[3]

Once upon a time, Collinsville Avenue was the fulfillment of a shopper's dream, with stores selling everything from furniture, clothing, music, pharmacy items as well as entertainment at the ornate Majestic Movie Theater. Today, that is as much ancient history as the Egyptian Pyramids or The Sphinx.

That's because all of these factors, seemingly, took East St. Louis from boom to doom overnight and, over 50 year later, time and changes in leadership and racial demographics have produced zero results or progress toward a real solution.

But, "violence is as American as cherry pie", as former Black Panther H. Rap Brown once stated.[4]

America exists because of violence: from the American Revolution to the slaughter and displacement of the Native American population, to the capture and enslavement of Africans who were used to build this country and create her wealth. From the assassinations of President Kennedy to Dr. Martin Luther King, Jr. and Malcolm X, violence has always been America's legacy and, *de facto*, change agent.

So, in a real sense East St. Louis, Illinois, has learned her lesson well, all too well, consistently leading the state, the metropolitan region (and, on occasion, the nation) in violence and murder statistics and infamy as a "most dangerous" city.

Yet, and equally as American, East St. Louis, per capita, is unmatched in terms of producing excellence on a national and international scale.

Who is the world's greatest female athlete of all-time? That would be East St. Louis native and Olympian Jackie Joyner-Kersee. Oh, and I'd be remiss in failing to mention that, just by mere coincidence, her brother Al was also an Olympic medalist.

Their example would, later, inspire another East St. Louisian, Dawn Harper, to win gold at the 2008 Beijing Olympics.

NFL Hall of Famer and legendary San Diego Charger, Kellen Winslow, never played football prior to gracing the halls of East St. Louis Senior High. Left to his own devices, he would have been an elite chess player. But he now owns the distinction of being one of the most prolific tight ends in professional football history.

Darius Miles, former NBA star, leaped into the professional ranks fresh out of East St. Louis Sr. High, parlaying his acrobatic dunking style into a lucrative career.

Unfortunately, that promising basketball career later became more associated with run-ins with the law, drug violations and a propensity for being in the wrong place (with the wrong people) at the wrong time.

Still, "only in America" (to quote boxing promoter Don King) could a Darius Miles be catapulted from the depths of the ghetto to millionaire status in the blink of an eye, then (with the same speed) squander his golden opportunity.

Perhaps, Miles should have consulted with another prominent East St. Louis native, sports sociologist Dr. Harry Edwards, who completed his PhD at Cornell University and is a widely sought after author, speaker, panelist and consultant for professional athletes and sports organizations. But, in Miles' case, that would mirror responsible behavior, which would be out of character with the troubled ex-NBA star.

And East St. Louis' athletic dominance even extends to the

world of tennis, with the verbal ferocity and longevity of the original "bad boy" of tennis, Jimmy Connors, who (despite his claims of Belleville, Illinois as his "home") was born in East St. Louis on September 2, 1952.[5]

Connors' regular, profanity-laced outbursts, foul temper and courtside tirades were his calling card. Yet it's interesting and, yes, hypocritical how tennis star Serena Williams was criticized over her use of profanity during a much publicized outburst, when Connors' potty-mouth was accepted as par-for the-course.

The only distinction: Connors is a white male and Williams is a black female. That sort of hypocrisy is as American as the legacy of slavery.

Then there's the world of music, and few musicians can rival the style, the swagger and artistry of East St. Louis great and international jazz icon Miles Davis. From East Boogie to Paris, Davis' reputation as the personification of "cool" is unmatched and unquestionable.

In the world of politics, East St. Louis (before I deal with her shameful past and present) has been a producer of world class

leadership.

Donald Franchot McHenry, who grew up in East St. Louis, was the 15th United States Ambassador to the United Nations (from 1970-1981) under President Jimmy Carter, after serving as a member of Carter's transition staff at the State Department.[6]

Senator Dick Durbin, born in East St. Louis and a graduate of Assumption High School, is the 47th U.S. Senator from the state of Illinois. The senior senator holds the seat which was formerly held by his mentor, the late Paul Simon and, at this writing, serves

Spivey Building entrance, 2010   Powell Photo

as the Assistant Majority Leader or "Majority Whip", the Senate's second highest position. But it doesn't stop there.

Even in the world of Hollywood, the Hudlin brothers (Reginald and Warrington), Harvard and Yale graduates, respectively, learned much of their flair for depicting "the hood" and African-American culture in such colorful terms, from their East St. Louis upbringing, only to showcase it in such classic Hollywood films as *House Party, Boomerang, BeBe's Kids, and Serving Sara.*

The roll call could go on, but the point is clear; that it is virtually impossible to name any significant field of achievement or endeavor, on the American (or world stage) without there being some significant contribution by someone with East St. Louis roots.

Now, I began with all of these East St. Louis paragons of achievement, realizing that even an element as precious as a diamond begins with humble roots, first as chunk of coal subjected to immense pressure which, ultimately, results in a sparkling gem of extraordinary value and beauty.

I've always maintained that it is this humility, day-to-day pressure and "underdog" status of growing up in East Boogie that has (aside from my parents) been the motivational and driving force in my life.

Yes, I grew up in an East St. Louis nuclear family with 3 siblings and parents married over 52 years (at this writing), with grandparents who were married nearly 60 years.

Our family activities were traditional: Shopping for groceries at National Food Store

or the A&P with my mother and grandmother, followed by browsing for sales at the old W.T Grant's department store at the now defunct Shop City.

Mornings near 23rd and State Street were hectic affairs, with the delivery of diapers to new mothers. Milk, butter and cheese were delivered fresh daily and I vividly remember my grandparents having their farm fresh eggs delivered to them every week.

Mr. Foggy, their neighbor, made his own pork sausage and was the "Jimmy Dean" of East St Louis, with rolls of his sausage prominently displayed in every market and corner store.

Family entertainment (for us) was at the old Cahokia Drive-In on Saturday nights. I joined the Okaw Valley Cub Scouts, Webelo Troop, then Boy Scouts. Recreation consisted of bowling at Shop City Bowl or skating at the Skate King Memorial skating rink. Sundays were spent in Sunday school, youth choir, and usher board at my church. Cardinal games with my friends, with earnings from my paper route, became a personal passion and diversion from my academic endeavors.

My neighborhood was eclectic, with parents who ran the gamut from school teachers and principals to blue collar workers (like my parents). My peers and I would eventually go off to college. Same would attend engineering school at places like Northwestern, Boston University, and Rolla. Others went on to become teachers or entered the military.

Yet, on that same block, were mentally challenged children and one particular household which

produced a pimp, a Marine (who just happened to be gay), and a felon. Unfortunately, two other neighbors became overwhelmed by drug addiction; one an honor student and the other a once immaculately dressed pre-med student at Howard University who, later, became homeless and, finally, succumbed to his addiction.

There were also three white families living on our block, as my family played our role in integrating our neighborhood. One of those families, the "Gleeson", was a large family with kids who were, roughly, in my age range. One of the Gleeson kids became a frequent playmate of mine and, years later, (after moving away to Belleville) became an attorney and is now, an Associate Judge for St. Clair County, Illinois.

Our next door neighbors Lillian -Moberg, a Jewish palm reader, and Albert Phelps, a self-employed upholsterer, played the role of surrogate grandmother and grandfather figures who provided my siblings and me with intricately decorated Easter baskets and Halloween bags loaded with candy. They remained in that neighborhood until I enrolled in college, at which time the crime in East St. Louis was becoming a major concern.

That was my neighborhood: diverse, progressive (despite the circumstances), yet as dysfunctional as are most "All-American" fairytale characters.

Yet, despite these Norman Rockwell-like descriptions of various aspects of my coming-of-age in East St. Louis, I also vividly remember being robbed at gunpoint after collecting the money from my daily *Metro-East Journal* paper route.

The robber, donning a stocking cap, waited patiently until I had collected my last dime, and then instructed me to lie face down and count to 200 as he fled. Interestingly enough, to this day I know who this lazy imbecile was, a fact made easy to discern by the gleaming gold tooth that betrayed him from beneath his mother's old stocking.

It was so devastating (but not surprising), that my father insisted upon escorting me (packing his trusty pistol) for quite some time following that experience.

Maybe one day my robber will have the opportunity to read these words from prison, which is where he has resided for most of his worthless life. That's provided, of course, that this miscreant can read.

Unfortunately, my robbery wasn't my first (or last) exposure to East St. Louis criminality. From having my first car burglarized outside of the old Regal Room nightclub to having a bullet shatter my bedroom window (at my parent's home), lodging itself in a wall where, normally I might have been sitting, were other instances. Such was life in East Boogie.

However, my understanding of historical criminality in East Boogie was the product of actually *reading* the *Metro-East Journal* before delivering it to my paper route patrons.

So, even at the age of 15, I wasn't oblivious to East St. Louis' reputation for violence, from actual gangster-like activity to her many political criminals (white and black) who had contributed to the demise of a once stellar community.

From indictments at city hall and the board of education, unlike many of my young peers, I knew the names of East St. Louis' movers, shakers, the famous and the infamous.

Like Charles Merritts, the once powerful black political powerbroker that was groomed under the tutelage of Alvin Fields (East St. Louis' last white mayor), John T. English, Tom Lewis and

Stately house on Bond Avenue, 2010   Powell Photo

Esther Saverson (one of the early black political big shots in East Boogie).[7]

Merritts would eventually become school board president, but was later crushed in his bid to become East St. Louis' first black mayor by James Williams, who would rob Merritts of his greatest political ambition.

Compounding that loss was Merritts' eventual indictment for allegedly taking kickbacks as president of School District 189, as well as for allegedly putting out a contract for the murder of Clyde C. Jordan, publisher of the *East St. Louis Monitor* and a fellow school board member.

There were other names as well: Elmo Bush, Mayor William Mason, et.al., some felons, others unindicted co-conspirators and, yet others, social climbers and "society" celebs . I followed their records, achievements and misdeeds in the same way that my teenage friends followed the St. Louis Spirits (of the old ABA), the "Big Red" (Old St. Louis football Cardinals) and the St. Louis Cardinals.

Then, I was, also, equally aware of the legacy of Frank "Buster" Wortman, Al Capone's counterpart in East St. Louis, who monopolized everything from nightclubs, illegal gambling to prostitution from the 1940s -1950s after the demise of the Shelton brothers crime family.[8]

And what's more American than the good old fashioned romanticizing of organized crime? From Al Capone to the modern-day mafia, in the person of the John Gotti, America just loves a good gangster tale.

That's why movies like *The Godfather* and *Goodfellas* and the TV series *The Sopranos* will go down in history as American Hollywood classics.

East St. Louis is no different in its recollection and embellishment of folklore regarding Buster Wortman and the gang. Wortman's Leavenworth and Alcatraz pedigree may as well have been Harvard and Yale degrees if you listened to the old timers; but isn't that the case with most American gangster tales?

And, while the East St. Louis

East St. Louis City Hall, 2010   Powell Photo

criminal status quo may no longer be the exclusive domain of the white mafia types, the present-day African-American leadership (in East St. Louis) seems to have learned their deviant lessons from those who once ran East St. Louis' political and criminal plantation.

Take, for instance, Charlie Powell, who was East St. Louis' most recent political boss. Two years removed from a federal prison stint, Powell was once the head of East St. Louis' democratic machine (and a city councilman) before being sent to prison for a conspiracy to buy votes in the 2004 general election.

Another, recent department head, Kelvin Ellis, a felon who originally served prison time for extortion, was returned to East St. Louis city government, upon his release, only to return to prison after running a prostitution ring from city hall and attempting to have a federal witness murdered (which turned out to be one of his prostitutes).

And despite the fact that the city of East St. Louis reports to a financial advisory authority and the school district was under oversight only a few years ago, public outrage seems tepid at best.

The street mantra of "don't hate the player; hate the game" is the rule of thumb in East St. Louis "politricks". It's a slogan that discourages whistleblowers and those who would expose the bloodsuckers of the poor.

As a columnist covering the East Boogie political scene for nearly 20 years, I can always identify

those who benefit from East St. Louis political dysfunction, because they tend to be my only critics.

In general, words of appreciation and "thanks" (for my columns) invariably come from either those who don't live in East St. Louis or from those who are victims of the politics of East St. Louis.

Unfortunately, despite my exposes and journalistic rants, seldom do those victims make their presence known at the city council meetings or school board meetings, where their very presence is the one thing that would create real and lasting change.

Yet, even their indifference and apathy are all–American in that, with the exceptional voter participation experienced in the election of President Barack Obama, most local, state, and national elections reflect the mass indifference, frustrations, and apathy of the American public by the absolute lack of voter participation at the polls.

So, what do we do in America (and by extension in East Boogie) when corruption and ineptitude are rampant and public apathy has become the normal coping mechanism for dealing with the poverty and decay that has become an overwhelming reality? In the fictitious 2004 graphic novel, *Birth of a Nation*, by *The Boondocks* cartoon creator, Aaron McGruder and East St. Louis native and Hollywood writer/ director Reginald Hudlin, the authors pose the question: Would anyone care if East St. Louis seceded from the Union? The

authors create an imaginary plot in which the national election hinges on East St. Louis' electoral votes. Subsequently a black billionaire and mayor of East St. Louis devise a plot to secede and arrange an offshore bank (albeit in America) to finance the new "Republic of Blackland", whose national anthem is sung to the tune of "Good Times".

The satire, while absurd and hilarious, in many ways mirrors the hilarity of East St. Louis city government, its schools, its buffoonery and the almost cartoon-like manner in which East St. Louis leadership has mismanaged this very American slice of reality for over 100 years, while her citizens sit on the sidelines as spectators to their own demise. The same scenario played out after George W. Bush, with the help of the U.S. Supreme Court, literally stole the American presidency in 2000. Filmmaker Michael Moore, in his 2004 film *Fahrenheit 9/11* did a brilliant job of exposing that fact; but Americans returned the inept Bush to the White House in 2004, allowing him to lead America to the brink of near financial ruin.

So, the answer to East St. Louis' woes (as is the case for America's ills) lies not in the politics or the leadership, but in the people. When America, when East Boogie, when the *people* become "sick and tired of being sick and tired", then all of these "American" problems will become a distant memory. The real question is when will "America" (which includes East St. Louis) FINALLY become "sick and tired"?

End Notes:

1. Steve Heckel, "An All-American City," *LAS News Magazine*, Winter, 2008.

2. Elliott Rudwick, *Race Riot at East St. Louis*. (Carbondale, Illinois: Southern Illinois University Press, 1964).

3. Jonathan Kozol, *Savage Inequalities*. (New York: Crown Publishers, 1992), 7.

4. Jamar Edwards, Plot Summary for American as Cherry pie http://www.imdb.com/titile/tt0462178/plotsummary

5. Bud Collins, Biography of Jimmy Connors, http://www.atpworltour.com/Tennis/Players/Co/J/Jimmy -Connors.aspx

6. Donald McHenry, http://en.wikipedia.org/wiki/Donald_McHenry

7. Andrew J Theising, *Made in USA; East St. Louis*. (St. Louis: Virginia Publishing, 2003), 25.

8. Ibid, 143.

9. Aaron McGruder, and Reginald Hudlin, *Birth of a Nation*. (New York: Crown Publishers, 2004).

Gambling on the Economic Future of East St. Louis: The Casino Queen

Anne F. Boxberger Flaherty, Ph.D.

Department of Political Science
Southern Illinois University Edwardsville

The Casino Queen has been a significant source of financial support for the city of East St. Louis since its introduction in 1993. The Casino Queen has generated more than $160 million in tax revenue for East St. Louis between 1993 and 2009. In addition to these direct funds, Casino Queen, Inc. has also contributed money, support, and services to the city, non-profit organizations, and residents as part of its ongoing commitment to the social and economic development and future of East St. Louis. An issue that the city needs to address in the future is the large proportion of its operating budget that comes from taxes generated by the Casino Queen. Casino revenues—and the resulting taxes—have been reduced in East St. Louis and across the country in the wake of the economic downturn that began in 2007. This has meant challenges for many urban and state governments, including East St. Louis and the state of Illinois, that anticipate and rely on gaming related funds to provide basic services to citizens.

The casino entrance on Riverpark Drive, 2010   Powell Photo

State Oversight and Gaming in Illinois

The city of East St. Louis faced a deep economic crisis during the 1970s and 1980s. The loss of industrial and manufacturing businesses, employment for residents, and mismanagement in city government nearly resulted in bankruptcy. The loss of businesses meant that the City of East St. Louis was left without a steady source of tax revenue or even sources of employment. The city resorted to levying extremely high property taxes for the same residents who were now increasingly unable to meet those burdens. The late 1980s and early 1990s were a low point for the government of East St. Louis, which faced a budget crisis so severe that it was essentially unable to function. The city could not provide basic services such as garbage collection for residents, supplying police and fire equipment, or meeting payroll for employees.[1] With the city in precipitous economic decline, the state government intervened in 1990 with the Illinois Financially Distressed Cities Act (IFDCA). The IFDCA prevented the city from declaring bankruptcy and authorized a state loan to pay off the city's debts of nearly $75 million. The IFDCA also appointed a state panel named the East St. Louis Financial Advisory Authority (ESLFAA) to oversee the finances of the city until it could produce and implement balanced budgets for a ten-year period.[2]

At nearly the same time that the State of Illinois was dealing with the decline of East St. Louis and other urban industrial governments, the state was also facing its own serious economic problems. Many government entities (from local to national) faced economic challenges during the 1980s and sought alternate means of generating income. In this environment, states began to explore the option of gambling and the accompanying taxes to generate additional revenue.[3] New Hampshire had been the first state to reintroduce the lottery in 1963, the first time since the 1800s that lotteries were considered legal, and many other states followed suit. As a form of entertainment tax, lotteries were considered more politically palatable than income taxes or other compulsory tax increases for all citizens. Illinois adopted a statewide lottery in 1973, earmarking the funds generated for education in 1985.[4]

Riverboat gaming and casinos were also considered by lawmakers across the country in the late 1980s as a means of aiding both state and urban communities falling into economic trouble.[5] Nationally, plans for casinos were supported by politicians as a means of generating much-needed tax revenue for both local and state governments. Iowa allowed casino development in 1989, prompting Illinois lawmakers to act as the residents of Illinois (and their money) left the state to gamble at the new facilities in neighboring Iowa. In February 1990 the Illinois Riverboat Gambling Act (IRGA) was signed into law. Ten casino licenses were allowed, and gambling had to be conducted on riverboat facilities. Specific tax schedules were laid out (and later modified) defining the percentage of revenue to be collected as taxes by the state and by local communities. The first riverboat casino operation in Illinois opened in Alton, about 30 miles north of East St. Louis, in 1991.[6] The plans for a casino operation in East St. Louis were not far behind.

The Development of the Casino Queen

After the passage of the Illinois gaming law, the idea of a casino was floated as a potential solution to some of the economic problems of East St. Louis. Private investors applied to the state for a gaming license at the same time they entered into discussions with government and property owners in East St. Louis. The original home of the Casino Queen was a four-story riverboat made to resemble the riverboats of the 19th century. The boat could carry as many as 1,800 passengers and 200 crew members.[7] The development was supported by the ESLFAA as well as local investors with the hopes of encouraging broader economic development and growth in East St. Louis. Investors and the city of East St. Louis were reported by *Bond Buyer* magazine to have put in $43 million to help develop the gambling boat and the administrative complex.[8]

The Casino Queen began operations in East St. Louis in 1993. It was the biggest new employer to enter the city for decades, and many East St. Louisans sought one of the 900 jobs available when it opened.[9] The casino remains a significant source of jobs in the city, second only to the city school district in terms of number of employees. At the time of the casino's opening, the proportion of employees who would have to be residents of the city was a matter of contention.

While the owners initially promised 30 percent of the jobs to local East St. Louisans, they were under pressure from city officials to bring the number to 50 percent. The Aldermanic Council made a statement that locals should get 80 percent of the jobs.[10] A report from early 1993 shows that about 350 of 1,100 jobs were held by East St. Louis residents, meeting the 30 percent threshold but far short of the 50 percent or 80 percent goals.[11] Given the lack of employment opportunities in East St. Louis at the time, this was a significant number in terms of employment. For employees, a job with the Casino Queen meant not only direct employment and income, but also benefits for themselves and their families, patronage for local doctors and the hospital, and additional money redistributed into the local economy.

The Casino Queen proved its viability as a source of direct revenue for the city almost immediately. Only open for a portion of the year, casino taxes brought nearly four million dollars into the city in 1993. This allowed the city to reduce its property taxes for businesses and residents, which had been among the highest in the state. The city was able to put together a budget (in itself a political feat in the early 1990s) that added firefighters and policemen, paid bills, restored basic services, and began to pay off state loans.[12] The first full year of operations in 1994 pumped over ten million dollars into East St. Louis. This more than doubled the city's general fund from $9 million to $19 million.[13] The tax revenue generated for the city has hovered between $9 and $11 million every year since then (with the exception of 2007), and has continued to make up a huge proportion of the city's income. A *St. Louis Post-Dispatch* article in 1994 entitled "Seeds of Hope" reflected on the positive changes in the city: "The Casino Queen, the largest new employer in decades, swept into town, bringing jobs and millions of dollars for the city's treasury. The raft load of money from 'The Queen' has resulted in new fire trucks, more police and firefighters and a lower property tax rate ...."[14]

There is a flip side to this success:

TABLE 1:

Casino Queen Receipts and Distributions to the State and City of East St. Louis

Year	Adjusted Gross Receipts	Local Tax Collected	State Tax Collected
1993	51,541,276	3,793,015	8,947,142
1994	129,785,446	10,161,155	23,139,700
1995	128,197,800	10,293,069	23,112,849
1996	128,987,975	10,555,319	23,454,116
1997	116,590,371	9,437,080	21,096,117
1998	116,486,988	9,254,006	25,895,369
1999	138,202,218	9,719,782	31,762,447
2000	156,880,385	9,954,810	36,681,103
2001	155,082,587	9,780,703	36,063,984
2002	156,943,162	9,895,991	40,184,130
2003	158,033,927	9,926,617	52,995,840
2004	166,262,134	10,483,185	63,224,264
2005	168,724,765	10,545,446	54,343,093
2006	174,279,291	10,820,363	53,995,657
2007	188,624,732	11,738,204	59,547,076
2008	160,194,391	10,292,397	44,166,962
2009	147,539,524	9,623,667	39,343,475

(Data from the Illinois Gaming Board Annual Report 2009)

the health of the city's budget is now closely tied to the health of the casino's revenue and the accompanying taxes. The tax revenue from the casino has consistently been a major source of income for the city, in some years constituting as much as 50 percent of the general fund, so when the casino suffers there is little buffer for the city's often precarious finances.[15] This has come into play during the economic recession that began in 2007, and was cited as a major concern about the city in the 2005 report of the ESLFAA, a scathing document which offers a dismal view of the city's economic future. The authors warn in the report that without additional development, attentive management, and long-term planning, East St. Louis stands

in grave danger of backsliding into another period of economic turmoil.[17]

The State of Illinois has also relied on gaming as a source of revenue. After the initial law, the state raised taxes on gaming operations multiple times. In 1998, the state of Illinois passed a gaming law that increased state tax rates and included a "boat in a moat" provision that allowed gambling facilities to move off rivers into land-based moats. The Riverboat Gambling Act was amended in 1999 to allow riverboat gaming operations to remain permanently moored at dock sites without conducting cruises. This meant that patrons could board at any time and stay as long as they wished, rather than having to hold to set cruising times. The

change increased overall gambling revenue (people gambled and spent more in the casino) and sent far more money to the state, but actually decreased head tax amounts going to East St. Louis. The reason for this is that head tax was now only being paid once. Previously, the head tax was paid for every gambler each time a two hour-cruise began. So, while the change brought immediate payoffs for the state, it also resulted in a loss of revenue and resulting layoffs for East St. Louis.[18]

Illinois raised taxes for gaming facilities again in 2002, lifting the top tax rate from 35 percent to 50 percent. Then in 2003, the legislature approved another hike and raised the top tax rate to a staggering 70 percent for those in the highest category for income.

CHART 1:

State and Local Tax Dollars Paid by the Casino Queen

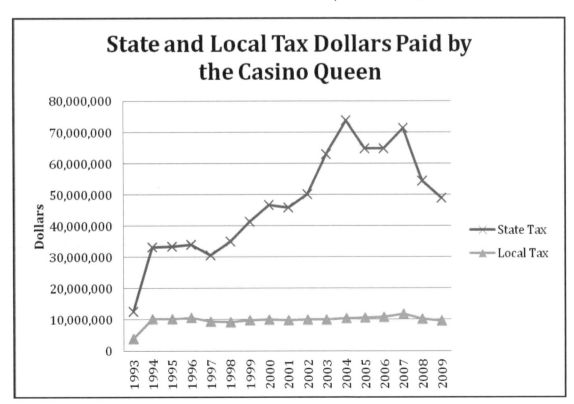

(Data from the Illinois Gaming Board Annual Report 2009)

For those facilities in the lower revenue ranges, taxes were raised as much as 7.5 percent. Along with the 5 percent guaranteed to East St. Louis, therefore, the Casino Queen now pays a state tax rate of around 45 percent based on its revenues. The state's willingness to increase gaming taxes has been a major challenge for all casino operations in the state, which have struggled to keep profits high enough to make ongoing business worthwhile.[19] Increases in state taxes have cost the Alton Belle and Casino Queen millions of dollars, decreased profit margins, and made it harder to compete against competitors on the Missouri side of the Mississippi River, which have lower tax rates and operate under different state regulatory requirements.[20]

The Casino Queen was developed as an enterprise that would offer economic benefits for the city of East St. Louis as well as the state of Illinois. As discussed above, the needs of the state budget have meant several increases in taxes for casinos. In 2010, the nine gaming operators in Illinois are expected to contribute over $500 million to the state's General Fund, which is used for purposes such as education, human services, healthcare, and family services. This makes up about 3.5 percent of the total general fund budget, or 3 percent of all appropriated funds for the state.[21] Just as there are concerns about the reliance of the city on gaming funds, the state has increasingly relied on and taxed casinos in an attempt to balance budgets. While the demands of the state have increased, there have been no increases for the city's benefit.

At some point, there is the danger that the State of Illinois (which again faces a massive deficit and budget crisis in 2010) may increase taxes again and lean too heavily on gaming for revenue. This may put gaming operators out of business, harm the state, and devastate cities such as East St. Louis or nearby Alton, which have come to count on casino taxes for funding day-to-day operations.

The Casino Queen has continued to pursue new avenues for development in order to increase revenues in the face of city, state, and market changes. A related area of success—both for the gaming facility and for the city in general—has been the addition of services for tourism, such as an RV park and the Casino Queen hotel. In 1998, the Casino Queen added an RV park, which was immediately popular and saw more than 12,000 visitors in 1999, its first full year. While many of the RV park visitors gamble, others come primarily to take advantage of the park and its services as a stand alone destination.[22] In January of 2000, the Casino Queen also opened a 157-room hotel as part of a larger plan for development.[23]

After the state law was changed to allow gaming to leave rivers, the owners of the Casino Queen began to develop ambitious plans for a new land-based casino and entertainment complex.[24] The new, modern facility was expected to generate increased business. The plan for a $150 million project on 80 acres was the largest development project in the city for 50 years that proposed a

park, lookout and other outdoor

facilities.[25] The plans were put on hold when Illinois raised taxes for gaming operations in 2002 and 2003, but ultimately the project continued. Another hindrance in the development of the new facility was local politics, which again caused a delay. After the initial deal was made with the city government—which had promised $11 million in support—Mayor Carl Officer said the agreement was not finally approved and could be changed. His attempt to renegotiate the terms was met by disagreement within the city government itself, and ultimately the original agreement prevailed.[27] The actual cost of the final Casino Queen development project was around $92 million.

The new Casino Queen was seen as a way to compete in a market that was expanding rapidly, with several new facilities having opened on the Missouri side of the river in the 2000s. The new land-based facility expanded the Casino Queen's casino floor from 27,000 square feet to 38,000 and floated in a ten-foot-deep moat. Importantly for the city, the anticipated increase in business meant that tax revenues were expected to bring in an additional $1 million to $1.5 million per year.[28] After about one year of construction the 207,500-square-foot facility opened on schedule in August 2007.[29] There was a push to open the new facility before the opening of the new Lumière casino on the St. Louis side of the river in the fall of 2007. The timing of the new Casino Queen reopening and its appeal gave it a market edge and a banner year. The casino brought in more business than ever before and also generated more money than ever before, over $11.7 million in taxes for the City of East St. Louis.

Since 2007, however, the Casino Queen (along with the other gaming facilities across the country) has seen a downturn. In 2008, the Casino Queen distributions to the City of East St. Louis declined 12 percent, from $11,738,204 in 2007 to 10,292,397 in 2008. They continued to decline in 2009, with a decrease of 6.5 percent to $9,663,627 in taxes distributed to the city. For 2008 and 2009, however, the local revenues for the Casino Queen did decline less than the state average of almost 20 percent in 2008 and 7.75 percent in 2009. In 2007, all casinos in the state sent $115,727,277 in taxes to local governments; in 2008, taxes to local governments came out at $93,095,279 and in 2009, it

was down to $85,885,708. This dramatic decline has meant challenges for both casino operators and local governments in dealing with the inhospitable economic climate, a trend that is continuing into 2010. The state has also been hit hard, with the total state tax payments from casinos going from $718,157,094 in 2007 to $473,648,638 in 2008 (a drop of over 34 percent) and $409,510,245 in 2009, a further decline of 13.5 percent.[30]

The downturn in gaming revenues across the state of Illinois has been attributed to both the overall decline in the national and state economies beginning in 2007 as well as the passage of the Smoke Free Illinois Act in 2008, banning smoking from casino floors.[31] The Casino Queen, as part of the metropolitan St. Louis region, has also faced stiff competition

from other area casinos. The Argosy Alton and Casino Queen both operate in Illinois, while the Missouri side of the river is home to the Ameristar, Harrah's President (closing in 2010), and the two most recent casinos, the Lumière (which opened in 2007) and the newest facility, the River City Casino, which opened in March 2010. Another hit for Illinois operators has been the repeal of the loss limits in Missouri, which had previously steered those who wished to gamble with larger amounts of money into Illinois.

The decline of tax flow from the Casino Queen to the City of East St. Louis has combined with the loss of other tax revenues to create pressing economic problems for the city. In the beginning of 2009, the city was forced to eliminate six unfilled

Side view of the casino hotel, 2010 Powell Photo

police positions and struggled to continue to provide fire services as the operating budget failed to meet expectations.[32] In June 2010, members of the city government proposed the reduction of the police force by laying off 27 of the 62 officers because of declines in business, property, and gaming taxes. The proposal was initially rejected and met with a public outcry.[33] In July the plan was revisited and on August 1, 2010 the city eliminated jobs for "37 employees, including 19 of its 62 police officers, 11 firefighters, four public works employees, and three administrators." The layoffs were a response to a massive budget shortfall, due in part to tax revenues from the Casino Queen that were nearly $900,000 below expected levels in 2009.[34] The situation clearly points to the city's need for diversification of income and better long-term economic planning.

Community Involvement

The commitment and contributions of the Casino Queen to East St. Louis have gone beyond taxes. The corporation has also remained invested and involved in various projects to benefit the city and non-profit organizations that serve the city, and its residents. The Casino Queen Foundation became active in 1994 to support the surrounding community, citizens, and businesses through investment and support.[35]

From its inception, the Casino Queen Foundation began a program for distributing low-interest small business loans for East St. Louisans, setting the minimum five-year total investment at $2.5 million. A major problem in East St. Louis

had been the lack of available capital; new businesses or programs struggled to get off the ground and were unable to secure loans. The Casino Queen Foundation's small loan program was designed to offer loans between about $10,000 and $15,000 at low interest to help encourage business development, particularly in needed business areas such as family restaurants or a farmers market.[36] The Foundation also contributed to the early development of the East St. Louis Small Business Development Center, designed to provide training, services, and counseling for small business start-ups.[37]

The Casino Queen Foundation has also remained committed to its pledge to continue to bring money and support to the broader East St. Louis community, donating to groups such as the Big Brothers Big Sisters, scholarship foundations, musical and dance troupes, and other community groups.[38] The Foundation has offered a great deal of support to and through the school system, such as a $25,000 donation to the Lion's Club for vision screening through local School District 189.[39] Other involvement within the East St. Louis school district includes a range of educational and training programs that promote leadership, community involvement, and good citizenship among students.[40] Contributions have also been made to surrounding communities, such as a $1,000 grant to a Catholic school in nearby Belleville, Illinois, to help provide computers for families that could not afford them on their own.[41] The Foundation has also regularly sponsored

a Holiday Toyland program, distributing toys and gifts to up to 3,000 children in East St. Louis each Christmas season.[42]

In addition, the management and owners of the Casino Queen have partnered in programs that work more directly with the city. In 2007, the Casino Queen joined Mayor Alvin Parks and representatives from the city and School District 189 to work on the physical clean-up of the city. This was seen as both a short-term goal and part of encouraging community service and volunteerism over the long term. The Casino Queen has also offered physical support for the partnership, providing supplies such as lawnmowers and trash bags.[43]

Ongoing Issues

Wherever there are gaming establishments, regardless of the good that they bring to the surrounding community and economy, there are often concerns about the negative repercussions. In East St. Louis, faced with so many challenges before the casino was introduced, it may be harder to attribute problems directly to the casino. Still there are ongoing concerns and challenges that face the Casino Queen and its relationship with the city and residents.

Political conflict and change have been a recurring concern for all businesses in East St. Louis. One specific example, mentioned above, was the disagreement with Mayor Officer during the development of plans to build a new facility. Political disagreements and transitions have been an issue for East St.

Louis over an extended period of time, and have at times been a hindrance to bringing in other business development or addressing the challenges that the city faces. Political changes and economic demands from the state have also hindered the growth and development of the Casino Queen as it has been forced to contribute more and more to state taxes.[44]

As has been discussed, even with the support of the Casino Queen's tax revenue the City of East St. Louis has continued to face economic struggles. The city government went into a crisis in 2002 in response to a massive budget shortfall in 2001. Since the Casino Queen opened in 1993, this was the first time that the city had faced a shutdown; revenues dipped in 2001 and did not meet expectations, which had been optimistically factored into an increased budget.[45] The

severe cuts to the city's workforce in August 2010 show all too starkly that the tenuous economic situation of the city has not improved. The heavy reliance on the tax revenues from the Casino Queen make the city extremely vulnerable to any economic downturn.

Lack of additional economic development in East St. Louis continues. Certainly, some new businesses have opened since 1993, but nothing on the large scale that was envisioned or hoped for at the time.[46] While the Casino Queen's investment in the city government and involvement in the community have had major effects on the self-sufficiency of the city, the Casino Queen itself remains a main source of income for the city with few other current alternatives for major economic support. This is not necessarily an unusual situation for urban-

based casinos. As they tend to draw gamblers from the local area, urban casinos do not often prompt the same level of economic development that destination-style casinos (such as Las Vegas) may spur.[47]

In East St. Louis, further economic development has also been hindered by business concerns about the political and economic security of an investment in the area. Among earlier failed attempts to spur development was a 1985 plan that would have included $500 million for barge traffic and a recycling plant; instead it resulted in lawsuits and criminal indictments.[48] The combination of city political turmoil, problems with perceptions of crime and insecurity, and the lack of a strong supportive infrastructure have limited interest or investments in large-scale development in East St.

The new casino building, 2010   Powell Photo

Louis for many years.

Opponents are often link to crime and the introduction of moral concerns.[49] East St. Louis faced problems with high crime rates long before the arrival of the casino. Because of this, the facility has given ongoing attention to the security of its patrons. While there have been isolated incidents of theft, age violations, and a handful of violent incidents related to Casino Queen patrons, crime in East St. Louis generally has not been adversely affected by the introduction of gambling into the community.[50] In fact, given the influence of the tax revenue from the Casino in allowing the city to support the police force, fire department, and basic infrastructure, the Casino

Queen's presence has likely made the city a safer place. As with any gaming enterprise, there may be concerns about the role of the casino in questions of morality, social issues such as gambling or alcohol addictions, or family issues, but these are difficult to track. In the case of the Casino Queen, however, the positive effects of gaming on funding government, employment, and supporting community businesses and development far outweigh any concerns in terms of its contributions to East St. Louis and the city's residents.

Conclusion

The Casino Queen and East St. Louis continue to face uncertainty in the still shaky economy of

2010. The economic viability of the Casino Queen is important not only as a business, but to the success of the City of East St. Louis. The revenue from the Casino Queen is an integral part of the operating budget of the city, and has proven fundamental to its economic success. This means that as the business of the casino prospers or suffers, the city and its residents do as well. Since 1993, the casino has been and will continue to be an important element in the economic development and success of the city. For true stability, however, the City of East St. Louis needs a greater range of economic development and sources of revenue.

End Notes:

1. City of East St. Louis Financial Advisory Authority (ESLFAA), "Report of the City of East St. Louis Financial Advisory Authority 1990-2005," 2005. Kenneth M. Reardon, "State and Local Revitalization Efforts in East St. Louis, Illinois," *Annals of the American Academy of Political and Social Science* 551 (1997): 235-247.

2. ESLFAA, Report of the City; Reardon, "State and Local Revitalization Efforts"; *Andrew Theising, Made in USA: East St. Louis:* (St. Louis: Virginia Publishing Company, 2003).

3. Audie Blevins and Katherine Jensen, "Gambling as a Community Development Quick Fix," *Annals of the American Academy of Political and Social Science* 556 (March 1998): 109-123.

4. Patrick A. Pierce and Donald E. Miller, *Gambling Politics: State Government and the Business of Betting,* (Boulder, Colorado: Lynne Reinner Publishers, 2004).

5. Pierce and Miller, *Gambling Politics,* 57.

6. State of Illinois, *Illinois Gaming Board 2009 Annual Report,* 2009.

7. Ray Malone, "Casino Project is hailed as East St. Louis Rebirth," *St. Louis Post-Dispatch,* November 18, 2002.

8. Reardon, "State and Local Revitalization Efforts"; April Hattori, "East St. Louis Hopes Its Luck Will Change with Help from Mammoth Riverboat Casino," *Bond Buyer,* July 12, 1993.

9. Margaret Gillerman, "Nearly 2,000 cast lot with Casino Queen," *St. Louis Post-Dispatch,* January 22, 1993.

10. Margaret Gillerman, "Casino Jobs Pledged for E. St. Louis," *St. Louis Post-Dispatch,* February 2, 1993.

11. Margaret Gillerman, "East St. Louis businesses get gambling boost," *St. Louis Post-Dispatch,* June 24, 1993.

12. Margaret Gillerman, "E St. Louis Budget calls for property-tax cut," *St. Louis Post-Dispatch,* November 2, 1993; Reardon, State and Local Revitalization Efforts.

13. Bob Moore, "A New Cardinals Stadium Could be Catalyst for East St. Louis Development," www.swi-news.com, September 18, 2002.

14. Margaret Gillerman, "Seeds of Hope," *St. Louis Post-Dispatch,* March 27, 1994.

15. Moore, "A New Cardinals Stadium Could be Catalyst for East St. Louis Development;" Bob Moore, "East St Louis Mayor Plans Big Turnaround," *St. Louis Post-Dispatch,* July 8, 2007.

16. ESLFAA, *Report of the City.*

17. Denise Hollingshed and Michael Shaw, "East St. Louis loses money with change in casino boarding rules," *St. Louis Post-Dispatch,* December 16, 1999.

18. Christopher Carey, "On troubled waters," *St. Louis Post-Dispatch,* October 3, 2003.

19. Kevin McDermott and Alexa Aguilar, "Tax increase has casino owners in Illinois considering raising the odds," *St. Louis Post-Dispatch,* June 4, 2002.

20. State of Illinois, *Illinois State Budget Fiscal Year 2010.*

21. Ray Malone, "Casino Queen's RV park doesn't just attract people there to gamble," *St. Louis Post-Dispatch,* February 17, 2000.

22. Denise Hollinshed, "New Hotel at Casino Queen opens for business with views of St. Louis Skyline," *St. Louis Post-Dispatch,* January 4, 2000.

23. The Casino Queen is owned by a group of investors, including members of the Koman family, Charles Bidwell, III, Timothy Rand, Patrick Kenny, and Michael Gaughan. "Casino Queen," *St. Louis Business Journal,* March 26, 2010.

24. Doug Moore, "Queen prepares to build larger casino $150 million project could start this summer," St. Louis Post-Dispatch, March 29 2005; Mary Delach Leonard, "Park is in works for E. St. Louis riverfront," *St. Louis Post-Dispatch,* June 18, 2005.

25. Doug Moore, "Casino ties expansion to current deal Mayor Officer seeks new agreement," *St. Louis Post-Dispatch,* May 20, 2005.

26. Doug Moore, "Casino Queen project moves forward: Clayco Construction signs on to build 'boat in a moat' on East St. Louis riverfront," *St. Louis Post-Dispatch,* February 22, 2006.

27. Betty Moore, "East St. Louis Welcome Re-Opening of Casino Queen," SWI-news.com, August 2, 2007.

28. State of Illinois, *Illinois Gaming Board 2009 Annual Report.*

29. Tim Logan, "Casinos bet on bettors," *St. Louis Post-Dispatch,*

April 11, 2008; Illinois Bureau of the Budget, "Illinois State Budget Fiscal Year 2010," Illinois State Office of Management and Budget, www.state.il.us/budget, 2010; State of Illinois, *Illinois Gaming Board 2009 Annual Report*.

30. Doug Moore, "New Queen is rolling snake eyes. Lumière opening, end of loss limit, smoking ban, slow economy all combine to hit casino hard—and East St. Louis along with it," *St. Louis Post-Dispatch*, March 27, 2009.

31. Nicholas J.C. Pistor, "East St. Louis rejects plan to lay off 27 of 62 officers," *St. Louis Post-Dispatch*, June 12, 2010.

32. Nicholas J.C. Pistor. "Layoffs to Gut East St. Louis Police Force," *St. Louis Post-Dispatch*, July 30, 2010.

33. Margaret Gillerman, "Casino Queen to make start-up business loans," *St. Louis Post-Dispatch*, February 22, 1994.

34. Ibid.

35. Margaret Gillerman, "Dedicated; New Center Designed to put 'Go' Into Business," *St. Louis Post-Dispatch*, April 25, 1996.

36. Margaret Gillerman, "Foundation Gives $9,000 to Groups," *St. Louis Post-Dispatch* July 4, 1994.

37. Doug Moore, "Lions, Universities Provide Eye Care to Those Unable to Get it Elsewhere," *St. Louis Post-Dispatch*, September 11, 2000.

38. Gillerman, "Casino Queen to make start-up business loans."

39. "St. Clair-Monroe County Briefs," St. Louis Post-Dispatch, November 4, 1999.

40. "Santa's Gift," *St. Louis Post-Dispatch*, December 16, 2002.

41. "East St. Louis School District, City and Casino Queen Partner for Progress to Beautify City," *SWI-news.com*, July 8, 2007.

42. Carey, "On troubled waters."

43. Doug Moore, "East St. Louis runs low on supplies as workers face last checks," *St. Louis Post-Dispatch*, January 11, 2002.

44. Christopher Carey, "A decade after gamble, results are mixed," *St. Louis Post-Dispatch*, December 14, 2003.

45. William R. Eadington, "Contributions of Casino Style Gambling to Local Economies," *St. Louis Post-Dispatch* 556 (March 1998): 53-65.

46. Doug Moore, "Mayor has confidence in plan for riverfront," *St. Louis Post-Dispatch*, December 2, 2001.

47. Blevins and Jensen, "Gambling as a Community Development Quick Fix."

48. Donald E. Franklin, "Man is shot in casino queen parking lot," *St. Louis Post-Dispatch*, February 5, 2002; Valerie Schremp, "East St. Louis man is charged with killing man coming home from casinos," *St. Louis Post-Dispatch*, November 15, 2000.

A Call for Effective Leadership

Debra H. Moore, Ph.D.

St. Clair County Intergovernmental Grants Department

There are divergent views as to why East St. Louis, once designated an All America City, fails to experience the resurgence that it seems poised to experience. Proclamations of growth have been the hallmark of each twentieth century leader whose decision-making leaves the city short of the promise. This essay offers a perspective into the city that continually fails to capitalize on the potential it possesses. Plagued by the ills typical of many urban environments, East St. Louis has not had the leadership necessary to reinvent itself. It has been mired in a tradition of machine-style politics. The city's history chronicles the use of this industrial suburb's diminishing resources to advance an often-narrow and personal agenda. Developed as the back operation for St. Louis the adjacent urban center across the river, East St. Louis has long struggled for the legitimacy that would enable it to be a contributing force within the region. As an industrial suburb that ceased to be profitable, this struggle has become even more daunting over the last generation as business after business has left the city.[1]

Fountain of Youth Park, 2010   Powell Photo

Ideally, city leaders should have cultivated an entrepreneurial spirit, like other industrial suburbs, to identify a new niche that would have generated enough revenue to provide for the delivery of services to its remaining population. In East St. Louis, however, nearly every approach that has been tried has been grounded in self-serving politics and a reliance on revenue transfers from federal and state government. The result was recuring failure leaving the city fiscally stagnant , unproductive and on a downward slide , they were all doomed to failure, leaving the city closer to total collapse.

Why Is the City This Way?

The design of East St. Louis government was not meant to provide a viable quality of life for its citizens from the very beginning. Rather, government was designed as a business tool to promote industry and increase profits.[2] Although an incorporated place with an ability to formulate and enforce laws, East St. Louis was an industrial suburb created to facilitate the interests of industry rather than the interests of its citizens.[3] Throughout its glory days business dominated the city and wielded political control over government to ensure

maintenance of a pro-business environment.

De-industrialization exposed the problems inherent to city government. The departure of industry left East St. Louis "abandoned instead of dismantled but without the resources the city had depended on since its creation".[4] Although discarded by industry, a permanent institutional structure was left behind with people that "expect[ed] the municipali[ty] to be forever viable".[5] Interestingly, government leaders were also left without the direction that had been previously provided by business leaders.

City Hall parking lot sign, 2004   Theising Photo

Antithetical to governance by the people, with its overarching involvement, business leaders were able to limit government through the provision of the revenue stream that supported its continuation. Consequently when it was abandoned, an industrial suburb like East St. Louis was simply "unable to replace obsolete industries and associated disinvestment from its deteriorating physical environment."[6] Whatever limited funds had been present for the city to operate were no longer there. As a result, the city no longer had the revenue to provide for its citizens. Neither did the city develop a new economic niche th maintain the city's profitability. Instead, there was more often than not a business as usual attitude by new leaders as they learned how to function in their roles by often replicating behavior instituted by their predecessors.

East St. Louis has simply not had the political institutions or political culture to adequately respond to its changing economic state. Designed to grow an industrial suburb rather than to address the needs of the people, East St. Louis has always had a laissez faire attitude with respect to using government to promote the collective interest. East St. Louis' first mayor John Bowman openly "merged public and private prosperity."[7] As long as personal gain and company prosperity did not conflict, political leaders were pretty much allowed to take advantage of whatever opportunities came their way. This design condoned corruption and vice for personal gain, and became the typical behavior over time. Since Bowman's

administration, corruption has become the primary learned institutional behavior to which each leader seems to aspire once seated. Even after the collapse of the industrial economy, this toleration of corruption and incompetence continued. From the pillaging of the city in the late sixties by Mayor Alvin Fields forward, to the recalcitrant administrations of the twenty-first century.

The Need for a New Leadership

East St. Louis has long needed leadership that would deviate from the city's political traditions and culture to consider the greater good. With political leaders who have been more interested in personal gain rather than organizational competence, city hall often has been staffed with political operatives . As a result, city staff often lacks the basic skills and expertise in critical areas such as economic development— leaving departments unable to communicate, understand, or negotiate complex economic development deals that have the promise of leading East St. Louis out of its seemingly perpetual malaise. When political institutions are mired in corruption, potential deals often never make it to the table because developers are pressed for kickbacks and under-the-table financial transfers.

In this environment one of two outcomes occurs. The developer walks away, leaving the city in the same state as before, or the city becomes vulnerable to be exploited by the developer. If East St. Louis is ever to recover, the focus must turn toward aggressive policies that promote

economic development centered on the needs of the "citizens broadly and not to narrow political interest".[8] Years of mismanagement, disinvestment, and deindustrialization, however, make such a transition impossible without the engagement of power beyond the current capacity of the city.

Why Didn't Outsiders Intercede?

One would assume, by being located directly across the river from downtown St. Louis and having a central regional location, that economic, social, and political conditions in East St. Louis would have forced governments at higher levels to intercede. Rational actors would be guided by the consideration that the "greater the local fiscal stress in a city, the greater its salience to the responsible higher level of government".[9] That was not the case. Instead of rallying in support of East St. Louis' recovery, governments at all levels stayed away. Governmental entities from the federal government, to the State of Illinois,, to St. Clair County were all reluctant to help East St. Louis adjust to the challenges exposed by de-industrialization. One reason may have been the lack of political leadership and the culture of corruption . The city had tainted itself and external leaders saw no reason to respond to East St. Louis' economic plight. Population and markets evolved around the city, making it of no value, economically or electorally, to any of these larger entities. As a result, there was no special consideration given to East St. Louis as the city declined.

The U.S. political system is

influenced by two factors that represent political power, "wealth controlled by a particular group and the size and distribution of its population"[10]. East St. Louis controlled no wealth, therefore its value to the political system was in its population as it related to the "one person, one vote principle that undergirds the American electoral process"[11]. With a declining population, where only a small percentage of the eligible population even bothered to vote, East St. Louis came up short and was left to accept what it was given with little recourse to advocate differently. The state could get by with the offer of many short-term remedies and until there was a higher potential to impact the state's interest and the interest of the region no substantive action was taken.

Does Race Matter?

Reluctance by outside governmental entities to get involved was not the only problem preventing action. East St. Louis political leaders were not responsive to overtures of assistance and feared intervention from outside entities. Racism became both a rationale and an excuse to maintain the status quo. In a way it was quite understandable. Arguing that outside governmental entities only wanted to intercede to keep African Americans from exercising power, East St. Louis city leaders maintained that racism was the motivator behind any offer of assistance rather than acknowledging it as a desire to positively impact the greater good. In retrospect, race was often a shield behind which the political leaders of East St. Louis stood to ensure their continued control of

the city and their ability to carry out their personal interests with little regard for the needs of their constituencies.

There was some legitimacy to the hesitancy of East St. Louis residents and politicians to be readily responsive to overtures from outside interest. Relations with higher governmental powers were not always cordial. East St. Louis had staunchly supported the Democratic Party at every level of government. When East St. Louis became predominantly African American in the seventies and began electing African American mayors, these mayors anticipated membership into the coalition. This representation would have equated to an acceptance by the larger machine to which the city had been steadfastly loyal. However, the St. Clair County machine was reluctant to accept city elected

19th Street, 2009   Powell Photo

officials, even when they initially showed promise. For the early group of young minority mayors, there was an expectation that a win even at the local level would show an ability to build electoral coalitions sufficient to become a partner. However, no desire to admit the city into the larger political process was shown by the machine coalition .

An argument can be made that the "arms length" politics that excluded African Americans from the coalition was racist and that East St. Louis officials were justified in believing that outside entities acted from racist motives and would act to minimize their power. It was then natural that city leaders would develop a posture to hold on to every aspect of city governance and administration since this was

apparently the only political platform over which they would have power and control.

However, as Grimshaw argues, this stance distorted the perceptions by East St. Louis political leaders of the true motives of the county machine and eventually became self-serving for them. According to Grimshaw, their initial response to outside political actors emanated from a natural predisposition to view the actions of the coalition from a racist or sociological perspective. The perception of racism prohibited East St. Louis political leaders from perceiving that as an organizational entity the coalition was merely acting from the economic interests of machine politics.[12] By framing their rejection in racist terms, East St. Louis politicians could

justify their own quest for power from a political perspective. Since the external political elites operated according to the political perspective, they held a "distinct interest in acquiring power, maintaining, and enhancing their positions of command in the organization".[13] and beyond. As a result, the problems of East St. Louis were not a priority and were only superficially addressed when necessary.

Eventually, the city's financial condition threatened the state and regional interests forcing the State of Illinois to act. As a creature of the state, a city must often seek redress from its creator where "there is an unspoken responsibility of the state to ensure cities function in the public interest".[14] State intervention at this level typically steams from

Former Walgreen's site, Missouri Avenue, 2009   Powell Photo

a conception of necessity due to potential impact on the state's financial future rather than a preference and will to fulfill the obligations of its role.[15] In East St. Louis' case, the redress came in 1990 in the form of imposed oversight as a result of continuous institutional failure and fiscal crisis. Unfortunately, the oversight continues today with no evidence of removal.

The Will of the City

Even before the imposition of state oversight, East St. Louis' political institutions have consistently operated autonomously, failing to address the demands of the city these institutions were created to serve. Leaders are preoccupied with wielding influence rather than being rational actors who maintain control and order in the face of "recalcitrant socioeconomic circumstances".[16] In most American political contexts, political will is evident when "politics is organized by a logic of appropriateness".[17] Where interrelated rules and routines that have proven successful are learned and followed whereby political institutions realize "order, stability and predictability".[18] East St. Louis' political institutions instead have adapted a logic of consequentiality where behavior is willful and reflects an "attempt to make outcomes fulfill subjective desires".[19] Absent an understanding of the rules of political institutions, institutional capacity is not sufficient to develop, maintain, and distribute available resources.[20]

The logic of consequentiality is not limited to city operations. The typical companion to dysfunctional city government

is a dysfunctional school district, and such is the case in East St. Louis. East St. Louis School District 189, like the city, experienced mandated oversight from 1994 until 2004 and has been under academic watch for nine years. Despite multi-million dollar reserves available at the termination of financial oversight and nine new schools on line or under construction for a dwindling student population, the District remains academically troubled.

Like city hall, the culture of the District is more "concerned about providing jobs for local political associates and less concerned about improving the learning environment and academic performance of students".[21] It is reported that only nine percent of the District's approximately 7,500 students met or exceeded state minimum academic standards in 2009. The District excelled, however, in contracting by spending $3.1 million on paid consultants for the academic years 2005-2010.[22] The oversight panel concluded that absent some type of governance reform, the District was likely to revert to its past practices negating the work and successes realized by the panel.[23]

The District was saved from financial insolvency during the period of oversight but remains one of the lowest performing school districts in the State of Illinois. The 2002 Annual Report of the Financial Oversight Panel concluded that the "leadership needs to be free from concerns about the political pressures of local employment and contracting".[24]

Clearly, East St. Louis' governing institutions struggle under

leadership that fails to respond to the needs of the greater good but defaults to its political traditions and culture. Until leaders develop local coalitions that are prepared to engage external interest with no expectation of compliance with unscrupulous activities, the city is destined to continued decline. Progress can only begin with effectively retaining and redistributing revenues sufficient to operate the city, and political leaders focused on governing logically.

Viable Remedies

A leadership style must emerge that improves the quality of public decision-making and pursues strategies that advance rather than diminish the city. These strategies can only come about—and the image of the city restored—if strong leadership prevails. Change can only come if the norm is radically challenged and the electorate holds its politicians accountable in terms of their success to grow the city. Real change can only occur if the citizens demand it. The commitment to improve the quality of life within a community is of greatest interest to those who are part of the community and feel the effects of its inefficiencies.

The response of city leaders to problems faced by the citizens of East St. Louis should be rational and decisive. City leaders should not hesitate to pursue policies fundamental to addressing the needs of the city at the risk of disturbing traditional boundaries of power. An example of such a rational policy would be the implementation of residency requirements for city employees. Requiring city employees to live in East St. Louis would strengthen neighborhoods, generate more taxable revenue, and foster civic responsibility. Another rational policy would be shortening the hours of liquor stores in the city. Early closure of liquor-dispensing establishments would improve the image as well as the landscape of the city. The proliferation of such establishments is counterintuitive to basic quality-of-life initiatives voiced by city leaders over time. The tradition of being an all-night town not only leads to increased crime and gun violence, but acts as a magnet for purveyors of unscrupulous behavior. Criminal justice professionals have consistently called for early closure of liquor dispensing establishments in the interest of shaping and sustaining a city that is safer and family friendly. There is no benefit to the continuous award of liquor licenses that benefit the individual holder over the interest and safety of the city.

Many of the city's practical remedies already exist and are codified in volumes, but are not enforced by city leaders. Relaxed regulatory enforcement cultivates a laissez-faire environment where violations are tolerated and leniency is expected.

The remedy is not complex or difficult. Until the city's political leaders are willing to function according to the rules and routines that define appropriate actions, and until the city's institutional arrangements are shifted toward a more responsive function and culture, order and credibility will not be realized and the common good will continue to be sacrificed.[25]

End Notes

1. Andrew J. Theising *Made in USA: East St. Louis.* (St. Louis: Virginia Publishing. 2003), 11.

2. Ibid., 1.

3. Ibid., 8.

4. Ibid., 197.

5. Ibid., 197.

6. Susan S., Fainstein, Norman I. Fainstein, Richard Child Hill, Dennis Judd, and Michael Peter Smith, *Restructuring the City,* rev. (New York: Longman Inc. 1986), 4.

7. Theising, *Made in USA,* 133.

8. Moore, in Theising, *Made in USA,* 222.

9. Robert Ted Gurr and Desmond S. King, *The State and the City,* (Chicago: The University of Chicago Press 1987), 89.

10. Lucius, Barker, J., Mack H. Jones, and Katherine Tate. *African Americans and the American Political System* 4th ed. (Upper Saddle River, NJ: Prentice Hall. 1999), 21.

11. Ibid, 21.

12. William J. Grimshaw, Bitter Fruit: *Black Politics and the Chicago Machine 1931-1991.* *Chicago*: (University of Chicago Press, 1987), 6-7.

13. Ibid, 10.

14. Debra H. Moore, *When Cities Fail and States Intervene: Camden, New Jersey and East St. Louis, Illinois*: (University of Missouri St. Louis unpublished dissertation, 2004), 21.

15. James G. March, and Johan P.

Olsen. *Rediscovering Institutions*: (The Organizational Basis of Politics. New York: The Free Press.,1989),161.

16. Theda, Skocpol "Bringing the State Back In: Strategies of Analysis in Current Research." In *Bringing the State Back In,* eds. Peter B. Evans, Dietrich Rueschemeyer, and Theda Skocpol, (New York: Cambridge University Press, 1985), 9.

17. March and Olsen *Rediscovering Institutions,* 160.

18. Ibid, 160.

19. Ibid, 160.

20. Debra H. Moore and Andrew J. Theising, "The Hollow Prize of East St. Louis: How Institutional Function and Institutional Culture Limited a City's Future," Journal of Illinois History 11 (Spring 2008): 17-38, 22.

21. Annual Report of the Financial Oversight Panel for School District Number 189. 2002, 1.

22. Baran, Maria and George Pawlaczyk "East St. Louis Schools Spend $3.1 Million on Consultants," Belleville News Democratic, April 25, 2010.

Gurr, Robert Ted and Desmond S. King. 1987. The State and the City. Chicago: The University of Chicago Press., 2010.

24. Ibid, 1.

25. Ibid, 3.

26. March and Olson *Rediscovering Institutions,*160

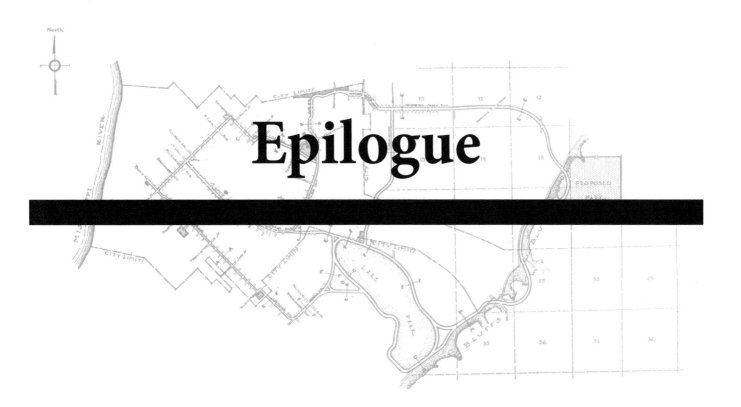

Epilogue

A Tale of Two Captains & Two Avenues in the Life of East St. Louis

Eugene B. Redmond

Poet Laureate of East St. Louis

I
ode to disaster

first All Hell came--& went;
then High Water did too.
what's left?—just the scent--
natural/human do do.

II
presences

> **we arrive, we arrive**
> **we cross-fertilize**
> **we derive, we survive**

The former Lincoln High School, 2009
Powell Photo

Between bluffs & plains,
quakes & rains,
flesh & veins—
    & before the births of James Piggott & Bloody Island,
St. Clair County & Illinoistown, John Robinson & East Boogie--
    a river-spiced gumbo of Afro-oboes, Indigenous percussive soulos
& Euro-immigrant flo' shows
    dots the pioneerscape like a born again Old World orchestra
& trumpets arrival of a "miles-ahead" Lincolnknight
    coolly bopping like a blue-note from the land of "so what(s/!/?)."
The *ark-estra's* voice chorus doo-wops the coming of Lincoln High's
    "Leaping" Leon Thomas, who can be funnier than a valentine,
yodeling his Bond Avenue/jazz-throttled sermons
    about the mating of the Mississippi & the Nile.
Blending like Southern Harmonizers, these creole crooners also exult
    in another Lincolnlight, Jackie Joyner *cum* Kersee,
who hurdles Lincoln Park's Mary Brown Center
    from 15th Street & Piggott Avenue. On her flight to Los Angeles, Seoul, Tokyo
& Barcelona, an aboriginal cheering squad
    is layen down the skinny on lacrosse & "hidden-ball."

And way-way (back) before son-settlers & daughter-settlers
        squat in Little Egypt's "Cayro"/ Land of New Pharaohs;
& even ahead of Crispus Attucks' freedom *cum* death cry
            on Boston Commons
                (conjuring his namesake elementary school
                    on Kansas Avenue in East St. Louis) . . .
ancestrails & life-tales & robust nature-hails of a city yet-to-be-born
        begin fermenting among Cahokia moundbuilders & soul-tillers,
spinners & weavers, drillers & quilters, dancers & healers,
        shakers & shamans whose ancestors' ancestors
name them Algonquin, Illinois, Mississippi, Michigamea, Iowa & Iroquois.

III
incarnation via migration: confluences

Floods of ethnic dreams, named for First Peoples,
        missionaries, immigrants, soldiers, settlers, chattel & Old Testament players
--& nicknamed for unpronounceables--
        follow explorers, water-ways & commerce. Then come Africans,
first in the form of an early 1700's trickle—up-river
        from a Louisiana French colony—& next as fugitives, rebels & migrants
flowing full-up from Southern fields of cotton & cane, tobacco & rice.

        Starting in the East, they beat three drum-routes/roots to the Promised Lands:
        from the Atlantic Seaboard w/their West African yam festivals prefiguring kwanzaa: North to Boston;
        from Mississippi, reborn as Arkansippians: haulin' acres, head-wraps & box cars of blues: headin'
Memphis-way, maybe a Chicago-stay, 'least East Boogie by-day;
        from Louisiana/Texas: a-moverin' wes' to California, jukin' gumbo, Cajun,
jazz & Juneteenth.

        Many of these "drummers" are cross-routed &, whether by book, hook,
crook, incident, mishap or accident, end their northern pilgrimage
        at an un-appointed place. Like the Merritts Family, an Oklahoma-stocked
"gumbo" of African, Choctaw, Irish & creole: They de-train here by mistake.
        But, shy of funds to ride 'cross the 'Sippi to St. Louis,
they create their "fortunes" in East St. Louis,
        making their proverbial way outta no way.

17th and Piggot, 2010   Powell Photo

IV
a century apart: men of moment & monument:

The Captains:

(1) Late1700's Territorial Judge James Piggott bridges Illinoistown's
      Cahokia Creek (foreshadowing invention of East St. Louis
     & Eads Bridge), dams Bloody Island & ferries commerce—
         flesh, coal, produce & hardware--across the Mississippi.
     The latter so named for a classical civilization, a river, a State
         (& state/s of mind)
     & an Avenue that parallels the river
         & interchanges appellations with 8th Street on the north,
     Illinois Route 3 on the south
         & a namesake boulevard in the middle
     where it cruises or rushes thru Rush City
        (a ward of Monsanto Chemical Company like Sauget)
     between the river (on the west)
         &12 sets of railroad tracks (on the east).

     These ubiquitous tracks are early/mid-20th Century conduits for food,
         coal, detergent, soldiers, hobos, livestock, deadstock, army tanks, trucks
     & varied vehicles, "flammables," Pullman cars & even WWII German POWs
         enroute to a Tennessee "holding" camp.

     So let's snap-to for a two-century salute:
         a true sentry: Revolutionary War vet, "Indian fighter"
     (captain in a regiment commanded by Gen. George Rogers Clark),
         pioneer, patriarch & jurisprudent merchant, his namesake,
     Piggott Avenue, runs westward-- like blood--
         from a 15th Street center toward the river
      (engaging *ritual ground*: hunting ground, flood ground, immigrant ground, slavery ground, dueling
     ground, riot ground, ancient burial ground (& mini-mounds), roundhouse ground, water(ing) ground &
     railroad tracks contiguous w/ Franklin School & Park, 6th Street Bottom, the Red Light District
     & light industry).

MacArthur Bridge trestle, 2010
Powell Photo

As Piggott about-faces at the river, the18th &19th centuries--
running eastward like wine—catch up w/the 20th (& 21st):
    15th Street's Mary Brown Center [1968/2006] in Lincoln Park
& [Poet] Paul Laurence Dunbar Elementary School (1910/2005),
an educational-literary delight sandwiched between Piggott & Tudor
    Avenues at 19th Street (whose official opening, four years after the poet's
death, is attended by his mother) . . . all while flowing over the shores of
    numbered streets between--& fore & aft-- aforementioned wonders.

Continuing east from its ancestral "grounds,"
    Piggott Avenue's lore runs through a deep-veined ore
ala lodes of scientific, cultural, artistic, athletic & crafts wizardry.
    It crosses 8th Street's multi-named strain, pausing
at 10th, where foot- , horse- , & motor-drawn life merges
    with a 1940's Coca-Cola distributorship & Harley Davidson sales.

Here, the foot of MacArthur/Free Bridge parallels 10th
    & slides like a sled, in a weird & optical-illusionary/northward
way, into the gaping/glistening mouth of Piggott's 10th Street Fire Station.
    A door or so east of the station rests the home of
teacher-coach Douglass Clark whose new namesake
    Middle School now sits (like a wakeful & wonder-filled sentry)
atop a new century on outer State Street.

As centuries & the Captain's sentries march with--& mark--
    Piggott's historical rise from animal, foot & wagon path
to paved Avenue, the fabled 11, 12 & 13 hundred blocks unload their lodes:
    children-cuddly Moody's Drug Store faces a
a brick-faced but welcoming George Washington Elementary School
    & both embrace Coffman's Market at 12th while tolerating talkative
sisters Rose & Lily Coffman. A block away the Avenue yields to the Harper House
    (nurturer of educators & scholars, including literati leader Clifford)
& Scotia Calhoun Thomas' Shrimp Shop, Apartment Building
    (first Black-owned in East St. Louis) & Beauty Shop.

Scotia's business "combo" is a hot-comb across from
    [first Black Illinois legislator] Aubrey Smith's Dental Building.
The "Smith" building's second floor façade
    inspires w/its huge engraved numbers: "1938," its founding year.

Lincoln Park, 2010   Powell Photo

At Piggott's 1400 block, the "mine" is glowing w/veins of cultural,
    intellectual, ethnic & entrepreneurial ore,
beginning with two sets of brothers of the 1940's-'50's vintage:
    Jesse & George Brazier (businessman & musician/drummer [w/"The Blue
Devils"]) & McHenry & Charles Richard Robinson
                    (public educators par excellence),
Charles serving as an early Black assistant superintendent of city schools.

    These four-runners are center points of an extended block family
including the Milton Green dynasty of skilled craftsmen.
    They gladly toss gauntlets to James Rosser, hoop star, chemist,
college executive, Black Studies architect, renaissance scholar &
    sight/site-lifter who criss-crosses the USA as a higher education leader
& becomes President of California State University-Los Angeles (1980-);
    late Linda Green, daughter of Milton & a world-circling
teacher-thespian-scholar
    (who teams for a while w/native son Charles Means, a provost at
Bowling Green University, Ohio); & Olympians Jackie & Al Joiner
    (more snap-to salutes to Lincoln Park's Mary Brown Center!).
This block-long mother lode ends w/the Lincoln "picture show"
    across Piggott Avenue from Banjo Candy sto'.

Pausing, before accessing more easterly lodes,
    but without exhausting previous precious veins,
15th & Piggott offers decades-long hives of diverse businesses,
    morning-come-evening debaters
(depending on the season & timing), pool sharks, dice players,
    holy rollers & street corner orchestras. And mid-block south
on 15th between Piggott & Tudor Avenues, yet another
    rare-jewel-of-a-face-off features Lavelle Sykes' Drug Store
& "Wink" Falconer's Vet's Club, the "knight" of night spots where jazzerati
    "dig" bassist John Mixon, drummer Ben Thigpen & pianist "Albino" Red.

But not before "locating" the "Black Bridge"--subject of a "blues" poem
    by Southend native Darlene Roy--as it spans 15th
at the Malones & Dixons' Boismenue Avenue & snakes across
    & behind Pearl Gregory & (R&B singer) Bobby McClure's Colas Avenue.

[Here's "East Saint Oxymoron," one local poet's regional rendering:
from the pith-deep end of a pitch-dark Southend
comes the day-breaking din of a gambling den,
rising to perch like a steeple on a church,
wee-wee mornin' catching last night in a lurch.]

U-turning northward at this busy trestle brings Eugene O'Connor's Hardware
    (at 15th & Russell near Spencer/Stewart homes)
into rear-view-relief. Then the advancing mindscape reveals Ruby's
    Lounge; & activist Mary Martin, writer Arthur Dozier & the Perrys
& Bonners' Baker Avenue. Next crossing/sighting: Tudor Avenue,
    home of Truelight Baptist Church
& the Teer (as in National Black Theatre founder Barbara Ann),
    Campbell, Mason & Nicholson families.

Veins now strain right on Piggott's Piggott, shinin' east, yo,
    & basking in the "loded" glow of Lincoln Park.
As Afro-East St. Louis' cultural/recreational/athletic hub,
    Lincoln runs two blocks--west to east/15th to 17th.
But it is a swamp in the late 19th/early 20th Centuries
    before becoming the Apple of the Southend's Eye
& equipped w/an indoor swimming pool in the 1930's.
    For Piggott Avenue families like the Hudsons, it is *utili dulce*,
a useful/practical asset of great beauty. But all Piggott families
    are magnetized by this useful/beautiful center: the Nelsons,
the Sampsons, the Casons, the Walls, Dunbar School students & staffs,
    the McNeeses, the Perrys, the Stennises (maternal grandparents of
JJK's trainer Nino Fennoy) & even members of Hopewell Church,
    one of the oldest of such local Black beacons.

Indigenous architecture, 2010   Powell Photo

Negotiating set after set of rail road tracks, Piggott glows eastward,
    as street or trail or oral lore or dumping ground or a mind's eye-
image:
    Past the first one-room school house for "colored" children.
    Past Aluminum Ore's sub-cities Alorton & Centreville/Fireworks
        Station.
    Past former trading post/Village of Cahokia.
    Past "colored" people's Sunset Gardens of Memory Cemetery.
    Past the German-named city of Millstadt
    where native trumpeter's father, Dr. Miles Dewey Davis Sr.,
    hosts & harvests his early-to-mid-20th Century Davis Farm
    of Landrace Hogs (& horses), imported from Canada, Norway,
    Sweden & Denmark—to where the saga-song
    of Captain/Judge/Pioneer/Patriarch James Piggott
    is forever a part of the boogie-down history of ferries & bluffs.

35th and Bond, 2010   Powell Photo

(2) *"In the 1920's Bond [is] the premier Avenue for Blacks."*
                                        —Jeanne Allen Faulkner

"Captain" John Robinson, son of the 19th Century, surviving two
    decades into the 20th, knows about blood—old & new;
he's seen it trickle from & flood the body—& the body politic.
    Patriot, "colored" pioneer & patriarch, Robinson also knows a
warrior-leader's life-worth's only as reliable as his blood ties,
    that most reliable property of the species, evidenced in his
Civil War campaigns with the Union Army & at Harper's Ferry, Virginia,
    where, as he now regales fellow East St. Louisans with the story,
he bears witness to the execution of none other than John Brown.
    (Though he doesn't know it, he'll also live to see the city's 1917 "Riot.")

In the latter quarter of the19th Century, this former slave is now
    a professional plasterer, white washer & interior decorator;
& though illiterate, has set his brilliant oracular
    & oratorical sights on quality (public) education for Black children
& improvements within the broader Black family.
    "Passionate" & "possessed" by a "commanding" ethical, moral &
spiritual intelligence, "Captain" John reaches East St. Louis shores in
    1878, greeted by a Black population of 400 & zero schools for
children of his hue & history. However, when he withdraws from these
    mortal metro east plains & bluffs in 1919,
he regales/rallies fellow ancestors with good news:
    several elementary schools, including Dunbar, & an
Abraham Lincoln Junior/Senior High School.

No "John Robinson Boulevard" struts across numbered streets
or railroad tracks of former Illinoistown,
     like the annual Afro-American Emancipation Day Parade
he brain-childs & leads, starting in 1882 & lasting until his life
     ebbs at a pace faster than it flows.
But a west-to-east-running Bond Avenue,
     sliced south-to-north by 15th Street, like Piggott's Piggott,
boasts two edifices bearing the "Captain's" memory:
     John Robinson Elementary School at the corner of 15th where
Miles Davis, his sister Dorothy & brother Vernon matriculate in the 1930's;
     & The John Robinson Homes in Bond's 1200 block—
poised like a rescue vessel across the street from Lincoln High
     in its "third" incarnation (circa 1949).
This one, after an 1886 "first" birth at 6th & St. Louis Avenue
     (snap-to salutes, again, "Captain" Robinson, for protest marches/
sit-ins at school board meetings/persistence/persistence)
     & a 1909 "second" arrival at 10th Street & Broadway Avenue
(o effervescent famous fabulous flawless Forty-Niners, scholar-athletes!).
A "fourth" birth comes in 2005 when Lincoln returns to 10th & Broadway as a junior high.

15th, a.k.a. "Black Wall Street," spread-eagles at Bond Avenue,
     wing-spanning four blocks south to Piggott's spigot
& five blocks north to funky, soulfisticated & fabled Broadway.
     But two blocks beyond Broadway, the eagle's north wing
flutters over the corner of Kansas Avenue & 15th,
     site of the Euros' Washington Irving Elementary School & later,
per a population shift,
     the Afros' James Weldon Johnson Elementary School.
Meanwhile, back at Broadway's northwest corner,
     a business-civic-social magnet, holding Dr. Miles Davis'
Dental Office & domicile,
     perches on the second floor of Daut's Drug Store.
And less than a stethoscope away, an L-shaped complex,
     built by Dr. Henri Weathers II, commands the northeast corner.
On the third--& southeast--corner, yet a third Medical Office,
     that of Dr. A. M. Jackson, an early Black school board member, sits above
an immigrant-owned grocery store.

Indigenous architecture, 2010
Powell Photo

Enmasse, the Davises gather Sundays at St. Paul Baptist Church on Bond
    (a song & prayer across 15th from Robinson School)
where the Rev. John DeShields, whose namesake housing development
    occupies a three-block cut of Bond (resting on either flank
& behind Lincoln School), pastors mightily to spiritual & community needs.

    Enriched artistically & intellectually by the arrival—
in the second decade of the 20th Century—
    of Fannie & Lucy Turner, brilliant educator-granddaughters of
19th Century slave rebellion leader Nathaniel "Nat" Turner,
    Metro-East St. Louis in general & the Davis siblings super-specially
are exposed to these renaissance women at Robinson School
    & St. Paul Church, where Lucy Turner is an organist
& Fannie is a poet, St. Louis University Law School Graduate
    & historian. The Turner Sisters also share a home in the 1900
block of Bond Avenue.

    From Bond, the south 15th Street stretch of the eagle's wing,
reaching past Market Avenue to Piggott, hovers between Lincoln Park's
    western border & two1940's/50's grand-landmarks:
Police Captain Trainee Polk's proudly elevated (brown-brick) brick house
    & a teaser-of-an-example of "indigenous architecture"--thanks,
Hudlin Brothers--in the form of the home of Attorney Louie F. Orr
    [about whom a 1930's flash-b(l)lack reveals this morsel: Orr,
w/Attorney Frank Summers & the indefatigable leader Horace Adams
    (arriving from Corinth, Mississippi in 1919, the year Robinson dies),
helps found the Black-based Paramount Democratic Organization,
    headquartered in a "Wall Street" social-business-dining center
at 15th & Brady Avenue, four blocks north of Bond.}

    The Paramount lies on a jazz-weavin'/bop-duffin'/ping-pong-northward
approach to The Deluxe Theater (right). . . Dr. Henri Weathers III's
    Medical Office (left) . . . Paul Harris' Hat Shop (right) . . .
Bill Skidas' Liquor Store (left) . . . & Broadway Avenue, straight ahead.

Hudlin home, 2010   Powell Photo

Now take a sharp-as-a-tack left to the Peppermint Lounge
		(you might catch guitarist Grant Green or the Three Sounds!),
Hudlin's Drug Store, educator-activist Homer Randolph's abode &
		business, the Manhattan Club w/Ike & Tina plus Billy Gayles on
drums & the Broadway Movie Theater w/Katherine Dunham ala "Stormy
		Weather."...
Or a right, jazz-weavin', again, toward We-Three Restaurant,
		Dr. Leon Magarian's Dental Office w/terrazzo tiling, Sykes Drug Store #2
& the Horace Adams House (1535 Broadway)
		w/its wrap-around porch & glazed brick.

		The eagle's north wing reverses course to view-feel
the full kaleidoscopic-sensorial-confluent blast of sounds,
		smells, sights, motions & dreams that drape "Captain" John's
Bond Avenue, as 15th's intersection pulsates from the center
		to the circumference *cum* cardinal points—
& then returns to mirror its minor & major undertakings.
		Example: Ike Turner's early East St. Louis home at1420 Bond,
two doors removed from Robinson School, helps drive
		the area visual experience of "do-rags," "conks," "processes,"
silk-pastels, wigs, Stacy Adams/white bucks/wingtip shoes, suave sweaters,
		pinstripe/charcoal w/double-breasted everything
including belt-in-the-back "bennys,"
		topped off/in warm weather/w/pedal pushers on skates.
(And don't even mention the
		Sunday-go-to-/&-after-/meeting Big Hats!)
These sights (sites) unseen mix w/sounds of unloading/
		reloading musical instruments, rehearsals, strolling jaw-jerkers,
doo-woppers & the drag-grind of heavy trucks
		(heaving/bucking w/"goods" going everywhere).
This "wiring" of the intersection--especially at night--
		creates a "mesh" of down-home/upscale worlds.

17th and Bond, 2010   Powell Photo

Eyebrows--& "grapevines"---get raised considerably when Ike—
        w/Tina—"upgrades"
(mid-1950's style) eastward to 29th /off-Bond, one block north/
        & acquire a "mansion" on Virginia Place.
The move nestles them among a rainbow of neighbors including
        Warrington & Helen Hudlin & Brother Joe Mays,
gospel music's "Thunderbolt of the Midwest."
        (Warrington descends from riders of underground railroads,
        is a member of the Hudlin Brother builder-broker-educator-business/
        warrior [hero] dynasty & father of filmmaker-brothers
        Warrington III & Reginald.)

Back at 15th & Bond, barbeque scents--including those of "snoots,"
        an East Boogie specialty-delicacy--waft across the intersection;
& on the northeast corner, joining the sensorial kaleidoscope, Walter
        McDonald's Drug Store & "Shorty" Humphrey's (off-corner)
Rockway offer the "usual" w/milling room,
        a mix of "who you know"/"need-to-be-seen" passers-by
&, in Shorty's case, tongue hypnotizing ice cream with booths for
        ooglie-eyes, raconteurs, bobby soxers, signifiers,
balladweavers & smoochers—all b(l)ack dropped
        by the hive's ubiquitous juke box.

Doubling, tripling & quadrupling as thoroughfare, parade route
        & Highway 13/163, much of Bond Avenue is a concaving/
convexing window, yielding aforementioned vocals,
        back- & fore-ground sounds & visual delights--
as ancient & contemporary spirits traverse its surfaces,
        sub-surfaces & side surfaces.

Turner home, 2010   Powell Photo

Streaking eastward from ancestral rivergrounds toward ancestral
        bluffgrounds & beyond "zones" that even Captain Piggott's
Avenue cannot "ferry" you to,
        "Captain" Robinson's well-paved artery pauses at
other juke junctures, commercial cross streets & bloodshot
        corners. Right here, at 17th, the Lewis Brothers' Cosmo Club,
a night spot/eatery featuring young B. B. King
        & just-rising/early 1950's Chuck Berry,
is only a duck walk across Bond from W.K. Allen's
        Unity Insurance Company & residence
(where teacher-activist Jeanne Allen Faulkner is raised/still lives).

BBQ also flavors & favors this intersection & variegated side scenery:
        As 17th spread-eagles south, its wing hovers like a huey
(offering homage) at Market Avenue where wonder-lookers genuflect
        (like young dancers at Katherine Dunham's
North 10th Street Residence)
        in front of Attorney Frank Summers' "ruble" stone castle.

Built by the Hudlin Brothers in the summers of 1937/38
        (according to neighbor Annabelle Lukes of 1708 Market),
it "guards" Lincoln Park's northeast corner & engages eyes,
        skies & sighs as the best "model" of the city's
"indigenous" architecture.
        The eagle's south wing extends to its tip before it dips into
the smell of rib tips, the sounds/tastes of Friendship Baptist Church choir's
        Jubilee lips, & flips its hips as the belch of "Black Bridge"
trains & Monsanto smoke stacks nips then rips the clouds.

Summers home, 2010   Powell Photo

Under the eagle's northward-spanning wing, eyes, ears,
feet, pedals & wheels reel back to Bond, hop scotching
McCasland & Converse Avenues, railroad tracks & industries,
to behold the famous Blue Flame Club at 17th & Broadway
(hosting Herbert Jackson's Venetian Blind business on its top floor),
a night-bright "flame" (jazzaic/bluesaic) cattycorner
to Certain Teed Company. But just a blue-note-of-a-jazz-jog
to the right, 17th's tour resumes its northward "swing,"
under the eagle's wing, beyond Division Avenue
(w/an askance-of-a-glance toward 18th at "Tricky Sam's"
over- /under-ground Club that takes no prisoners)
before commingling with the corner of 17th & Kansas Avenue:
site of a deceptively small, two-story white wooden structure
housing the Davis family in a dozen-plus rooms.

The Davises move here (from 15th & Broadway) in 1939
when Miles is 13 & receives his first trumpet
as a gift from Dr. John Eubanks--
physician/civic centerpiece/descendent of an
East St. Louis Founding Family-- who builds a home on Bond Avenue
(w/hints of the Hudlins' signature architecture).

The eagle's wing tips down one block farther north
at 17th & Missouri (a.k.a. US-460/IL-15) & taps another oasis:
Blue Flame owner Welbon Phillips' DeLisa Club,
watering hol(d)e of the wild & wannabes, classy (fashionplates)
& country (cover-alled), dance contestants & politicians, Ike & Tina,
saxophonist Joe Enlow, DJ's spinning webs of hi-fi "soul."

U-turning under the eagle's canopy, the southward-swooning
senses re-encounter the cosmic Cosmo corner where a left or right
onto Bond Avenue treats them to a show-stopping "march" of
stately &/or modest homes, shops, stores & churches, hailing the progress
—& progression—
of Colored, Negro, Black & African American middleclass—
with a fading mixture of Euro-homesteaders & retailers.

Davis home, 2010   Powell Photo

An eyes-left "loop" eastward from 15th & Bond, for example,
        catches the Law Office of Richard G. Younge (in the Rockway
suites), Felix Williams' Coal & Ice Company &, strung like pearls,
homes of the Robinsons, Willinghams, "Little/s" (w/brick-tiled
        letters reminiscent of the "1938" engraved on Dr. Smith's Piggott
Avenue building), the Hoovers (Honorable Wyvetter Hoover Younge's
        parents), the (Maude) Kennedys & the Fennoys.

And an eyes-right scopes the tailored brick/stucco/variously paneled
        residences of educators John T. Caldwell, Ethel Graves
(Lincolnknight '57), trumpeter Elwood Buchanan (mentor of Miles Davis),
        Aurilla Taylor, James Gladden, Alta Mae Caldwell Russ & Irene King
(brilliant tutors of "maestro" Eugene Haynes, Miles' classmate
        at Lincoln & Juilliard School of Music).

Potpourri: Soul-weavin' east toward Alorton & numerous "elsewheres,"
        Bond hosts more homes & edifices: Doctors Baldwin, Eubanks,
Hunter, Jones & King, the Neely Brothers Hat Shop
        (across from St. John's C.M.E. Church
& cattycorner to Haynes Drug Store), Hudlin Insurance Company,
        the "new" Mt. Zion Baptist Church (after its 13th & Tudor tenure),
Leading Food Store & Alta Sita Elementary School
        (at the foot the 26th Street Viaduct,
        spanning multi-sets of railroad tracks
        between Bond & Kansas,
        coming to rest at Attucks Elementary School on the north),
an assortment of eateries & sleeperies
        &, at 29th, the Midtown Lounge/Restaurant
featuring "soul"-spinning by DJ Robert "BQ" Louis
        & a delectable index of recipes
Xpress from 'Sippi's Soular System.

Cosmo site, 2010
Powell Photo

Outer Bond also gifts mid-20th Century East St. Louis
        w/homes of West Indian-accented Dr. Fingal,
night club owner/politician Welbon Phillips, the Calverts, the Stallings
        & Mildred Louise (Sammons) Business College.

Bond Avenue, a grand promenade w/grander promise,
        is a measure of "Captain" John Robinson's "bond"
w/Black neighbors & the "gumbo" of kindred cultures within
        metro-"East St. Louis toodle-oo," as Duke Ellington,
who loves to play the Harlem Club in next door Brooklyn (IL),
        wings & swings it.

Abandoned tracks, ESL HEC, 2010
Powell Photo

INDEX